RHODES OF VIET NAM

Father Alexander de Rhodes

RHODES
OF VIET NAM

The Travels and Missions of
Father Alexander de Rhodes in China
and Other Kingdoms of the Orient

TRANSLATED BY SOLANGE HERTZ

The Newman Press • Westminster, Maryland
1966

Nihil obstat: Rt. Rev. Msgr. Justin D. McClunn, J.C.D.
   Censor librorum

Imprimatur: Most Reverend John J. Russell, D.D.
   Bishop of Richmond
   February 14, 1966

The *Nihil obstat* and *Imprimatur* are official declarations that a book or pamphlet is free of doctrinal and moral error. No implication is contained therein that those who have granted the *Nihil obstat* and *Imprimatur* agree with the opinions expressed in the book.

Translator's Introduction

WHAT ALEXANDER DE RHODES thought of travel books is no secret. He didn't have much use for them. "A way of crossing the seas without danger," he sniffs, and "satisfying the curious rather than the devout."

Thus the intrepid seventeenth-century Jesuit who emerges historically as the "Apostle of Viet Nam" warns his readers to expect nothing of the sort from him. And with that he proceeds to write one of the most fascinating travel books ever penned: *Divers Voyages et Missions du Père Alexandre de Rhodes en la Chine et Autres Royaumes de l'Orient, avec Son Retour en Europe par la Perse et l'Arménie,* offered here under the title RHODES OF VIET NAM.

Despite the author's protests to the contrary, his account turns out to be highly satisfying to the curious. The larger part of it, dealing as it does with the geographical area that is modern Viet Nam, could hardly be overlooked by any serious student of southeast Asia. As a historical document bearing on the all-important wedding between East and West whose anguished courtship is even now in progress, and which must somehow reach its consummation if the peace of the world is to be insured, *Divers Voyages* proves to be an invaluable mine of information. One can only wonder how it could have taken so long to make its appearance in English.

Looking through Fr. de Rhodes' eyes, even the most casual

reader will discern in the three highly hostile and competitive little kingdoms of Tonkin, Cochinchina, and Champa, which composed the Viet Nam of 300 years ago, the main roots of the baffling disunity that plagues and retards her as a nation today. The marvel is that she has held together at all, but *Divers Voyages* answers part of this question too, for Fr. de Rhodes uncovers to our gaze the tensile strength of the oriental family system that in our day, as in his, has been the unifying force providing cohesion on all levels to the otherwise "granular society" of the East. Even today the foreigner is struck by what remains of the mystique of the *gia dinh,* or family community, to which the beautiful little religious shrines in every home, whether pagan or Christian, all bear witness, along with the universal respect for the aged, the position of the wife and mother as undisputed "general of the house," and the duty to ancestors. These aspects will delight the historian, the sociologist, the political scientist, and as we have said, the just plain curious.

To the curious we therefore offer this translation, but like Fr. de Rhodes, we offer it especially to the devout—for whom he insists he wrote particularly. To tell the sober truth, RHODES OF VIET NAM is a travel book of the kind St. Luke wrote when he set down the *Acts of the Apostles.* It tells, in short, the travels of the Holy Spirit—how the Holy Spirit set out for Viet Nam and what He did there, and it explains in depth what is really transpiring in Viet Nam today behind the wars and rumors of wars.

Even so its message deals in universals far transcending Viet Nam itself, or indeed the whole Orient, for it is addressed to anyone who hears the divine injunction to "go into the whole world and preach the Gospel to every creature" and who intends to do so wherever he may be. Certain luminous principles emerge from Fr. de Rhodes' pages that speak even louder in our day than they did in his. Like his fellow Jesuits Ricci and de Nobili in China and India, de Rhodes was never guilty of evangelization by condescension, nor did he confuse the accidents of his own culture with the word of God. He never looked on the oriental as "underdeveloped" or even as just plain hungry, benightedly awaiting the benefits of Western technocracy and superior social structures.

He inveighs against missionaries who force their Christian converts to cut off their pigtails. "I used to tell them," he says, "that the Gospel obliged them to lop off their spiritual errors, not their long hair!" He deplores preachers who use interpreters instead of learning the native language, as he admires the French layman in Persian dress near Shiraz who edified every pagan he encountered by the purity of his faith. He is amazed at the fasting prowess of the schismatic Armenians. He is wildly enthusiastic about tea and oriental medical practice. As a matter of fact, he fell quite shamelessly in love with many foreign ways and tells us all about them.

He wasn't above bribing the Lord Trinh-Tráng, King of Tonkin, with mechanical clocks to win his favor in true oriental style, but he never proffered potential converts material gadgets (or foreign aid) to enlist their allegiance. He offered them the only thing eternally capable of moving men: the truth, and the opportunity of living and dying for it.

That those he came to save were capable of such sacrifice he never doubted for a moment. He recognized in them the highest natural virtues, finding them already providentially prepared by the Holy Spirit for the gift of supernatural life. It follows that when he first planted the faith in Viet Nam, it wasn't to Jesuit headquarters in Macao that the good Father looked for continuing support, but to the new Christian community itself, whose moral and economic resources he took entirely for granted, except—like St. Paul—where his own personal needs were concerned.

The Church he founded in Viet Nam was no branch of the European one now open for business, but the Vietnamese one that had existed from the primordial beginning in the mind of the Blessed Trinity and became happily manifest through his efforts in the fullness of its time. It is this one that is even now fighting for its life and the souls of men in southeast Asia, and which already boasts over 100,000 martyrs.

Inevitably lacking a native clergy in the early days, de Rhodes managed nevertheless to spread his sacerdotal power over an incredibly large area by using the laity to its utmost. Through the lay catechists and other helpers he trained, and countless others he did not have to train, this lone priest (for years at a stretch he never met another to hear his own confession) brought thousands effectively to the faith. Speaking of the job done by the young Tonkinese layman Simon, he himself marvels that "in the town where he lived there was not one pagan; all the devils had been driven out. There were at least a thousand Christians who were living very holy lives, *although they had never seen a priest.*" In just such fashion did St. Peter marvel after Pentecost "that on the Gentiles also the grace of the Holy Spirit had been poured forth," and asked, "Can anyone refuse the water to baptize these?"

It's evident that these early Vietnamese laymen were free men, not rubber-stamp puppets ever waiting for Father's nod of approval before making the slightest apostolic move. Nor had they any artificial societies to run to when the going got rough. They carried on the same devastating apostolate the Christians of *Acts* did, by daring to live their ordinary lives to the hilt in the fire of the Spirit.

Fr. de Rhodes himself had no qualms whatever about deferring to them. Hard pressed in a public debate with pagans at the Cochinchinese court, he found "the more obstinate ones sometimes interrupted me and put forward some nonsense from their idols and their books, so I besought Ignatius (his head catechist), who was present, to refute them, because he was very well versed in all their books and *possessed special grace* for disproving all the errors of these idolaters. He did so with such vigor and enlightenment that all those gentlemen remained at a loss."

He finds nothing unusual in this. He is quite undismayed at the charismatic gifts cropping up in his new laity, feeling this is to be expected wherever the Holy Spirit is laying important groundwork. He is never guilty of silly scientism either. In all humility he permits himself to be edified by their visions and revelations, and praises God for the miracles He performs through them, mobilizing everyone in the Christian community. One newly converted idolatrous priest alone brings in 500 converts, many of them former colleagues.

Some of the most ruthless apostles are women, toward whom the good Father is not the least fearful, suspicious, or condescending. He finds it quite proper that the former pythoness now baptized Teresa should be possessed of a most useful gift of exorcism for the common good, and he commends the old lady who makes fools of her torturers. He makes firm friends of several women to the great benefit of the Church, notably two high-born princesses both baptized Marie Magdalene and both referred to on occasion as "Madame Marie." One was the Princess Minh-Dú'c, concubine widow of Nguyên Hoàng, founder of the Nguyên dynasty, who is revered today as the great matriarch of the South Vietnamese Church. The other, also very influential, was the Princess Ngoc-Liên, who was this same Nguyên Hoàng's granddaughter and later wife of the governor of Phu-Yen province.

Two centuries before Cardinal Newman unsettled the hierarchy of his day by his controversial *On Consulting the Faithful,* Fr. de Rhodes was making no bones at all about consulting his, newly converted pagans that they were. Why not? As he says, all were of one heart and mind, moving as one, as did the Christians of the *Acts.* He is very much aware of the striking re-creation of the atmosphere of the primitive Church in his own budding communities, and he remarks on it frequently.

He quite naturally expects martyrs, and they duly appear, bearing the famous "cross of Cochinchina," the curious ladder-like yoke with which criminals were loaded in those climes. His eyewitness account of the martyrdom of young Andrew of Phu-Yen, whose cause is even now before the Holy See, has all the eloquence simplicity can lend. It is powerful hagiography

and brings to a climax the great message latent in Fr. de
Rhodes' unique "travel book": the missionary vocation of the
layman.

There are many things in this book that will make the modern reader smile. Fr. de Rhodes' piety may often appear naive
and overly credulous to many today. He might also be accused of viewing things more in blacks and whites than in
the more modern shades of gray, of promoting unduly material
forms of devotion; but whatever he did, it was suited to his
mission, for *it worked,* and never for one moment did he fall
into a far more grievous error rampant among more sophis-
ticated clerics who came after him: contempt for the religious
vocation of the ordinary man.

He makes a point of the fact that the first person to promote
a mission to this part of the world was not a religious, but the
Portuguese nobleman Ferdinand da Costa who "on returning
to Macao from a trip he had taken to Cochinchina, came to find
our Fathers and told them about what he had seen, and the
excellent likelihood there was of converting that kingdom." He
also cites the layman Philip d'Oliveira as the zealous missionary to Ceylon.

Pious literature tends to picture fervent religious like St.
Francis Xavier dashing off alone ahead of the laity, crucifix in
hand, into a hitherto unpenetrated wilderness of foreigners to
be saved, whereas history clearly shows the exact opposite to be
true. The religious missionary in the past has normally followed, not preceded, the Christian trader and the Christian
soldier into terrain whose avenues have been prepared by the
Holy Spirit working through laymen. As Fr. de Rhodes' own
pages prove, these are the first to carry the faith, like da Costa
bringing the Jesuits.

It would be tedious to enumerate the instances of close co-
operation between religious and laity de Rhodes gives. He deplores French lack of interest in oriental trade, well realizing
the apostolic possibilities this would open up to his compatriots.
It is true that a most regrettable identification of colonial and

ecclesiastical interests developed in the missions, the growing seeds of which can easily be detected in this book, and which reached disastrous proportions by the nineteenth century, but this doesn't mean that laymen as individuals shouldn't normally co-operate with religious in extending the kingdom of God, each in his own sphere, as did Lydia the dye merchant, Simon the tanner, the seamstress Dorcas, and the army officer Cornelius in the days of the Apostles. Who but the laymen Mary and Joseph were first entrusted with the Word on earth and took Him to Egypt?

It remains, however, that the most fervent laity is helpless without a worthy priesthood, and Fr. de Rhodes demonstrates this too between the lines. If his laity was charismatic, so was he. His gift for languages alone is most remarkable, a near gift of tongues. As it stands, his story is the utterance of an extraordinary man in whom we find reconciled the paradoxes existing in the God-driven. He is both enthusiastic and hardheaded, softhearted and ruthless, uncomplicated and shrewd. His optimism and sense of humor never fail. Expecting death by drowning on the king's orders, he limits himself to one drink of water the night before, remarking wryly that he hadn't wanted to overdo things.

Generous and fiery, he has a talent for friendship and personal contact quite beyond the ordinary. He would excel today as a public relations man, a born "publisher" of the Gospel. Withal, he is utterly lovable, weeping shamelessly at all partings and being forever "touched to the heart" by any kindness. On a galley deporting him on one occasion he converts twenty-four of his pagan guards, plus the captain, and eventually takes over the ship. Even in print one is captivated by him. Being a child of his century, he is distinctly pre-ecumenical in his attitudes and speaks his mind on Dutchmen and heretics; yet he finds it the most natural thing in the world to make close personal friends of them, as he does of the Dutch governor of Malacca and his English shipmates. And he has no patience with people who say Moslems can't be converted.

He has a disappointing lack of appreciation for Confucius, whom he regards as a false god, but he is sympathetic to the cult of ancestors and encourages prayers for them. Moderns may gasp a bit at his part in the forcible abduction of fatherless pagan children in order to give them a Christian education, but he firmly believed all the unbaptized go straight to hell, as we are sorry to hear him tell the sorrowing young Vietnamese widow who has just lost her pagan husband. But such was the current conviction in his day.

He was himself descended from converted Spanish Jews called Rueda who came to France from Aragon in the first part of the sixteenth century to engage in the silk trade in Avignon. Thus he was technically not a Frenchman by birth, but a papal subject, for Avignon then still belonged to the Holy See. It seems his father Bernardin and his elder brother Raymond ranked among the nobility of Avignon and that the family had maintained relations with the Society of Jesus for some time, making it most probable that he received his education from the Jesuit Fathers in his native town. At any rate, his younger brother George also took vows and eventually became rector of the theological college in Lyons.

The main facts of de Rhodes' life are best learned from him as he relates them in his own incomparable idiom. The Viet Nam he knew so intimately was not so extensive as at present, but comprised then as now a northern and a southern segment, on opposite sides of the Gianh River: the Xu Bac, or northern kingdom of Tonkin, and the Xu Nam, or southern kingdom of Cochinchina. Southernmost Viet Nam as we know it today was then roughly the kingdom of Champa he speaks of, and part of Cambodia.

He evangelized Tonkin, as he tells us, only from 1627 until his banishment in 1630, after which he never returned. He spent far longer, twelve years in fact, in China; but he mentions his work there only in passing. By his own admission, his heart belongs to Viet Nam, and no doubt still does. His most significant activity was carried on in Cochinchina between the years 1640 and 1645 in the district around Hué and Danang. The latter is the "port of Cham" he calls Kéan, or Cahan, the ancient port of Ke Hán or Cu'a Hán, which the French later dubbed Tourane. The proto-martyr Andrew of Phu-Yen met his death farther south, at a place called Go-Xu in the village of Vinh-Phuoc in Quang-Nam, in the actual parish of Mang-Lang.

All comes to life in Fr. de Rhodes' account. His only fla-grant omission is not telling us that Pope Innocent X tried to make him a bishop on his return to Europe. (He refused.) Nor does he dwell on his hidden role as founder of the French Foreign Missions, which Fénélon ascribed to him publicly thirty years later in a commemorative service. He died in Persia, at Isfahan, in 1660 or 1661, a missionary to the last.

His readers will see that his favorite words were *great, good, beautiful, glorious,* and *immediately.* He was an energetic, prac-tical man with an iron constitution who said all he wanted to say by stringing together as many simple sentences as necessary. It's a standing temptation to his translator to vary his vocabu-lary a bit and improve his syntax considerably, as some later editors, alas, did. This being the case, we learn with some sur-prise of the heavy literary output of this man of action, and even more surprise of its nature.

No doubt building on the work of Portuguese Jesuits in Macao, he was actually responsible for the publication of the first Vietnamese dictionary, with Latin and Portuguese equiva-lents, as he himself tells us, together with a grammar that formed part of it but was distinct from it. The dictionary not only provided future missionaries with an indispensable tool of their trade, but equipped the Vietnamese themselves with the flexible Roman alphabet, thereby giving them a 300-year head start over their neighbors in the Orient who are still shackled with cumbersome Chinese characters in a breakneck world.

He also wrote an admirable catechism in Latin and Viet-namese, divided into eight days of instruction suited to the temper and psychology of the oriental catechumen. Far from being outmoded, it appeared in a new edition in 1961 in honor of the tricentenary of the author's death and is currently in use, a living monument to his genius for practical pedagogy and the fruit of his own solid experience.

In 1650 he published in Rome a *History of Tonkin* designed to awaken zeal for the missions. Five years later he produced the *Relation of What Transpired in the Year 1649*, concerning the Jesuit martyrs in Japan, and subsequently another *Relation* about the Jesuits in Persia. There were other hagiographical works, notably the *Glorious Death of Andrew, Catechist of Cochinchina*, whose martyrdom he recounts briefly in the present volume.

RHODES OF VIET NAM, or *Divers Voyages*, was itself first published in Paris by Sébastien Mabre-Cramoisy in 1653, following on the heels of a shorter version published earlier that year by Florentin Lambert. Later editions appeared in 1666 and perhaps 1688, sadly tampered with by editors seeking to embellish his style. In 1854 Fr. Auguste Carayon, S.J., put out a new edition purporting to reproduce the original faithfully, and Herder published a German translation in 1858.

This English translation was made from the modernized Desclée de Brouwer edition of 1884, which also follows closely the 1653 original. Fully aware that all translation is betrayal, I lay no claims to its being either polished or scholarly. Spellings of a few place names have been modernized and stabilized, but the reader will look in vain for elaborate footnotes. Those interested in tracking down details will, I fear, have to look elsewhere or wait for a better edition. Following the luminous example of its author, I haven't attempted to make a fine book for the curious, but a timely, serviceable one for the devout. It is offered barefoot and lively, as much as possible in the same spirit in which Fr. de Rhodes offered it to readers in his day, to be read adventurously and with the heart.

I wish to thank Fr. André Gélinas, S.J., and the Jesuit Fathers of the Centre Alexandre de Rhodes in Saigon, Viet Nam, who so kindly encouraged my meager talents and supplied my ignorance with much incidental information, plus a portrait of the author—besides lending me a copy of the book to translate from. I wish particularly, however, to thank my husband, Gustav Hertz, whose idea this translation was in the first place, who implacably set me to work on it, and who first borrowed the book from the Jesuits. It so happens that he is at this writing a civilian hostage of Communist guerillas in that same beloved Viet Nam to which Fr. de Rhodes lost his heart and Andrew his head, and to which all three men, each in his own way, wanted to convey such very Good News. To this triad my rendition of RHODES OF VIET NAM is respectfully, lovingly, and gratefully dedicated.

SOLANGE HERTZ

At the "gia dinh" near Leesburg, Virginia
In the time after Pentecost, 1965

Contents

Preface

BY ALEXANDER DE RHODES

After I put out a little summary of my travels, several very worthy persons who took the trouble to read it have urged me to put the whole work before the public, which I took on when I began the synopsis. But I must confess in all honesty I had a hard time making up my mind to it, because I realize that in all these treks I made mistakes at every step, and my mind is so occupied with devising means of getting out of Europe and getting back that neither time nor inclination for reminiscing is left me.

Moreover, inasmuch as the objective I kept before me in my travels was not viewing the wonderful, but rather accomplishing the worthwhile, I took not the slightest pains to notice, nor often even to look at, the great curiosities found in all those places in the world through which I passed or where I stayed. I have always held views far broader and more elevated than those of earth, where, after having seen the better and greater part of it, I find nothing that isn't both pretty piddling and contemptible when compared to the many souls whom Jesus Christ valued, as it were, above His blood, which He poured out to the last drop to save.

I commend the purpose of so many persons of rank who, after traveling in various quarters of the globe, put together fine books in which they relate all the things they have observed and thereby supply those having neither strength nor inclination to leave homes where they are quite comfortable with a means of crossing the seas without danger and finding themselves in all the most beautiful cities of the world without losing one whit of their ease. I admit these books are exceedingly fascinating and that their authors deserve much credit for locking up the rarest things in the world within a volume that can be read in a few days.

Speaking for myself, I admit I'm not the type, nor have I ever had any intention of writing such fine books, nor of getting rich from such commentaries. My sole ambition in my travels has been the glory of my good Captain Jesus Christ and the profit of the souls He conquers. I travelled neither for the sake of riches, nor for knowledge, nor to amuse myself. Through God's mercy I sought no other pearls but those Jesus Christ glories to set in His diadem, no other knowledge but that which St. Paul preached on returning from the third heaven, no other amusement beyond giving joy to the angels by converting not a few sinners.

Therefore, dear reader, don't expect from me all those fine tales told by those highly talented people who tell you about the customs of nations beyond our hemisphere, about land fertility, the whereabouts of towns, the laws of kingdoms. I know that sort of thing satisfies the curious rather than the devout and produces more wonder than edification. What I have to say concerning thirty-five years of travelling deals with the ways of grace in the conversion of souls. These are the triumphs of faith victorious over error, and the establishment of the Church in several more lands where devils were worshiped.

And because I went by way of Rome to China, remaining there several years and returning to Europe by a different route, this little work will have three parts: the voyage, the stay, and the return.

Part 1. The Voyage

1. Departure from Rome by Way of France and Spain

WHEN BY pure grace our Lord called me to join the Company, He gave me at the same time the resolve to leave Europe and go to the Indies. This was my main purpose in choosing this holy Order rather than others, because in it I thought I would find it easier to go to those great lands where so many souls are perishing for want of preachers; and so happily did God guide me in the design with which He inspired me that He caused me to leave my country for Rome at the age of eighteen to take on the livery of the Apostles, entering the Company in that great city where so many martyrs gave birth to the faith by their deaths.

On completing my novitiate, I began laying plans for Japan at the very time the persecution began there. I presented a memorandum to that effect to Reverend Father Claude Acquaviva, our General, then I continued to importune his successor Reverend Father Mutio Vitelleschi throughout my four years of theology, constantly commending the matter to God. And to acquaint myself better with His will, which I took as sole rule for my own, I made a pilgrimage to Loreto, where I wholeheartedly besought the Mother of God to act as my Mother on this occasion and to dispose of me as her exclusive possession. On my return to Rome from Loreto I discovered my holy Lady and Mother had worked powerfully in my favor. The Reverend Father General called me to his quarters on Easter Sunday, 1618, to give me the good news I had so long hoped for. He told me that he had prayed to God a long time to

3

learn whether my desire of going to Japan came from Him, or whether He had other plans; that the more he prayed to God and considered the matter, the more he felt inclined to satisfy me; that I might leave in good time, for he thought God would look after me.

I can never look back on the joyous stirrings I felt at that instant without my heart flooding with consolation. There was hardly any reply I could make except through my eyes, and the tears which ran plentifully for very joy. I threw myself at his feet and thanked him with all my heart for the favor he was according me, and straightway began to prepare for my departure, which was to be in September.

My principal occupation during the ensuing six months was studying mathematics, which has since stood me in good stead. Hardly a day went by that I didn't say Mass in some holy place in that great city, imploring the help of the great saints honored there and begging a share of their spirit.

A few days before leaving, I was privileged to kiss the feet of our Holy Father, the then Paul V, and to receive his blessing. I confess I received very great consolation thereby, for once he learned I was headed for Japan, the Pope gave me extraordinary tokens of affection, and not content with giving me the blessing I had requested of him, gave me of his own accord a very large number of indulgences and told me to go to work in these new lands where I would find so fair a field for winning souls to God, and that he would pray for me. These words of our Lord's Vicar have stuck in my heart ever since, and I credit their efficacy with every success God has bestowed on my meager efforts in those missions.

I therefore left Rome in October of the year 1618 and journeyed overland as far as Lisbon. The first thing I did was return to Loretto to thank the Blessed Virgin for the favor she had granted me, and ask her yet another in accomplishing the work I was undertaking. We were in Milan for the Feast of St. Charles, crossed the ice- and snow-laden Alps without mishap, and by the express order of my superiors I went to Avignon

to see all my relatives. I spent a few days with them, whereupon I bid them adieu, firmly believing we would never see
one another again on earth.

But both going and coming from my native town, I found
myself in danger of ending my travels in the Rhone River.
Coming down from Lyons, I got into a boat with some highly
insolent Calvinists, who began at once to read aloud from a
heretical book that contained a thousand blasphemies against
the sacred mysteries of the Catholic faith, causing these errors
to be heard and this venom tasted by several who were present.
I spoke up immediately and began refuting the false teaching
they were uttering. This made them so angry they wanted to
toss me overboard, and they would have done so if the Catholics
hadn't resisted them. As for me, I didn't offer them any resistance beyond telling them that I would be very much obliged to
them if they were to give me on the spot what I was going to
the ends of the earth to seek; but as for the heresies they wanted
to read, that I would oppose them while I had breath. They
quieted down, and God willed they leave off that evil book.

When I left Avignon, we were supposed to cross the Rhone
by boat to reach Languedoc, but when we got midstream, the
north wind rose so strong it overpowered the combined strength
of the boatmen and drove our skiff against the remains of the
bridge, which had recently collapsed. We all thought this blow
would shatter the boat, which crashed against the stones with
unwonted violence, but God willed it not to sunder, and the
wind carried us forcibly a league's distance with no further
trouble on our part but fearfulness. It was there that several
persons of rank and some of my relatives—who had nearly met
their deaths by taking the trouble to accompany me—bid me
their last farewells with many tears; and having offered thanks
to our Lord, I proceeded blithely on through Languedoc toward Spain, which we crossed in its entirety.

I arrived in Barcelona on Christmas Eve. I went immediately
to Manresa to see the holy grotto that our great patriarch St.
Ignatius had hallowed by his first fervors of devotion. I stayed

there a while, after which we visited the devotional church of Our Lady of Montserrat, and on the first day of the year 1619 we entered Saragossa, capital of Aragon. Among the wonders we beheld there my greatest consolation was seeing that famous column where tradition claims our Lady appeared to St. James during her lifetime and lent him courage for the labors he was undertaking in the conversion of those people, until then idolaters. This column is enclosed by a most beautiful chapel on the banks of the Ebro, and many pilgrims gather there.

From Aragon we passed into Castile, where I avoided entering Madrid lest, being recognized as French at the Spanish court, I be prevented from going on to the Indies. We went by way of Toledo, and after visiting the famous church of Our Lady of Guadalupe, we arrived in Portugal around the middle of January, where out first stopping place was Villa-Viciosa. There we met His Serenity the Duke of Braganza, who indulged us as only a prince can indulge poor religious. Then we went to the royal college of Ebora, and finally to Lisbon toward the end of the month of January, 1619.

2. Our Stay in Lisbon and the Boat Trip to Goa

LISBON is a city so well known throughout Europe that I need say nothing of its size and beauty. Its circumference seems to me to be a little under that of Milan's, but I was told there were a good 40,000 souls there. The harbor is marvelously beautiful, but the approach to it is difficult. There are always large numbers of ships, and what is really magnificent is the quay, which is very long and as well suited to trading as to relaxation. We have four houses in that beautiful city, where our Fathers work most profitably at all the things proper to our

Company, which generally includes anything that might contribute to the salvation of souls.

I stayed there about two months, during which I helped as much as I could all the French who were there in great numbers for commercial reasons. To please me, Fr. Nugno Mascaregnas, whom I had known in Rome while he was there as Assistant for Portugal, insisted that I go see our University of Coimbra. I found there an altogether admirable college, and although I have seen many other houses of our Order, I never saw any so magnificent or so well arranged for maintaining order in a religious house as that one. There are sixteen large residential buildings with four lovely courts, without counting the church, which is hardly inferior to Rome's *Gésu;* and besides all that there is the refectory, which easily accommodates 300 religious who ordinarily live at this house. The classroom building is really splendid and isn't included in the sixteen dormitories I mentioned.

Reverend Father Francis Mendoza was rector of this fine academy at the time and lent it luster by the light of his holiness and teaching, to which the wonderful books he compiled bear solid witness. He received me with all the charity one might expect from a saint, and a few days later I returned to Lisbon in time for sailing.

It was the fourth of April of the year 1619 that we left with three fine ships. Ours was called the *Saint Teresa,* boarded by us six Jesuits, three of us priests, and three others who were studying philosophy. Foremost was Fr. Jerome Majorica, a Neapolitan, of whom I shall often speak hereafter as a most illustrious person, one of the best workers we have seen for a long time in the Orient, where he has been laboring without let up for more than thirty-five years and has produced marvelous fruit in Tonkin and Cochinchina. The second was Fr. Diego Mursius, who after a few years died as rector of the novitiate in Goa. I was the third. Two others were Portuguese, and one Italian.

And so we began this long voyage in high spirits, but after

a few days the storm grew so violent we were losing hope of getting through it. And actually one of our ships was forced to turn back to port, because the wind splintered its mast. The other left us, carried off by gales that forced it to follow another course. We alone remained, and God willed the tempest to subside eventually; and escorted by our good angels, we proceeded gaily on over the waters, several hundred leagues removed from land, seeing nothing but the heavens that guided us and the waters over which we traveled.

Our main concern was to see to it that God was served on shipboard and sin outlawed. Every day at least one of us said Mass, provided there was no storm to prevent us. After dinner we always gave a long catechetical instruction attended by all; and even the Captain of the ship, Francis de Lirea, a person of high rank and great influence in Portugal, was the first one there and took great care that none dispense himself unless he was very busy elsewhere. We sought to ingratiate ourselves with that enormous troop of 400 people by treating everyone with kindness. We comforted them in their illnesses and rendered them assistance in their every need.

Our ship seemed like a floating monastery, and God granted that all be well ordered on it. One heard there neither swearing, nor quarrelling, nor dissolute speech. Several went to confession often, and during the six-month trip we distributed general Communion to those who were with us on the principal feasts as they occurred. On Corpus Christi we carried the Blessed Sacrament in procession on a large platform that was on the deck of the ship, which provided great consolation to all who had never seen processions take place at sea!

We made a big holiday of the Feast of St. Anthony of Padua on board. The morning was spent in devotions. In the evening we planned to hold some games in honor of this great saint, who was very dear to the Portuguese, but an accident occurred that distressed us very much. One of our soldiers, a very decent fellow who had just gone to confession that day in honor of his patron (his name was Anthony Francis), came so close to the rail at nightfall that he tripped and fell into the sea, and we were never able to rescue him or give him any spiritual help. We didn't even know he had fallen in. His greatest good fortune was that he had put himself in good condition a few hours before, which was a consolation to us and gave us occasion to exhort the others always to be ready to settle their accounts with God. Several drew profit from it and urged us to hear their confessions.

When we crossed the Equator, the winds abandoned us completely, and we were left in such great heat that even sitting still our perspiration turned us all to water. We had to suffer this discomfort twenty-five days. Of the four times I've crossed the Equator, only the first time was I uncomfortable. The three other times we hardly bothered to keep the sun off our heads because we had winds to relieve us.

After three and a half months of sailing, we arrived safely in sight of the Cape of Good Hope, around July 20. We were a good twenty leagues' distance from land and rounded it without mishap. All three of us said Mass in thanksgiving for having skirted this danger, considering our arrival in India already certain.

But our hope was soon changed into foreboding, near despair of ever seeing Goa, for on the twenty-fifth of July a storm so violent and prolonged arose that we never thought of anything but heaven. The waves battered us with such force we were kept practically buried in water. We did not, however, lose our confidence in God and the glorious Virgin, but we nevertheless redoubled our prayers, which through God's goodness were answered after eighteen days of storm. On the Feast of St. Clare the clouds, still very heavy, disappeared in the morning, the air cleared, the sea subsided, and the wind changed in our favor, which obliged us all to realize that the good Lord whom storms obey had had a hand in it.

Hardly had we escaped this danger before we fell into another no less great. We were in the wide channel that separates Madagascar (which we call St. Lawrence Island) from the

African mainland. Here and there at this point, there are numerous reefs and sand banks through which one must thread so skillfully as always to keep in the middle. If you go too far to one side or the other you're sure to run aground and perish. Those nearer the African coast are called the reefs of Sofala, whereas those by Madagascar are called the Judean reefs.

Our pilot had made a mistake, and trying to move away from the former, brought the ship too close to the latter. What alerted us to the danger we were in was that we saw practically on the surface of the water certain big fish called *tuberons* [sharks], which are never found any place where the water is deep. A sounding was taken revealing only twenty fathoms of water, which scared us all, and soon after we found only twelve, which led us to believe we would run aground in short order; but God willed the wind to blow so fair that once the prow was turned to port we escaped danger and went on our way quite uneventfully from then on.

But when the sea ceased vexing us, a contagious disease broke out on board and gave us much cause for practicing patience and charity. For five months God had granted us to be free of troublesome diseases, but from the outset of the sixth month we saw a great number of those plagues called scurvy and which the Portuguese call *loanda*. It's a strange sickness that putrefies the members of the body and particularly swells the lips and the whole mouth so horribly that they rot away. It's caused by the sea air and especially by a regular diet of salt meat.

Many soldiers and sailors were stricken. We assisted them with all the spiritual and corporal remedies available to us in a situation where we lacked everything, if not courage. Out of so many patients we lost only five, who died during the last five days of the trip, which lasted six months and five days. The havoc promised to be much greater, but God willed to bring us to the harbor we so longed for, where we forgot all our troubles. We came alongside at Goa on October 9, 1619, the Feast of St.

Denis, Apostle of the French, whom I've taken as my special protector in all my travels since.

❧ 3. Sojourn in Goa

GOA is a most beautiful city on the Indian Ocean, held by the Portuguese. It is situated in the Torrid Zone, fifteen degrees off the Equator, but that doesn't mean it doesn't have a very healthy climate and isn't filled with all the delights of Europe plus many more of its own. It is surrounded partly by the sea, partly by a river that encircles it like an island within an area three leagues in circumference which is marvelously secure and pleasant. It compares with our finest cities. Its size is about that of Lyons or Rouen. The walls are as solid as any fortifications built according to regulations, and there is a well garrisoned fort. The buildings are magnificent, and especially the churches, which are large and very beautifully appointed.

But nothing surpasses the harbor in beauty, which is wide and quite safe for all types of vessels. They come here from all over the Indies, from Persia, and from several large islands off the coast. The most costly goods of the Orient are brought in here. The viceroy lives there along with many of the nobility. There are many Portuguese merchants who, after becoming wealthy, prefer living in peace in that land to returning to Portugal, and they end their days there where they began their fortunes.

There is a large body of clergy there under an archbishop who has jurisdiction over all the churches in these parts as far as China, besides many fine monasteries for both men and women.

Our Company has three very fine houses there, filled with religious who work incessantly for the good of souls, and a large pool of reserves from which are drawn laborers for all the kingdoms of the Orient. It was there the great Apostle of the Indies St. Francis Xavier began his conquests, filling all those countries with Christians and all heaven with saints. He is credited with having baptized at least 3,000 to 4,000 persons with his own hand. We learn from one of his letters that in one year alone he baptized 100,000. Within 10 years he had journeyed and preached Jesus Christ over 300 kingdoms. The glorious deeds of his lifetime surpass anything that has ever been heard of, and the miracles he performed before and after his death are so numerous they can scarcely be counted. At any rate, we know twenty-eight dead were revived through his prayers, and as I write this I receive a letter from Rome assuring me that one of our Fathers in the kingdom of Naples, while on a mission last April, carried a picture of this great saint whereby God performed over 250 well-attested miracles, which we are promised to see published soon.

By the grace of God the spirit of this great saint is found in all the houses of this Company, but in the house of the professed members in Goa we have his holy body, still entire and fresh as if he were still alive. Pope Paul V evinced a desire to see the arm so often wearied in baptizing new Christians, but when he saw him thus whole, it grieved him to think of somehow cruelly severing this precious relic from the rest of his body.

He is encased reclining at full length in a silver reliquary. The venerable face can be seen, and as far down as the chest, through a large glass pane; and the devotion of people coming from all directions honors this great saint by all kinds of vows and beautiful offerings, but the graces the saint obtains for them makes them richer still, all the while they part so liberally with their goods.

There are still some pagans in the city and its vicinity whose conversion is still being worked for, but I can't gloss over two things that caused me acute distress when I found myself in

that district, and which to my way of thinking abets the ob-
duracy of the infidels to no small degree—concerning which I
well know I myself have often had trouble making explana-
tions to them. I saw that ordinarily much honor and kindness
are shown those who are still pagans, and then after they're
baptized they don't even rate a glance. And what's more, when
they become converts, they are forced to give up their native
dress, worn by all pagans. One can hardly believe how hard it
is for them, and I don't know why they are asked a thing our
Lord doesn't ask of them and that furthermore keeps them
from Baptism and heaven. For my part, I well know that in
China I vigorously resisted those who wanted to oblige new
Christians to cut their long hair, which the men all wear as
long as the women's, and without which they aren't able to
circulate freely about the country, nor have entry into society.
I used to tell them the Gospel obliged them to lop off their
spiritual errors, but not their long hair!

I can't tell the joy the Fathers displayed on our arrival
in Goa, and the kindness they showed us. After a few days'
rest, I began thinking of the trip to Japan, but our superiors
thought it wise to keep me working in Goa for a while until
the persecution of Christians in Japan quieted down a little. My
house chore was learning the Kanarese language, which is
spoken on the island and roundabout Goa.

But the worthiest project we engaged in was hunting up
pagan children who had lost their fathers. The kings of Portugal gave proof of their piety by reserving to themselves over
the heathen the right to take young orphans and baptize them,
and then placing them somewhere to be instructed in the Christian religion until they reached an age capable of voicing their
preferences. There is a large receiving home for that purpose in
Goa, of which our Fathers are in charge, and the fruit is very
great.

And inasmuch as these little innocents are often hidden, it's a
lot of trouble to find them. We went about searching everywhere, and we would get information from our friends as to

how to ferret out the quarry being concealed from us. I found seven in one house alone, whom I brought to our seminary. The mother herself insisted on following us both into town and to Baptism. On the Feast of the Conversion of St. Paul, the Baptisms were solemnized, as is done annually, and 600 were baptized, which proved to be fairly successful hunting.

🙢 *4*. Mission to Salsette

AFTER I had been in Goa about three months, God sent me a serious illness that brought me to death's door. I don't know whether it was the climate in Goa that didn't agree with me, or the sufferings we endured on the long trip over. At first the doctors thought I would hardly recover, but God wished to give me time to do penance and restored my health after a few months.

Nevertheless, to get me back on my feet our superiors, ever full of charity, deemed it advisable to send me to a neighboring island called Salsette, where the climate was very good and where our Fathers have a college that renders much service to the local inhabitants. It's there that Reverend Father Rudolph Acquaviva,* along with four other religious of the Company, suffered a glorious death in the battle of Jesus Christ in the year 1583 on July 15.** I don't know whether it was that blood shed in so good a cause that conferred a blessing on the whole place, but I do know that idols are outlawed there and that all the inhabitants have accepted our holy faith.

It was the Fathers of our Company who cultivated that fine vineyard and won it entirely to Jesus Christ. I've been told that

---

* Nephew of the famous Father General. (TR.)
** Rudolph Acquaviva and three companions were beatified by Leo XIII.

out of 100,000 inhabitants, not one remains who isn't a Christian. This was accomplished little by little, and our Lord so blessed the efforts of those good workers that Msgr. Christopher de Saa, Archbishop of Goa and Primate of the Indies, in the course of two visits to that beautiful island at three year intervals, gave this fine tribute to the virtue of our Fathers: that the first time he visited that Church there were 50,000 exceedingly well-instructed Christians, and on returning three years later he found 70,000; and things have gone on increasing ever since to the point that error finally gave way before truth, and the devils relinquished their position to the true God, who is now worshipped over the whole island.

Among other persons of note I ran across at the house of the Fathers of the Company, I was happy to make the acquaintance of Reverend Father Stephen Crucius, a Frenchman by birth who after spending his youth in Portugal was received into our Company and later sent to India, where he labored many years so profitably that he was considered one of the foremost personages of all India. He had learned the two native languages so perfectly—Kanarese, the vulgar tongue; and Mahrati—that he spoke them even better than the natives and published several books in both one and the other that are highly rated by all; and I saw an exceedingly fine poem on our Lord's Passion that the Christians sang in church every Friday evening during Lent; and the service lasted a large part of the night, with a gathering so large that ordinarily 10,000 to 12,000 men came even from Goa to attend this beautiful service.

But the reputation the good Father earned by his virtue far exceeded that earned by his fine mind. Both our Fathers and outsiders considered him a great saint. He was connected with several missions, and he held all the most honorable offices, wherein he always displayed a truly apostolic spirit, and finally in his old age he came to end his days among the neophytes, who all looked to him as their father.

I stayed three months with the good Fathers, among whom I tried to be of service to my neighbor. It was there I learned Kanarese, in which I developed such fluency that I was judged capable of hearing confessions and preaching.

ᘉ 5. The Return to Goa, up to the Departure for China

AFTER THREE months' stay in Salsette I was recalled to our professed house in Goa, where I was employed in the prisons, the convict ships, and in instructing all the Portuguese slaves.

But a mishap occurred in one of the prisons that distressed me very much, all the while bringing home to me God's providence in my regard. I was in the habit of going every Sunday to a prison set aside for those condemned to labor in the gunpowder works. I don't know why, but instead of going there Sunday I went there on Saturday. I gave a talk, after which I was surprised to have several request confession, and they did so with many tears. Neither they nor I knew whither this grace of God's was to lead, but God had His plans. The next day, around two o'clock on Sunday, precisely at the time I usually went there, it happened that through a prisoner's negligence a spark fell on the powder, which was on hand in quantity. It was touched off with such great violence that not only the prison and several neighboring houses were blown up, but even the big tower of the fort toppled over. One could see large sections of wall being thrown up with such force that they fell at a considerable distance and killed several people who were in a main square of town. It's said that many people there were badly knocked out.

The noise was so awful, one would have thought the whole

town was going to crumble, and although very far away, even our church was shaken by it. All our Fathers ran to the scene of the disaster to render assistance to the souls and bodies of those still living. All through the streets and particularly in the big square called *Mondoui,* we found heads, arms, legs, and half-living bodies. Our first thought was for the salvation of souls. We heard the confessions of many who were dying and baptized several pagans who were in the same state. Thereupon we arranged for transportation and carried those poor victims still alive to the hospital on our shoulders.

There was half of a house that seemed likely to fall in any minute, in which there was a poor old woman no one dared go rescue. One of our Fathers went in without regard for the danger threatening him, helped the good woman, and happily emerged just before the house caved in. All those killed were natives of Goa, with the exception of one Portuguese who had gone out into the countryside, where he was being carried on a stretcher. A fragment of a large stone happened to cross his path, and it struck him so hard in the side he died of it a few days later. As soon as he knew he was wounded he ordered his servants to take him to our house for confession. Our Fathers, seeing the stretcher come in, assumed it was I who was killed or wounded, knowing it was my day for going to the prison, but God had willed that I go a day ahead in order to save the souls of those who went to confession and to preserve me from that misfortune.

During the time I was in Goa, in 1621, we received the most welcome news of the beatification of St. Francis Xavier. Our Fathers wished to render their holy patron all the honor this great occasion called for. They had his holy body in its entirety transported in solemn procession, as I have said, from the former church where he had lain till then, called St. Paul's, to the beautiful church of the professed house where he was placed in the magnificent tomb prepared for him to the right of the main altar, where he lies to this day.

❦ 6. Departure from Goa, by Way of Cochin and the Pearl Fisheries

AFTER A stay of two and a half years, partly in Goa, partly in Salsette, I finally received the good news of my departure for Japan. I set sail the twelfth of April of the year 1622 with a Portuguese nobleman who was going to assume command of the fort in Malacca. Within a few days we got as far as Cochin, which is only about 100 leagues from Goa. It's a fairly large town and highly commercial, especially in pepper, which is found there in quantity. The harbor is very accessible, the churches very beautiful. We have a college there where all subjects are taught. It's the best in Malabar province, located ten leagues from Cranganore.

Our Fathers greeted me there with great charity and wanted to keep me until the departure of the Portuguese captain, who wanted to spend the winter in Cochin, thinking it impossible to reach Malacca in that season; but he stayed forever, for he died there, and while waiting for a chance to get away, he had to leave for heaven—as I trust he did, for he was a very good Christian.

I didn't judge it advisable to interrupt my trip by waiting so long. I took another ship on which I was promised to be taken to Malacca despite the bad time of year, but we were hardly out of the Cochin harbor before we witnessed that marvel related in so many books: Situated at Cape Comorin there is a mountain called *Mt. Gaté*,* which at one and the same time has winter on one side and summer on the other. We experienced to our cost how true this was, for at the spot nearest Cochin we ran into winds so violent and a storm so fierce that

* The "Mountain of the Healing Herbs," the tip of the Western Ghats. (TR.)

for thirteen whole days we considered ourselves as good as gone; but God granted us this favor in order to deliver fifty persons who, being till then infidels, asked for holy Baptism in the face of apparently certain death. I instructed them quickly and then administered Baptism to them, which they received with great devotion, and they were very good Christians thereafter.

Nevertheless, the sea didn't subside, and the wind drove us so hard we could neither advance nor retreat, but after the thirteenth day we finally rounded Cape Comorin, and suddenly we enjoyed balmy weather, a gentle breeze, and a very calm sea. This made us hug the Cape, and to avoid the storms on the open sea we headed for the Fisheries coast instead of going straight to Ceylon. Located there are the famous fisheries for the pearls drawn so plentifully from these waters. The natives know the right time of year for finding these beautiful heavenly tears, which are harvested and hardened in oysters. It's then divers put out to sea in boats. One of them dives in fastened to a rope running under his armpits, his mouth filled with oil, and a sack hung around his neck. He goes to the bottom and picks up whatever oysters he finds. He puts them in the sack, and when he can't hold his breath any longer, he gives a signal, pulling the rope to which he is tied. Those who are in the boat draw him up immediately, the oysters in the sack are opened, and usually a good many pearls are found.

Those divers are such good Christians they usually come to church after they've done fishing and often lay big fistfuls of pearls on the altar. I was shown among others a chasuble that was covered with them, and in that country its worth was reckoned at 200,000 crowns. I leave you to imagine what it would be worth in Europe.

The principal point along that coast is called Tuticorin, where the most beautiful pearls in the Orient are said to be found. The Portuguese have a fort there, and our Fathers a very fine college dating from the days of St. Francis Xavier, who was the founder of that Christian community and fished there for so many souls, which are the real pearls in Jesus Christ's crown. It later happened, I don't know by what misfortune, that this house was taken from the Company, and it is said that after our Fathers left, neither oysters nor pearls were to be found at that spot anywhere, but as soon as the king of Portugal ordered the house restored to us the pearls were seen to reappear, as if God had wanted to say that as long as fishers of souls were absent, good fishing could hardly be expected on that coast.

And so after fifteen days' sailing we arrived at the harbor of Tuticorin where our Fathers, seeing us so tempest-tossed and weary, received us with extraordinary kindness. But our stay was very brief. After a day's rest we continued on our way in a skiff in which we crossed the breadth of the channel lying between the island of Ceylon and the mainland. There are very dangerous reefs there, called Chilaw, through which our boat took us quite safely.

7. Our Arrival in Ceylon and the Kingdom of Negapatam

LEAVING THE fisheries behind, we went on toward the island of Mannar, which is a tiny one between Ceylon and the coast, but abounding in exceedingly good Christians whom our Fathers shepherd and instruct with great care. We were invited to put in there, but confined ourselves to merely greeting them, so as to push on to the kingdom of Jaffna, which is at the far end of the island of Ceylon.

This is the island so famous for its cinnamon, which Europe values so highly. I found it to be a shrubby little tree putting out several rather long hard stalks from the ground. It has no fruit other than its bark, which we call cinnamon. Every year these stalks are stripped of their covering, and every year it grows back. Thus it is that God has provided not only for men's necessities, but also for their delectation. The whole island is full of it, and none is found outside this territory. There is enough to make money for the whole country and particularly for the kingdom of Jaffna, which is well stocked with this condiment.

I found there some religious of St. Francis who overlooked no way of showing me kindness. The man in command of the Portuguese fort was Philip d'Oliveira, of a great family in Portugal, but greater still in the virtue and zeal with which he converted the infidels of that whole country. He worked unceasingly and insisted very strongly that I stay there a while until our Fathers from the Malabar country came to help him in this noble work. I told him I could have nothing more at heart than seconding so worthy a cause if I weren't called elsewhere, that those other good workers he had invited would soon arrive and do much better than I.

I was not deceived in my hopes, because our Fathers arrived the next year and worked with the good governor so successfully that they baptized up to 30,000 pagans in very short order in that kingdom alone.

After a few days' stay there I located a suitable ship for going to a strip of coast called Coromandel, where the seaport of Negapatam is situated, held by the Portuguese, who have a quite pretty town with a fortress and a college run by our Fathers. Most important, I found there a magnificent church that the Portuguese built, but a neighboring king heavily endowed it although he was still an idolater, which astonished me greatly. But I was very distressed to see several temples on the outskirts of town where idols were still being worshiped and sacrificed to because the king desired it—who was a benefactor to the churches of the true God but nevertheless still serving devils.

I wanted to go on next to Mylapore, called St. Thomas, which is on the Coromandel coast, eight days' journey from Negapatam. I passionately desired to see the famous tomb of the first Apostle of the Indies, the glorious St. Thomas, where every year can be seen the famous miracle of the stone on which it is claimed the Apostle was pierced by lances. It is said that this stone is ordinarily very white, without any trace of blood, but on his feast day during Mass it reddens bit by bit and becomes soaked with blood, exuding several drops.

It's there that the second Apostle of the Indies, St. Francis Xavier, praying night and day by these holy relics, reached his final decision to go to Japan, where he founded that great Church that has given heaven so many martyrs and has stood firm throughout the longest persecution we know of happening to the Church since the Apostles. I sorely needed to go draw on the spirit of those great saints at that place, but I was assured that if I went I would be obliged to stay six months, because everywhere in these waters the winds change at six-month intervals and those blowing for Mylapore having already started, the others required for the return trip wouldn't appear until six months later.

❦ 8. Our Arrival in Malacca, with Certain Particulars of the City

WE THEREFORE left Negapatam June 24, 1622, on the Feast of St. John the Baptist. Because the season was already far advanced the winds necessary for going to Malacca were beginning to fail us, which delayed us one month and some days at sea, whereas the trip ordinarily takes a fortnight at most.

But even so we had a lot of trouble getting there, and without obvious help from the Blessed Virgin we would have been lost. Coming in sight of the cape called Rachado, quite near Malacca, our vessel ran against a sand bank and stuck fast. We had no hope of extricating ourselves by human help. The pilot was in despair and yelling at the top of his lungs that he was lost. I bolstered his courage and that of all the sailors by telling them that God would help us through the prayers of His holy Mother and that we should all pray, which they devoutly did. As luck would have it I had a hair of the Blessed Virgin in my reliquary. I took it, and fastening it to a length of rope, I dipped it into the sea. It was quite plainly a miracle. Hardly had we said the Our Father and the Hail Mary once when our ship, without any help from any of the crew, after remaining motionless for a long time, emerged from the sand with extreme violence and was driven out to sea. Everyone shouted with joy and astonishment. We kissed one another, and overcome by the grace we had just received, we changed our prayer into a hearty thanksgiving from all of us to the great Queen of the Sea, our most honorable liberatrix.

The next day, July 28, 1622, we came safely alongside at the port of Malacca, where I was obliged to stay nine whole months because the winds necessary for going to China had already died. I'll relate later the work I was set to during that time, which to tell the truth seemed very long to me, but the reader will be pleased to have me speak briefly of what I saw worthy of notice in that famous town.

Malacca is a mainland town opposite the island of Sumatra. It has one of the most beautiful harbors in all the Indies, where one can put in at any time of the year, which isn't the case in Goa, nor Surat, nor Cochin, nor do I know of any other such harbor in the East Indies. Nobody can enter them from the beginning of June until the end of September, because the winds that last these four months render access impossible, besides the fact that the waves bring so much sand into the harbors they are closed up entirely until the October winds blowing from the other side drive all the sand out to sea again and reopen all the harbors.

This inconvenience isn't met with at Malacca's harbor. It is always accessible to incoming ships. Furthermore, trade there is very heavy. It was once called *Aurea-Chersonesus*. Silks and dry goods from China are brought there, and all kinds of food-stuffs and other riches from the Orient. A hundred years or so ago the Portuguese wrested it from the king of the Achinese, and after defeating him many times on land and sea, held it peaceably until the time the Dutch ignominiously drove them out, as I shall tell later.

When I came in I found a most beautiful city, which the Portuguese built, with a fort quite strong and well garrisoned. There were several richly appointed churches where the devotion of the people was admirable. It boasted only five parishes, but monasteries of religious were in far greater number. Our Company's college there was large and filled with several persons of note who did great good to the whole town, to which strangers came from all directions.

9. Various Kinds of Fruit Found in and around Malacca

ALTHOUGH MALACCA is only two degrees from the Equator and consequently it's very hot there, life is very good and the soil produces quantities of fruit, some of which are common to all the Indies. Others are not found outside this territory, which isn't extensive but is nonetheless very fertile.

Of the fruits we have in Europe there are very few, for they have neither apples, nor pears, nor plums. There are grapevines bearing grapes all the year round, but they never ripen well, and the wine made from them sours right away. The reason seems extraordinary, but it is true, and common to the whole Torrid Zone, where by a marvel greater still grapes cannot ripen for lack of heat and sun, which might seem ridiculous, but the reason for it is nevertheless natural.

The sun, shining straight down on the earth in this country, should burn everything up and make the land uninhabitable, as the ancients believed, but they didn't know the secret of Providence, which ordained this country to be the most densely populated in the world—because that's the time when the sun, being so strong, draws up such mists and vapors that this is the country's wintertime. The winds are strong, the rains continuous, which prevents the grapes from ripening because it's from June to September that the sun remains so hidden it can hardly be seen at all. At our house I saw a vine where there were always grapes at three stages, some in flower, some half ripe, and others entirely ripe, as can happen in that land.

I didn't see any of our best European fruits there, but there are so many other kinds that, finding myself once at table where I had been invited, I counted eleven different varieties of very excellent ones that I had never seen nor heard of. There are whole forests of those beautiful palms we call cocos, and which are so well known, because with these trees it is possible to build, fit out, provision and load a ship, as all stories about the Indies relate. But I found one thing wonderful above all others, which few people have noticed. It's that to render these trees really fertile, men must live beneath their branches. I don't know whether it's men's breath that's good for them or whether there is some secret sympathy that nature has concealed from us.

I won't bother to speak of the other fruits found over the rest of the Indies as well—pineapples as at Malacca; *jambis* as big as apples, very good for the health; mangoes, rather like peaches, but they salt them like olives; Indian figs, which last the year round and are longer but less plump than ours. The *carambola* is as big as our biggest plums. The appearance and color are different, but the taste about the same. The *papayas* are like small melons, but they grow on trees and all make their appearance at about the same time.

The finest of all these fruits is the *durian,* which is found only around Malacca. It's as big as our biggest clingstone peaches. It has a very hard husk and inside it's filled with a white liquid, thick and sweet. It's exactly like the *blanc-mange* served at the best tables in France. It's a very healthful thing and the greatest delicacy one could eat.

It would take me too long to tell all the other kinds of things that land produces. I know there are very few flowers, because the sun is too hot there, and I took note of one very special providence of God in the fact that hardly one fruit can be found in the whole Torrid Zone that isn't covered by a tough husk to defend itself against the heat of the sun.

✤10. My Nine Months' Stay in Malacca and My Arrival in China

WHILE WAITING for the proper winds for sailing to China to rise and make sea travel possible for us, our Fathers— who were few in number and had much to do—begged me to help them in their work, which I did very willingly both in town and in the country. In one as in the other we found so much to occupy us that this nine months' stretch never weighed on me.

I was associated with an excellent man, Fr. Gaspar Fereira, a Portuguese who was in charge of converting and instructing the heathen. We were together several months, and God granted us the grace of baptizing 2,000 idolaters. The good Father died later in the kingdom of Bengal, and common report had it that the holy Virgin came to see him and console him at his death.

The one who was rector at our college in Malacca while I was there was called Fr. Diego Rebellus, a man of very high virtue. At the same time, Fr. Pedro Gomez, taking leave of him and embracing him as he left for Bengal, told him, "I leave you now, good Father, to go where my superiors send me, but know that in a few months we are both due to find ourselves on a beautiful road on which we shall see each other and enjoy

very great consolation." What the good Father predicted shortly
came to pass. Both died on the first day of the year 1623, one
in Malacca and the other in Bengal, which leads us to believe
that the prophecy was completely fulfilled and that these two
good Fathers went to heaven in each other's company.

At that same time, Reverend Father Julius Caesar Margico
arrived from Macao and brought the good news of the victory
won by the Portuguese over the Dutch, who had come to attack
Macao with a powerful army, which the Portuguese had utterly
routed and put to flight after capturing the cannon and killing
many of these great enemies of the faith in the Orient. This
news marvelously cheered the whole Indies. Large bonfires
were lit for the occasion and general processions held in thanksgiving for so great a blessing.

Some time later the valiant Fr. Margico went to the kingdom
of Siam to preach our holy faith, which he did with such great
success that he won the king's heart, made friends of the chief
men of the kingdom, and founded a fine church. Some Spanish
soldiers who happened to be at that court at the time hampered the progress of the holy Gospel and irritated the king by
some serious treachery they perpetrated, but it served their purpose badly. They were taken by surprise and punished as they
deserved, but the king, who until now had favored the Christians, became their enemy, although he well recognized the
innocence of Fr. Margico, who didn't desist from his task of
preaching Jesus Christ until a bad Christian whom the good
Father had often rebuked for his evil life accused him before
the pagans, and after having him put in prison with irons on
his feet, gave him some poison that caused him to die within a
few days, destroying in one blow the budding Christian community the great servant of God had begun.

Finally, after waiting nine months for the proper time to
wend our way to China, Reverend Father Anthony Cardim and
I boarded a stout ship on its way to Macao. The trip took
only a month, but we narrowly escaped a great danger of being
taken by the Dutch. We ran into four of their ships along the

coast of Champa* that pursued us at a lively pace. We could never have escaped if night hadn't happily fallen, which gave us time to retreat to cover in the harbor of a small island we had already passed. That served us well because the Dutch, thinking we had gone on ahead toward China, followed us along that route, where they had no chance of ever meeting up with us. I attributed this good fortune to the intercession of St. Anthony of Padua, to whom we had recourse in a danger promising us little hope of escape.

We crossed without incident the whole breadth of the China Sea and the Gulf of Hainan, which I have since crossed fifteen times, and that often in great peril because of the heavy storms that are usual in that area where there is so large a number of islands, estimated at some 2,000. God gave us very good sailing. Finally, on May 29 of the year 1623 we reached the port of Macao in China, four and a half years after my departure from Europe. Think what a consolation it was to find myself in that great kingdom for which I had yearned so long!

❧ 11. Certain Particulars on the Kingdom of China

IN THE wake of so many able authors who have written at length on the beauties of the kingdom of China, which is without doubt the largest and in my opinion the richest in the world, it would be superfluous to write about it here at length. Still, my stay of over twelve years there and the uncommon rarities of that beautiful country would oblige me to say something of what I saw of its size, its wealth, and its culture.

---

* The region immediately south of Cochinchina, between Cape Varella and Phanthiet. (TR.)

China extends from the eighteenth parallel to the forty-eighth, so the temperature varies greatly, for some places lie in the Torrid Zone and the more remote lands fall well into the Temperate. It is divided into fifteen provinces, each of which, to tell the truth, is a fairly large kingdom. Also, the enormous size of their country and the abundance of goods they have there has made them so presumptuous they are persuaded that China is everything most beautiful in the whole earth, and they are very much surprised when they see our world maps where their kingdom appears so small as compared with the rest of the world. They do quite otherwise, for on their maps they show the world as square and put China in the middle (indeed they call it *Chung-quoc,* which means "middle kingdom"), and paint the sea underneath, in which they scatter a few small islands: one is Europe, another is Africa, another Japan—concerning which we certainly proved to them that they were far less well-informed than we.

The people of this kingdom are so numerous I believe I make no mistake if I say China has twice the population of all Europe. Those who have traveled to the limits of this empire say things that seem unbelievable about the principal cities, which are Peking, Nanking, and Hangchow, where they say there are 4 million souls in each. I won't say anything on the subject because I haven't gone that far into the country; but I saw the city of Canton, which is fourth in China, where I found people beyond counting. It is very large, the streets very wide and always so full of people that I had trouble getting through. And what astonished me most is the fact that the rivers are as densely populated as the solid ground. In this city of Canton there is one a good two leagues in width. I saw it entirely covered by boats whose masts looked like a thick forest, and I judged there were at least 20,000 of them, divided up into streets through which barges go carrying every necessity to those living in these floating houses.

There are estimated to be 250 million souls in China, a conjecture based on a levy from which no one is exempt, not even the king. Everyone pays one *jule,** which is about sixpence, for the maintenance of 700,000 soldiers who guard that famous wall 400 leagues long, counting the mountains that separate China from Tartary. Every year this levy amounts to 250 million *jules,* from which we guess the great number of souls there are in China, of which, alas, I have often figured at least 5 million go to hell every year. Could we sit with folded hands in the face of so great a disgrace to Jesus Christ?

❧ 12. The Wealth of China

THE RICHES of this country are beyond counting. There are several gold mines, a large quantity of beautiful silks from which those beautiful Chinese materials are woven. There is musk in great abundance. The soil is marvelously fertile in everything serving necessity or delight, with the exception of wine, which doesn't thrive there, not exclusively for the reason I alleged when speaking of the Torrid Zone, in which only part of China falls; but we know no other reason but experience, which has shown us that grapes never ripen well there, and that the wine we get from them becomes sour immediately. They have wheat, but they don't bother to make bread of it because rice seems better to them, and speaking for myself, I confess that all the while I was there I no more remembered or felt any concern over bread than I do now over their rice.

Don't think they eat it in soup as we do, nor that it's made into dough as we make bread. They eat it cooked, but in water so well regulated that when it's cooked it ends up dry, and the grains are still whole, but soft, and they say that in one lump

* The *jule* familiar to Fr. de Rhodes was a papal silver piece taking its name from Pope Julius II. (TR.)

they eat several fresh loaves. It seems to me their rice is very much better than ours. It doesn't swell so much and doesn't stuff you. With them the word which means dinner or supper means "to eat rice." They wouldn't think they had eaten if they hadn't had rice as we have bread. From their wheat they make a few cakes that they use as a supplement.

Their ordinary drink is plain water, but hot and cooked in the same pot as the rice. They laugh at us when we tell them we drink water fresh, and they say this causes us many diseases that they don't even know by name. I don't know whether they are mistaken, but I well know that in all the countries of China, Tonkin, and Cochinchina I've been in during the course of thirty years I've never heard tell of gout, the stone, or gravel. Of plague or epidemic disease there is no talk at all, and what is even more marvelous, during that time I never heard tell of any sudden death, but I attribute that more to the healthfulness of the climate and the quality of the foods they eat, which are very salubrious.

13. On the Use of Tea, Which Is Very Common in China

IN MY opinion one of the things that contributes most to the health of these people who so often reach a ripe old age is tea, used very widely throughout the Orient, and which is beginning to be known in France through the medium of the Dutch, who bring it from China and sell it in Paris for thirty francs a pound, which they bought in that country for eight to ten cents; and even so I see that it's usually very stale and spoiled. That's the way our good French folk allow foreigners to grow rich off the East Indian trade, from which they could extract all the world's greatest riches if they had the gumption to engage in it like their neighbors, who have less aptitude for succeeding in it than they do!

Tea is a leaf the size of that of our pomegranate trees. It grows on shrubs similar to myrtle. In the whole world there are only two provinces in China where it is found. The first is Nanking, where the best tea grows, which they call *cha;* the other is the province of Changchow. Harvesting this leaf in these two provinces is done with the same care we take with our grape harvest. It is so plentiful they have enough to supply the rest of China, Japan, Tonkin, Cochinchina, and several other kingdoms where the use of tea is so common that those taking it only three times a day are the more moderate drinkers. Many take it ten or twelve times, or rather all the time.

When the leaf is picked it is dried in ovens, then it is put into tin containers that must be tightly sealed, because if left open to the air it is ruined and has no strength, like wine that has gone flat. I leave you to consider whether our Dutch gentlemen much care about that when they sell it in France. To know whether tea is good, one must see whether it's quite green, bitter, and dry, so as to crumble under one's fingers. If it's all that, it's good; otherwise you can be sure it's not worth much.

Here is the method the Chinese use for serving tea. They boil water in a very clean container. When it's boiling hard they take it off the fire and put this leaf in it in proportion to the amount of water, i.e., a crown's weight of tea to a large glass of water. They cover the container carefully, and when the leaf sinks to the bottom of the water, that's when it's time to drink it, because that's when the tea has imparted its properties to it and has turned it reddish-brown. They drink it as hot as they can. If it gets cold it's of no use. The same leaf which is left in the bottom of the container can be used a second time, but then it is allowed to boil with the water.

The Japanese serve tea differently, for they powder it, then throw it in the boiling water, drinking the whole thing. I don't know whether this way of taking tea is more healthful than the former. I have always used and found satisfactory the one in common use among the Chinese. Both one and the other add a little sugar to the tea to offset its bitterness, which nevertheless doesn't seem to be disagreeable.

The properties of tea are principally three. The first is the cure and prevention of headaches. Speaking for myself, whenever I had migraine I would feel so much relieved on taking tea, it seemed as if some hand completely removed my headache from me, because the greatest effect of tea is overcoming the foul vapors that rise to the head and sicken us. If taken after supper it usually prevents sleep. There are certain people, however, who are put to sleep by tea because, overcoming only the cruder vapors, it leaves those conducive to sleep. As for me, I quite often experienced that whenever I was obliged to hear the confessions of my good Christians all night, as often happened, I only had to take tea at the time I would have gone to bed and I stayed awake all night without being pressed for sleep, and the next day I was as bright as if I had slept as usual. I was able to do this once a week without discomfort. I once tried to keep it up for six nights running, but on the sixth I wound up utterly exhausted.

Tea is good not only for the head; it has wonderful power for relieving the stomach and aiding digestion. Indeed many people habitually take some after dinner. One abstains after supper if one wants to sleep. The third thing tea does is purge the kidneys against gout and gravel, and that may be the real reason why this type of disease isn't found in those lands, as I said before.

I've expatiated a bit in discussing tea because since I've been in France I've had the honor of seeing some persons of high rank and proven worth, whose lives and health are extremely necessary to France, using it with profit, and they have had the kindness to desire me to tell them what my thirty years' experience has taught me of this great remedy.

~~~ **14**. Religion and Customs of China

T HE CHINESE are brilliant, and yet until now they have lived
in darkness and profound ignorance of the most important
thing in life, namely, knowledge of the true God and the proper
way of serving Him. There are three kinds of superstition
among them. The first is that of the king and the nobility, who
adore the material heavens, including the stars. At the doors of
their houses they usually have very tall handsome columns on
which perfumes are burnt every morning, because the smoke
rises to the heavens to which they pay this homage; and some
of the chief cities have at their four corners temples dedicated
to the sky, the sun, the moon, and the earth.

The second kind are idolaters, who adore certain special
deities who were once their kings. There are temples and
many idols among them, but to tell the truth the bonzes aren't
looked up to there as in Japan, nor even in Tonkin and Cochinchina, where they are called *saïs*. One of their false gods is a
certain Confucius who, as I said in my history of Tonkin, gave
them their laws and invented their letters. It's unbelievable how
much respect they have for him. We have trouble persuading
converted Christians not to genuflect before his statues, which
almost all have in their houses; and those who started the rumor
that the Jesuits permit their neophytes this idolatry are very badly
informed. And if they would like to take the trouble the Jesuits
take in going to that end of the world across so many oceans
to make Christians of the Chinese, they would soon see it's
wrong to calumniate the Jesuits, who never consider themselves
more fortunate than when they do good and suffer evil.

The third sect is that of the sorcerers, who are many and
very wicked. These are the ones who have waged the cruellest
war against us in all these kingdoms. I don't wish to repeat what
I have said of them elsewhere, but what delights me in China

is that the Christian religion is beginning to gain a foothold, and I hope that it will shortly drive out all false religions from that beautiful kingdom where there are 120,000 Christians since men of our Company first entered it. Thirty of our Fathers labor there, divided into seventeen residences, but at present there is far greater hope than ever of seeing all China Christian.

All Europe knew the great misfortune that befell this mighty kingdom in the year 1643. A great eunuch, a favorite of the king's, became so powerful he presumed to make himself king, and despite the fealty he owed his prince and benefactor, took possession of all the chief strongholds. Fearing to find himself at the rebel's mercy, the king followed a course of action unworthy of his rank: he put his children to death and then hanged himself and his wife. Having proved himself the stronger, the tyrant soon accomplished his evil ends, but the Chinese, unable to endure the shame of having a valet and a criminal as their king, decided to ask help of the Tartar, who didn't wait to be asked twice.

He seized the opportunity offered him in being granted free passage through the wall. He entered China with 400,000 men and 50,000 horses. First he drove out the eunuch, who has never been seen since; but after expelling one tyrant, the Tartars became so themselves. They found China much more worthwhile than their own country. They made themselves masters there and occupied fourteen out of fifteen provinces. The more courageous Chinese made a member of the same family as the lately deceased monarch their king, who with the assistance of a very brave general of the army, but a very good Christian, called Achilles, recovered seven or eight provinces. He became sympathetic to the Christian religion and on the advice of the good Achilles permitted his mother, his wife, and his eldest son to be baptized. Just recently I received word that the king himself has requested Baptism. This is what leads us to hope that all China will soon be worshiping Jesus Christ and will expel all the devils it has honored till now.

Up to the present all deference has been given to literature in this mighty kingdom, and the military profession has been devoid of honor. Everyone is aware of the great formality with which they hold examinations for the doctorate; but actually, to tell the truth, I find their scholarship quite confused compared to that of our European men of learning. They spend almost all their lives learning to read, and even then they don't know all they should. Because they have 80,000 characters, that is to say, as many as there are words, no one knows them all. To learn an adequate number of them our Fathers devote four years of study, with the same application as necessary for learning the whole theology course. I leave open to consideration whether this is very congenial to men whose minds are full of the great arts and sciences of Europe; but the desire of converting souls renders this labor very sweet.

All Chinese men wear their hair long and dress it, as do the women. They groom their hair with such care, they would as soon have their heads cut off as their locks. It is true that the women never go out, and their feet are so small they can't walk without support. When I returned to Europe I brought back some of their shoes, which are so small I find it hard to get two fingers into them.

15. My Year's Stay in Macao, a Chinese City Held by the Portuguese

ON MY arrival in this beautiful kingdom my first stop was Macao, where I was detained a year, during which I bent my every effort toward familiarizing myself with the language of Japan, where I proposed to go as soon as possible.

Macao is a seaport town in China that the Portuguese built and fortified with the permission of the king of China, to whom they pay 22,000 crowns tribute every year. It has been

100 years or so that this permission was granted. One of the chief founders was the valiant Peter Veillo who by his charity deserved to have St. Francis Xavier promise him he would know the date of his death. This was a strip of land near the sea to which certain pirates had retired and were making numerour raids in the province of Canton, which is the closest to the sea. In order to rid themselves of these robbers the Chinese called the Portuguese to their aid and allowed them to hold the position if they could drive these bad neighbors away. The Portuguese, who wanted nothing better than to set foot in China, sallied in force against this gang of thieves, easily drove them out, and began to build with the permission given them by the Chinese—without erecting fortifications there, however, because this was expressly forbidden by the treaty they had made. But some time later the Dutch attacked them in an effort to drive them out and would have done so without fail if God hadn't fought for the Portuguese, throwing a kind of panicky terror into the Dutch, who on hearing a few shots from a small cannon fired at random and rather as a last resort in holding the position, retreated in haste. But the Portuguese pursued them so effectively they cut them to pieces, whereupon they seized this opportunity of fortifying the position they had been granted, saying they couldn't maintain themselves there any longer if they weren't allowed to put themselves in condition to withstand their enemies.

They received permission and established a very good position where they installed 200 cannon, and they have lived in security ever since. The town isn't large, but it is beautiful and built in the style of Europe, where building is much better done than in China, where all the houses have only one storey. Trade in Macao has been very brisk, and the Portuguese were growing wealthy in short order, but since the persecution in Japan and the rupture with the Spaniards, who hold the Philippines, they have been left high and dry because it was the commerce with these two islands that was providing them with the best of everything they had.

Our Company has a very large college there, on a par with the finest in Europe. At least the church is among the most magnificent I've ever seen, even in all Italy, with the exception of St. Peter's in Rome. All subjects taught in all our great academies may be studied there. There those great workers are trained who are filling the whole Orient with the light of the Gospel. From there have come so many of the martyrs who are the crown of our province. I call it blessed because its glory stems from the fact that in Japan alone it numbers ninety-seven glorious confessors of the holy Name of Jesus Christ, who have sealed with their blood the fealty they swore to their dear Master.

Part 2. The Stay

Foreword

I NASMUCH AS God changed my original purpose, which had prompted me to leave Europe for Japan, and decreed that I work for several years in two kingdoms adjacent to China—where He established two Churches as flourishing as any our Company has seen in these new worlds, and where so many great men have labored so zealously—I shall speak briefly in this second part of what God gave me grace to see in these kingdoms, where I confess I still have my whole heart. I yearn day and night to return and see once again the host of good Christians I left there, who have the goodness to remember me by tokens of goodwill of which I am not worthy, but which I desire to reciprocate at least as well as I can.

⌘ 16. The Temporal Kingdom of Cochinchina

IT HAS been hardly fifty years that Cochinchina exists as a separate kingdom from Tonkin, a province of which it had been for seven years. The man who first threw off the yoke was the grandfather of the man now ruling. He was the governor sent by the king of Tonkin, whose brother-in-law he was. After living there a while he thought the title of king grander than a governor's, and the rank of sovereign superior to a vassal's. He rebelled against his prince and constituted himself master of the kingdom, wherein he thereafter maintained control by force of arms and left his children a heritage that has been disputed them on several occasions. The Tonkinese have gotten nowhere with them by their frequent offensives, so that at the present time there is apparently no likelihood of the royal power ever being restored to the rightful incumbent.

Cochinchina is in the Torrid Zone, in south China. It lies between the twelfth parallel and the eighteenth. I estimate its length at 100,000 paces, but its width is very much less. It has the China Sea on the east side; on the west, the kingdom of Laos; to the south, that of Champa; to the north, Tonkin. It is divided into six provinces, each having its own governor and its own special legal machinery. The town where the king resides is called Kehue [Hué]. His court there is very grand and the number of lords very large. They are gorgeous in their dress, but their buildings lack magnificence because they build only of wood. They are nevertheless quite comfortable and rather beautiful thanks to the exceedingly well-wrought columns that support them.

The number of people there is very large. Their natural disposition is very gentle, but they are nevertheless good soldiers.

43

They have marvellous respect for the king, who maintains 150 galleys at all times, which he keeps in three different harbors. The Dutch have experienced to their hurt how they can successfully attack their large vessels, in which they consider themselves masters of the sea.

Their religion is the same as that of China, of which they at one time formed part along with Tonkin. They have the same laws and practically the same customs. They have doctors like the Chinese, and the mandarins enjoy great prestige among them, but I find them less proud than the Chinese, more tractable, and much better soldiers.

They are very rich, for the soil is very fertile. It is watered by twenty-four beautiful rivers, which makes water travel marvellously easy, facilitating both commerce and transportation. These rivers overflow regularly every year during the months of November and December, and sometimes there are even three, enriching the soil and fertilizing it. At those times the country can be traversed only by boat. Their houses are so constructed that they can be opened up below to let the water pass through, and for this reason they are always perched on huge stilts.

There are gold mines in Cochinchina, great quantities of pepper that the Chinese come there for, and much silk, which is ordinarily used even for fishing nets and for rigging on the galleys. They have sugar in such abundance they sell it for never more than two cents a pound. They send a great deal of it to Japan, and although it's very good, I find nevertheless that they don't know how to refine it as well as we do. The sugar cane there is very good and is eaten as we eat apples. It can be had for practically nothing.

It's true the soil produces neither wheat, nor wine, nor oil, but one mustn't therefore think that living there is hard. They have things we don't have, which makes their fare no less good than Europe's. It's true they don't use so many varieties of sauces as we do. They are also much healthier for it and are free of many diseases we suffer from, as I said when speaking of China.

Of all the countries in the world, it's only in Cochinchina that the famous tree grows which is called *calambac,** whose wood is so fragrant and that is used in so many medicines. There are three kinds. The most valuable is called *calamba.* Its odor is wonderful. It is used to stimulate the heart and against all kinds of poison. Even in that country it's worth its weight in gold. The other two are *aquilla* and ordinary *calambac,* which are less potent than the first but still produce very good effects.

Also it's only in Cochinchina that certain little birds' nests are found that are put into soups and meat dishes. They are so tasty, they are a delicacy for the greatest lords. They are white as snow. They are found in certain cliffs near the sea, over against the fields where the *calambacs* grow, and none are found outside the area—which led me to believe that the birds who build those nests go suck those trees, and with this sap, perhaps mingled with sea foam, they make their nests, which are so white and taste so good, not when eaten alone, but when cooked with fish or meat.

It's in this country that there's a great number of those trees bearing big sacs full of chestnuts [jack-fruit]. A single one is a load for a man, and God's Providence didn't ordain them to grow on the branches, which couldn't support them, but they spring from the trunk itself. The sac is a very thick covering that must be cut open, and sometimes 500 chestnuts are found inside, very much bigger than ours. But the best part of them is the peel, very white and savory, which is removed before cooking the chestnut.

Pineapples, which are so much appreciated in France, are very common there. This fruit is very much bigger than our ordinary melons, and incomparably better when they are fresh. They grow somewhat like artichokes, to which their leaf is similar. The outer rind is red and yellow, filled with small eyes

* Aloeswood or eagleswood, the tree *aquilaria.* (TR.)

and spines. The inside is very sweet. A man can hardly eat a whole one, but it rather warms than refreshes.

I pass over the other fruit this fertile land bears, such as watermelons, similar to those I saw in Italy; three kinds of oranges, with which ours have nothing in common. Eating them, one would say, is like eating our muscat grapes. And now say that country isn't as good as ours!

17. Concerning the First Preachers Who Entered Cochinchina to Preach the Gospel

IT'S NOT the fertility of the soil that seemed so remarkable to me, but the great fruit that preaching the Gospel produced there in so short a time. I was a witness to it, and I can say after having been sent there five times that I always saw there the blessings of the land of plenty of which David speaks, on which heaven drops its dew, and where all fields produce every fruit in abundance.

The first to have the good fortune to be sent there to proclaim Jesus Christ in that kingdom—where as far as we know He had never been heard of—were Fr. Francis Buzomi, a Neapolitan, the real apostle of Cochinchina who spent himself there entirely, working for twenty years with a fortitude that couldn't be too highly praised. His companion was Fr. Diego Carvalho, a Portuguese who later went to Japan and suffered martyrdom there.

The man responsible for starting this mission was Ferdinand da Costa, a Portuguese lord who on his return to Macao from a trip he had taken to Cochinchina came to find our Fathers and told them about what he had seen and the excellent likelihood there was of converting that kingdom. Immediately after this speech Fr. Buzomi went and threw himself at the feet of his superior to ask permission to go to this beautiful land to which God was calling him. His request was soon granted him. He left at the beginning of the year 1615, arriving there on the Feast of the Chair of St. Peter at Rome, January 18. He bethought himself immediately of building a chapel at the entry to Kéan [now Danang], where his ship brought him on Easter Day. There he said a first solemn Mass and baptized ten new Christians.

From this port he extended his efforts over the whole neighborhood. There were 300 neophytes the first year, for whose greater convenience he built a second church, ministering in one and the other by turns for as long as he was alone. But he got fresh help from Macao with the arrival of Fathers Francis Barrett and Francis de Pina, both indefatigable hard workers who produced wonderful fruit among all these people in a short time.

But the faith was gaining too much ground not to encounter opposition from the devil, who is its chief enemy. There occurred a heavy drought that dashed all hopes of any harvest. The pagans thereupon maintained it was these new sorcerers who came to ruin their land under cover of showing them the way to heaven. In this deluded belief they proceeded to attack our Fathers, drove them out of their churches, and forced them to retire to a wilderness where they lacked everything but the grace of God.

Soon, however, help wasn't lacking either. Fr. Buzomi had won the heart of the governor of the province of Quinhin,* who was very much in the king's favor and consequently enjoyed great prestige throughout the kingdom. When he learned of the bad treatment meted out to his friend, he had him brought immediately to his palace, where he kept him and treated him very well for five weeks and then had a very comfortable house built for him, to which he had him taken in style, mounted on the finest of his elephants. All this fine treatment

---

* Modern Binh-dinh province, whose capital is Quinhon.

didn't prevent the Father from falling ill as a result of the discomforts he had endured in exile. Afraid of losing him, the superiors in Macao recalled him immediately to give him a chance of recuperating. He obeyed unquestioningly, but God willed that he recover his health just as he was on the point of leaving, so he thought no more of anything but work.

It was in the year 1618 that he assumed his first charge in the province of Quinhin, where he took Fr. Francis de Pina, and the two of them together set themselves to founding a new church, but it wasn't left in peace for long. With diabolic malice the pagans broke the arms and legs of several idols and brought them in pieces to the public square, accusing the Christians of having perpetrated the crime. The people believed it at once and stormed the Fathers' house, mistreating some of their servants, who were roughly dragged off to prison. Fr. Buzomi went to the court in secret, and having solidly established his innocence, returned with an order stipulating that the Fathers and the Christians were to be left to live in peace.

Throughout all the following years, 1620, 1621, and 1622, new workers continued to be sent to this lush vineyard that was beginning to spread over the whole kingdom. Fr. Emmanuel Porgez came there. I won't mention the others for fear of taking too long. It suffices to say that they were many and that they all worked with such success that they founded many churches in a short while.

18. How I Was First Sent to Cochinchina

CONTINUALLY PREACHING the holy Gospel, these apostles were filling their nets with so many fish they couldn't draw them in and were clamoring to their superiors in Macao to send some Fathers from that great college to help them; that even if they sent twenty or so, there would still be plenty to keep them busy in this great good fishing.

Seeing the doors to Japan closed, our superiors believed God permitted this misfortune that those to Cochinchina might be opened to the holy Gospel. In the year 1624 they sent Fr. Gabriel de Mattos—who until recently had been at Rome as Procurator for our provinces—as Visitor to the Cochinchina mission, and gave him five Fathers from Europe as associates, of whom I had the honor to be the fifth, and one Japanese who was well versed in Chinese characters.

We left Macao in the month of December of this same year 1624, and within nineteen days we all arrived in Cochinchina eager to do a good job there. We met Fr. de Pina there, who had thoroughly mastered the native language. Entirely different from Chinese, it is used in the kingdoms of Tonkin, Champa, and Cochinchina, and is heard in three other neighboring countries. As for me, I confess to you that when I first arrived in Cochinchina and heard the natives speaking, especially the women, it seemed to me I was listening to birds twittering, and I lost all hope of ever being able to learn it.

All the words are monosyllables, and their meaning is discerned only by the different tones given them as they are pronounced. One single syllable, for instance the one *dai*, denotes twenty-three entirely different things depending on the various ways of pronouncing it, which means one can speak only by singing. I discussed this at greater length in my history of Tonkin, where one can see how difficult it is to learn the language well.

Thus we found Fathers Emmanuel Fernandez and Buzomi currently preaching through interpreters. Only Father Francis de Pina was without one and speaking the language very well, and I noticed that his sermons were far more effective than the others'. This constrained me to devote myself to a serious study of it, distressing as it was, but it seemed to me that the profit would outweigh the pain. I began taking the task to heart.

Every day I was given lessons, which I studied with the same application as I once studied theology in Rome, and God willed that within four months I know enough to hear confessions and within six months to preach in the language of Cochinchina, as I have continued to do for many years since. I would advise all those zealous for coming to our province to convert souls to take this trouble at the outset. I assure them that the fruit produced by presenting our mysteries in their own language is incomparably greater than through an interpreter, who tells them only what he pleases and couldn't speak with the efficacy of words coming from the mouth of a preacher animated by the Holy Spirit.

One who helped me wonderfully was a little native boy who taught me all the different tones of this language in three weeks, and how to pronounce all the words. He didn't understand my language, nor I his, but he was so bright he understood right away everything I wanted to say, and as a matter of fact in this same three weeks he learned to read our letters, to write, and to serve Mass. I was astonished at his quickness of wit and dependable memory. He has since served as catechist for our Fathers and has proved a very good instrument for the honor of God in that Church and in the kingdom of Laos, where he worked with great success for many years. He has such love for me he wanted to bear my name.

Since my return to Europe I had printed in Rome, through the kindness of the gentlemen of the Propagation of the Faith, a Cochinchinese–Latin–Portuguese dictionary, a grammar, and a catechism embodying the method we advocate for presenting our mysteries to pagans. This should be useful to any wishing to come help us preach Jesus Christ in these tongues, which until now have been employed only to honor devils.

19. Some Remarkable Conversions, and Two Royal Edicts against Christians

BY THE year 1625 Christianity had been preached in all the major centers of Cochinchina. There were ten of us religious there who were kept plenty busy, and our labors were in no way burdensome to us, for the Master we were serving showed us visibly that grace was working with us with a success far beyond either our abilities or our expectations.

Some were in the province of Quinhin with Fr. Francis Buzomi, who was a man on fire and whose zeal had already set everything ablaze. I was with the wonderful Fr. Francis de Pina in Cham [Quang-Nam] province, where a great number of idolaters received Baptism. From there we went to the court, and on the way we stayed a while in Hoa [Hué] province, where one of the foremost ladies of the kingdom, a close relative of the king's and much attached to idols, was enlightened by the Holy Spirit on hearing Fr. Pina preach and renounced her errors so sincerely that after being baptized and named Marie Magdalene, she became the mainstay of this whole new Church. Her example and influence were wonderfully instrumental in converting unbelievers and sustaining the faith of those who had already received Baptism.

I saw her constantly the whole time I was in these parts, and I believe that after twenty-eight years she still perseveres in the practice of every Christian virtue. She has a most beautiful chapel in her palace that she continued to maintain through the most severe persecutions, where she is daily at her devotions, and to which she admits all Christians in the province—where she gives orders without fear of contradiction. By her wise admonishments she converted many of the most influential idolaters in the kingdom to our holy faith, among whom even the king's relatives were numbered. She is today still the refuge of all our Fathers, and there is no Christian she wouldn't help in any way she could.*

In the midst of the great success God accorded our labors we suffered two calamities almost simultaneously that would have crushed us had a power greater than that of men not upheld us. The first was the loss of Fr. Pina, one of the captains of our little army. It happened by an accident that stunned us all, in the same year 1625. The good Father was asked to go visit the Portuguese, who had arrived within sight of the port of Cham where their ship lay at anchor. On concluding his visit he got into a boat to return to his flock, but a storm arose with such violence it upset the craft. The Father, finding himself hampered by his cassock, wasn't able to save himself by swimming like the others. He found burial in the waters and later in the tears of every last Christian in the whole country.

Another storm came from the direction of the court. Seeing the Portuguese hadn't come that year with their ships laden as usual, the king easily gave ear to the Christians' enemies, who didn't miss the chance of calumniating them and ruining their reputation in the king's eyes. Among other crimes of which they accused them, the major one was their having no interest in succoring or paying respect to the souls of their departed relatives, saying that ours was a barbarous rule that obliterated all sentiments of gratitude toward parents from the heart, which nature impressed in every one.

What provided the excuse for this ugly talk was the indiscreet zeal of a certain party who with scant prudence had tried to abolish all ceremonies performed in that country for the relief of the departed. I described them at length in my history of Tonkin, and really, although there are a few in

---

* "Madame Marie," matriarch of the South Vietnamese Church, was the Princess Minh-Dú'c, concubine of the fourth rank to Nguyên Hoàng, founder of the Nguyên dynasty. She rose to the position of Vu'o'ng-Thái-Phi, "most honored concubine of the Lord King," and at the time of which Fr. de Rhodes speaks occupied a most exalted position as the Lord's only surviving widow, she having entered his harem at a very early age when he was quite old. (TR.)

which Christians can't indulge without sin, most are quite innocent; and we decided they might be retained without prejudice to religious purity.

And so, persuaded by these evil representations, the king published an edict, first against us, and then against all the Christians in the kingdom. They ordered all our Fathers to quit the churches they had built and to withdraw to the town of Faifo [Hai-Phô], under the pretext that we would find greater security to life and limb there and greater freedom for our ministry. We found a way of warding off the blow by courting the favor of his eldest son, who obtained permission for us to stay in our house 100 days longer so we could hold funeral services for Fr. Pina. In the interval we had time to win the king over and persuade him to change his mind.

We had far greater trouble finding a remedy against the order he had given all his Christian subjects to take off all the images, crosses, and rosaries, that the neophytes habitually wore around their necks. We would never have been able to prevent the enforcement of this edict if God hadn't put a provincial governor on our side who in this instance rendered us all the good services we might have expected from one of our best Christians, who had the promulgation of the edict postponed, and gave us time to caution our neophytes to keep all emblems well hidden and not wear their rosaries around their necks any more. There were many who were ashamed to pass up this fine opportunity of bearing witness to their faith, and considered it cowardice unworthy of the name of a Christian to conceal the insignia of their profession and the glory of Jesus Christ.

But when we informed them that Christian law forbade us not to be brave, only to be foolhardy, they bowed to our judgment, for which reason the king's edict caused no stir on publication and gave unbelievers no excuse for showing disrespect for the piety of our Christians.

20. How I Was Sent to Tonkin to Preach Jesus Christ, Unknown There Till Then

H ERE IS where I adore with all my heart the loving providence of our Lord, who deigned to use the most miserable and faithless of His servants to make a beginning in one of
the greatest projects undertaken in many centuries. As for me,
I know myself to be unworthy of the great task God entrusted
to me, in order to show that it was He alone who wished to
accomplish it, and I freely confess I have done nothing, but
have only impeded God's work.

I had been in Cochinchina about eighteen months, extremely
gratified to see the number of God's children increasing, when
Fr. Julian Baldinotti of the Company of Jesus was sent from
Macao to another kingdom where up till now none of ours had
ever been, because our Fathers all had their sights set primarily
on Japan. It was to the great kingdom of Tonkin that Fr. Baldinotti went in March of the year 1626, taking the ship that
traded there.

The good Father was filled with zeal and was extremely annoyed at being forced to remain mute in such propitious circumstances through want of knowing the language, which he could
neither speak nor in any way understand. He saw the king,
presented him his modest gifts, and was quite well received at
court. He was struck by the size and beauty of the kingdom and
the natural goodness of the people no less than by their wonderful intelligence. It was then he regretted with all his heart
not having learned the language so as to be able to implant the
faith in ground that seemed so well prepared.

He had to be content with baptizing four little children he
discovered on the point of death. These were the first of that
fine Christian community, going like four advocates to plead

their nation's cause before the throne of God. The good Father, finding himself useless in so great a work for lack of knowing how to speak, wrote urgent letters to our Fathers in Cochinchina, begging and entreating them to take pity on a whole nation that was being lost for want of someone to rescue it from error and set it on the right road. At the same time, he wrote and went in person to Macao to ask them to send him someone as soon as possible who could make himself understood in Tonkin.

In His infinite goodness God ordained that this job be given to me because I wasn't so indispensable to Cochinchina, and the language I had learned caused them to light on me to go give battle to all the idolatry in Tonkin with the weapons of Jesus Christ. I was overjoyed to receive this charge, and I was immediately ready to go where I was being sent. But there was thought to be some danger in going directly to Tonkin from Cochinchina because these two kingdoms were at war, and the king of Tonkin would have taken great umbrage had he known I was coming from his enemy's soil. This forced me to head straight for Macao, so as not to arouse any suspicion on the part of the Tonkinese. I left Cochinchina with this design in July of the year 1626 and left behind so many valiant Fathers in that kingdom, to which I was to return only fourteen years later—as I shall relate after describing briefly the wonderful progress of our holy faith in Tonkin, of which I spoke at much greater length in the history I wrote three years ago.

⁓ 21. The Temporal State of the Kingdom of Tonkin

I WOULD WILLINGLY forego relating all I saw in that mission, inasmuch as I told all I know in another book; nevertheless, I have been advised to give a brief summary here, considering

I've talked about all my voyages, and I'm told that those who haven't read the history of Tonkin would be pleased to learn something about it here.

I don't know how it happened that this beautiful kingdom should be so little known that our geographers in Europe didn't even know its name and hardly mention it on any of their maps where they locate all the countries of the world. They confuse it with Cochinchina and tell what amounts to outright lies about all those countries, often a cause of laughter to people who have been in those parts, whereas those who have learned about the world only through their books consider themselves educated for having pored over these writers' fabrications.

So, Tonkin is a kingdom bordering on China, of which it was a province for 800 years along with Peking and Nanking. It became separated from it as a result of the revolt of a captain who made himself king and entrenched himself so well there that the Chinese were finally forced to make peace with him in consideration of a small tribute paid them every three years.

It is four times larger than Cochinchina and in my opinion as extensive as France. It extends from the eighteenth parallel to the twenty-fourth and consequently lies entirely in the Torrid Zone. It is nevertheless beautiful and fertile, intersected by more than fifty rivers, and it also has the sea on two sides.* The temperature, the floods, the agricultural products, laws, customs, and disposition of its people are entirely the same there as I described in the first chapter of this second part. Also I noted that it has hardly been a century since Cochinchina formed one kingdom with Tonkin.

This state is a true monarchy, yet there are two kings; but one, called Bua [or *Vua*, king], is so in name only. The other, called Chúa [Lord], wields all the power and has absolute jurisdiction over all provinces, with the exception of the doctoral

* Fr. de Rhodes's knowledge of western Cochinchina was evidently sketchy. (TR.)

degrees, which Bua confers at the appointed time, and a certain show of homage that is rendered him at a ceremony taking place at the beginning of every year. Beyond that he makes no appearances and lives shut up in an old palace where he spends his life in idleness while Chúa manages all affairs of peace or war.

The latter is really king now that the usurpation of his predecessors has become a right no one disputes him. I was charmed to see the respect that his subjects all accord him and the alacrity with which they obey him. He has a guard of 50,000 men at all times. Every day 12,000 take up their sentry duty with wonderful precision. All wear the same livery, which the king gives them at the first of the year. When they take the oath of allegiance the usual color is a deep purple, which is also worn by all the doctors, and no one would dare enter the king's presence unless attired in this color.

The soldiers' weapons are muskets, lances, and scimitars, but they never carry more than one type of weapon, which they handle with great dexterity, especially firearms. Nevertheless their cannons are not cast iron, nor the size of ours. One thing I can truthfully say is that in spite of the fact that they are usually together and that in wartime they fight hard against the enemy without sparing their lives, they nevertheless love one another like brothers, and I've never heard tell of a soldier using his weapons to wound a companion.

I must say to my own embarrassment and the shame of us Christians that a Frenchman came to Tonkin and running into a Portuguese who was a friend of his wasn't long in picking a quarrel with him. Our pagan soldiers seeing them both with weapons in hand were amazed at such passion and told me indignantly they had never seen such barbarism. I leave you to consider what they would say if they could see our good fellows in Europe.

Since my return many people have thought I was telling tall tales when I told them, or when they read in my books, that the king of Tonkin always maintained 500 galleys. Or else they thought I was passing off a small boat as a galley, because all European potentates, who have ten times the wealth of the king of Tonkin, could hardly keep 400 of them equipped in all respects.

Everyone is free to believe what he pleases, but I will nevertheless say that by God's grace I don't care for exaggeration and that I hate lying to the point of horror. Still, I'm not sorry for having told what I saw, and on one occasion I very carefully counted 400 galleys in the king of Tonkin's forces, all exceedingly well outfitted, a bit narrower but longer than those I saw not long ago on my return from Rome in the harbor at Genoa and the one at Marseille. It's true these galleys have no galley-crews or convict-gangs like ours. It's not criminals who do the rowing, but soldiers, who make it a point of honor to do so. Furthermore, the king's customary recreation is watching his galleys drilling in the harbor, and the soldiers rowing the most skillfully always receive some reward from their prince's bounty.

The king usually leaves his palace four or five times a month for diversion, but he always keeps with him at least 10,000 to 12,000 men and 300 elephants on which are set beautifully painted or gilded towers. These are the ladies' carriages, which proceed very slowly and can each carry at least ten or twelve. I sometimes saw the king mounted on an elephant and controlling it very gracefully. Except for these amusements, he is continually busy with his affairs of state and never omits giving audiences to his subjects for a single day. Every morning you would see all the great men of the kingdom coming to court with their soldiery to attend the audience, to which they are obliged to come, even though there are many subsidiary judges in every province and even in every village.

22. Concerning Some Special Customs of the Tonkinese

I COULD RELATE many rather curious things about the Tonkinese religion, their courts of justice, commerce, banquets, and marriages, if I cared to retell what I've already written elsewhere. I'll merely touch at random on a few things that seem of consequence to me, by which may be recognized how well this nation is predisposed toward accepting our holy faith.

I noted one custom among them that, it seems to me, might lead us to believe our holy faith had been preached at one time in that kingdom, where nevertheless all memory of it has been obliterated by now. As soon as children are born, I often saw the parents put a crossmark on their foreheads with charcoal or ink. I asked them what good this was to the child and why they daubed this mark on its forehead. "That," they used to tell me, "is to chase away the devil and keep him from harming the child." I immediately rejoined, "But how could that frighten devils, who are spirits?" They admitted to me they knew nothing more about it, but I didn't neglect to disclose its secret to them and explain to them the power of the holy cross. This often served me as a means of converting them.

They have among them the same three types of religion as the Chinese, but the piety they display toward the souls of their relatives surpasses anything we could imagine in Europe. They go to incredible lengths to find suitable places for their tombs. They believe the happiness of the whole family depends on the respect they show the dead. They spare themselves neither trouble nor expense, nor any of their friends', to lay out banquets for them for several days after their decease and every year thereafter on the anniversary of their death, which they do without fail for all their ancestors back to the eighth or even the tenth generation. I say nothing about the other good works they perform to this end, which I related in my history.

When I began preaching, ere the aforementioned king built me the first church, a young lady relative of his who had recently lost her husband, whom she loved very much, heard tell that I recommended prayers for the dead. She summoned me and besought me to tell her whether I had some remedy for the relief of her poor husband who was some months deceased, that she would spare nothing for that purpose, and that I could simply charge her whatever I liked.

I told her in reply that I was obliged by the law I came to proclaim never to lie on any occasion whatsoever, and that concerning the request she was making of me, I couldn't truthfully tell her anything that wouldn't be distressing to her, that I had come to that kingdom to offer a sure remedy to the living, provided they wanted to use it, but that for the departed who had died in error I had no relief to offer them beyond regretting their misfortune.

The good lady answered only with her eyes and by her sighs, without considering conversion, but God ordained that another high-born lady who was present at the interview should reason thus: "If this Father here were lying about what he preaches, surely he would have told this lady he could help her husband. She would have given him a large share of her wealth, and no one could ever prove him guilty of having lied. Inasmuch as he stuck to telling the truth despite so excellent an opportunity of getting rich, one must believe he doesn't deceive concerning the law he preaches and that what he says is true. I intend to follow him and enter into the way of salvation he is pointing out to us." She came to find me not long after, told me all this, and disclosed her decision to me. I began instructing her on the spot and then baptized her in due time, ever wondering at the power of grace and the good inclinations of these people.

In my opinion justice is administered as well there as in any country in the world. It's the king who appoints all the judges, and they are forbidden to accept anything from the litigants in any lawsuit whatever, so that no one may spend anything in defense of his rights. Furthermore, there aren't so many formalities nor so much of the recording that eats up the parties in expense and chicanery. These are utterly unknown among these pagans, whom we call barbarians. I leave you to consider what they might say of us if they knew the conditions obtaining in the palace and all the rules of chicanery.

But I found among them one law that is kept inviolably and that seems to me wonderful above all others. It's that one relative may never bring a lawsuit against another relative that isn't settled in the bosom of the family and with the approval of the relatives. The judge, being a stranger, mustn't know of it. If this were the case among us, three quarters of our lawsuits would be eliminated. There is another law that no lord may ever be governor of the province in which he was born. None of the king's relatives may hold office in the kingdom for fear they might get the urge to make themselves king.

Finally, their marriages take place with very great ceremony and in the presence of the magistrate. All clandestine marriages are forbidden. They may have several wives, but adultery is nonetheless so severely punished that if a woman is convicted of having broken her vows she is invariably punished by death. The punishment inflicted on her is to lead her into a field; she is laid on the ground completely bound; an elephant is commanded to throw her into the air with his trunk, to catch her on his tusks, and finally trample her underfoot.

23. My Arrival in Tonkin and the First Fruits of the Gospel

AND SO it was the twelfth of March that I left Macao, and after eight days' sailing, in the course of which a heavy storm nearly wrecked us, we arrived without mishap at the harbor of Cua Bang, in Sinoa [Thanh Hôa] province on March 19, the feast of the glorious St. Joseph, whom I took for my patron in this great work, and we named the port after him, known since as Port St. Joseph.*

Our ship had no sooner come alongside than we found it besieged by a large number of people who came crowding to see the fine wares it was carrying. I immediately began hawking my own, telling them I had merchandise far more valuable at a cheaper price than any other, that I would give it away free to anyone who wanted it, that it was the true law and the true way to happiness. I delivered a little sermon on the subject, because in their language the one word *dang* means both law and way. God willed that before we even set foot on land two quite shrewd persons be caught in this first cast of the net and decide to receive baptism, which I later administered to them and their entire family.

We stayed at this port a very short while, and every day someone came to the truth God made known to him from hearing our sermons. We were taken to the king, whose mind was entirely taken up with thoughts of war. He was at the head of a fine army of 120,000 men and 400 galleys. The Portuguese paid him their respects and offered him various gifts. I was with them, and I gave him among other things a mechanical clock and an hourglass, but the king didn't have time to look at all that, so eager was he to make war on the king of Cochinchina. He ordered us to await him in Sinoa province, where he kept all his accoutrements and his wives, and provided us a good escort for our protection.

Our stay lasted two months, during which we had ample leisure for filling our Lord's storehouses. We baptized 200 pagans, and the harvest would have been much greater, but on the king's return from battle, in which his army suffered a heavy defeat, we were forced to go along with him. This time, being free of preoccupation, he received us with very good

* South of Haiphong, roughly coinciding with the modern city of Thanh-Hôa.

grace. I presented him a beautiful book on mathematics, heavily gilded, printed in Chinese characters. This provided me matter for a talk on the heavens and the stars, from which I was able to pass easily on to the Lord of heaven. The king listened to me for two hours running although he was very weary from travelling, and declared himself so pleased to have heard tell of our holy faith that he urged me to come to the court often. This first sermon wasn't entirely useless. A ranking lord felt God's touch on hearing it and came to ask me for Baptism.

The king did me the honor of summoning me several times and even of inviting me to eat with him following the native custom, where each one has a table to himself. He had me seated near him and had the kindness to serve me of the best dishes he had. But I was nevertheless in some straits to discover a way of staying on in the country after the Portuguese ship left, because it was due to sail soon. I looked everywhere for a friend who would put in a good word for me, but while everyone was making excuses, God spoke up for me and arranged matters without anyone taking a hand in it.

The king had me summoned to find out from me what the clock and the hourglass were for. On making my first obeisance, I wound the clock and made the hours strike, turning over the hourglass at the same time, telling the king that by the time the sand ran out to the bottom, the clock would strike the next hour. The king thought that wonderful and wanted to see whether I was telling the truth. I withdrew at a distance from the clock for fear I might be thought to be touching it. I began talking about eclipses to pass the time. The king was keeping his eye on the hourglass, and when he saw it nearly run out, he picked it up. "Here it is run out," he said, "and your clock isn't striking." As he says this, the hour strikes as I had predicted. The king was enchanted and told me that if I wanted to live with him a couple of years he would be happy to see me frequently.

"Not just two years, sire," I told him, "but all my life. I would consider myself fortunate to be able to serve so great a prince." He had a galley assigned to me on the spot so as to take me with him. I went along, daily receiving a thousand tokens of his kindness. On the way we had some opportunities of making war on Satan. Of fifty rebels the king had condemned to decapitation, I followed one whom I exhorted to receive Baptism before dying. When he was ready to receive it, I found myself without means of administering it to him because I didn't have any water. As I was in this perplexity in the middle of the field where we were standing, I discovered almost under my feet a little hollow that the preceding night's rain had filled with water. I scooped it up quickly with both hands and I baptized him, whereupon his head was immediately chopped off. I trust his soul went straight to heaven. I ran immediately to the others, but none remained alive. These are the impenetrable secrets of Providence.

24. The Great Strides Made by the Faith in the Kingdom of Tonkin

IT'S TO the glory of the great Father of light that I shall recount the victories that grace carried off over error in a very short time in a kingdom where the devil was making conquests every day, unopposed by anyone. As soon as we arrived in the capital of Tonkin, called Checho [Kè-cho, Hanoi], which is a very large, very beautiful city where the streets are broad, the people numberless, the circumference of the walls at least six leagues around, the king had a house and a lovely church built for me. News of it spread throughout the kingdom, and such crowds gathered that I was forced to preach at least four and more often six times a day.

The fruit was so great I could hardly believe it. A sister of the king and seventeen of his close relatives were baptized. Several famous captains did likewise, and many more soldiers.

Those baptized the first year numbered 1,200; the following year there were 2,000; and the third year 3,500.

Nothing so astonished me as the ease with which I was able to convert the idolatrous priests, who are usually the most obstinate. I found them marvelously open to reason. I baptized 200 of them, who will be of unbelievable help to us in converting the others. One of them alone brought me 500 of those he had disabused of error by teaching them the truths of the faith, and they have since become our most fervent catechists.

They were all delighted when I pointed out to them our religion's conformity to right reason, and admired above all God's Ten Commandments, finding that nothing more reasonable could be uttered or more worthy of being laid down by the Supreme Monarch of the world. My favorite method was to propose to them the immortality of the soul and the after-life. From thence I went on to proofs of the Divinity and then to Providence. Advancing thus from one degree to the next, we arrived at the more difficult mysteries. Experience has shown us that this way of instructing pagans is very practical. I have explained it at length in my *Catechism,* which I divide over the course of eight days, wherein I try to propound all the main truths on which idolaters require instruction.

Besides the interior graces that were at work in this noble endeavor of converting so many people, the constant miracles taking place at the birth of this Church were an important factor in the fortunate results I've been telling about. I say constant, because it's true they were so numerous, our catechists gave up bothering to count them. I know how grievous is the sin of those who counterfeit or relay false miracles, and may God preserve me from committing such, but I can speak truly of what I saw and of what the very people to whom the things happened told me.

By means of the holy cross and holy water, those good Christians drove away devils as a matter of course and cured all sorts of diseases. By giving them four or five drops of this sacred water to drink, they cured some blind people and even brought two dead people back to life. One pagan lord with a Christian wife came to beg me to send some of my Christians to a little town belonging to him, where several of his subjects were very sick and where someone succumbed every day. I sent six catechists there, and admonished them above all to accept absolutely nothing of whatever people might want to give them in return for any cures that might be effected.

They started out weapons in hand for making war on the devil, who was held to be the cause of these ailments. These were the cross, holy water, blessed palms, holy candles, and pictures of the Virgin that I had given them at Baptism. They went, planting crosses at the entrance, the middle, and the end of town, and visited the sick, saying a prayer and giving them a few drops of holy water to drink. In less than a week's time they cured 272 sick people. Wind of it spread throughout the kingdom. The lord of the place came to thank me with many tears. This heartened the Christians greatly, and many pagans were thereby convinced of their errors.

But there befell a sad accident that caused us both pain and edification. One of the Christians who had gone to that town and had been the leader of the others died a few days after his return, and I learned from their mouth that he had not heeded the warning I had given him to take nothing for any favors God might bestow through his prayers. He had taken a beautiful damask robe that the lord had given him. When I heard that I feared that God had chastised him like Giezi, who hadn't obeyed Eliseus. This gave me cause to deliver a sound warning to the others to be careful and never allow themselves to give in to desires for earthly goods.

A most virtuous Christian woman called Benedicta, mother of a young man only recently baptized and named Benedict, died in my absence and therefore without confession. Her poor son, very grieved over the death of his mother, was inconsolable about her having died without confession. While drowning in tears, bewailing this double misfortune, finally, by an interior motion of the Spirit of God, he begs several Christians who had come to comfort him to give themselves the prayer beside the body of his good mother, already cold and motionless six hours. They all get on their knees. Benedict recites the *Pater* and the *Ave* out loud, then puts a few drops of holy water on his mother's face. At that very moment she opens her eyes and finds herself not only alive but completely cured. She gets up, and then getting on her knees with the others, they sing all together a concert of praise that they offer God for so evident a miracle. I arrived in this village a few days later, where I learned from the mouth of mother and son of the grace they had both received.

I pass over the rest because I would be too long. Those with leisure to look up what I said about it in my history will find matter for praising God, who accords this new Church the same graces He showed the Christians of the first centuries.

❧ 25. The Outstanding Piety of the New Christians in the Tonkinese Church

THE PIETY and innocence of life practiced by new Christians in this Church offer even more visible proof of the hand of God than the miracles. I can truthfully say that nothing ever struck me so palpably to the heart as seeing that in this kingdom there are practically as many angels as there are Christians, and that baptismal grace inspires them all with the same spirit that appeared in the Apostles and martyrs of the primitive Church.

They have a faith so solid nothing could tear it from their hearts. A young lady called Daria preferred to forfeit her life rather than comply with the evil desires of a lord who wished to violate her honor. She made no difficulty about meeting death so as not to be sullied with a crime that would have caused her to lose baptismal grace.

Another Christian called Francis, who usually served the king's brother as bearer of his sedan chair, as was the custom among the great lords of the land, made no difficulty about dying rather than leave off practicing a good work in which he spent all the free time his master's service left him. He was particularly devoted to burying poor Christians, and this charity cost him his life. That beautiful death was the richest recompense he could have hoped for.

The love they bear their faith gives them incredible respect for the smallest ceremonies connected with it. They look on the Fathers who preach it to them as angels, and consider it an honor to obey them in the minutest particulars. I never showed them the holy crucifix that I didn't see them all dissolve in tears. They come from a distance of two weeks' journey to go to confession or hear Mass. Whenever they are no more than five or six leagues from the church where it is said, they never miss it on feast days. They arrive the night before and return the next day after the service, i.e., in the evening, having stayed in church from dawn till quite late at night. They always remain kneeling, and that with such wonderful modesty I couldn't contemplate it without tears.

They each wear two crosses, one on the breast and the other up their sleeve; and they say the former serves as their shield, the latter as their sword. They never travel abroad that they don't take their little oratories, which they open up as soon as they reach the hotel. Every morning without fail they pray a half hour, and most of them spend it meditating on some mystery, wherein they experience all the sweetness God gives pure souls to feel.

They have such reverence for holy water they come to fetch it from five or six days' journey away. They carry some in porcelain receptacles fastened to their arms on beautiful bracelets. They give it to all the sick to drink, with marvelous re-

sults. Every Sunday I was obliged to bless at least 500 large jars
of this sacred water to satisfy their pious desires.

Nothing delighted me more than the care they took in preparing themselves for confession and Communion. They have a
love and veneration for these sacraments that I have marveled
at a thousand times. They always fast the day before, and they
take the discipline. If I hadn't restrained them they would have
received Communion more than once a week. They make their
confessions shedding as many tears as if they had committed
great crimes, and yet I can say that usually in hearing their
confessions I would have trouble finding matter for absolution,
not with just a few people, but sometimes with a whole town,
and I very well realize this wasn't through ignorance but
through a praiseworthy fear of God.

What helped me wonderfully in the cultivation of this fine
vineyard and spreading our holy faith was the assistance of the
catechists who, to tell the truth, accomplished everything under
God in the great strides made by this Church. Seeing I was the
only priest who could preach, because the Father I was with
didn't know the language, I decided to keep some Christians
with me who were not married and who were filled with zeal
and piety, to help me in the conversion of souls. Many offered
me their services, but I chose those I thought most capable and
started a seminary, which succeeded so well we might say it's
what kept us going.

The first I selected were Francis, Andrew, Ignatius, and
Anthony, who promised publicly during Mass to spend their
entire lives in the service of the Church, not to marry, and to
obey the Fathers who came to preach the Gospel. All the Christians who witnessed this beautiful ceremony were delighted,
and since then have held the servants of God in great respect,
who truly acquitted themselves so worthily of their ministry
that we are indebted to them for a large part of all that was
accomplished in this kingdom. There are now over 100 in that
seminary, which the Christians maintain at their own expense,

for as far as our Fathers and I are concerned, we have always affirmed that we wanted to take nothing from them and that we were only after their souls. Consequently we ask them for nothing, and even when they want to make us presents, we always refuse them even though this annoys them, because if we wanted, they would give us everything they had; but they are nevertheless delighted about it, and it's an argument that is very useful to them against the pagans, who are convinced by it. "Why," they tell them, "would those Fathers want to deceive us? They come from far away, go to a great deal of trouble, and get nothing from us. They are people of good sense and virtue, who own property in their own country. What could they gain by abusing us? You have to believe it's God who is behind them and that what they are saying is true." I couldn't begin to tell how many pagans this argument converted.

❧ 26. How I Was Obliged to Leave Tonkin and Return to China

THE FAITH was making too great strides in Tonkin not to be opposed by the devil, who is its sworn enemy. For about a year and a half I lived in this tranquillity, during which it was a pleasure to see Peter's bark filling with the kind of fish that are the delight of Jesus Christ.

The first storm sprang from the same cause that originally put disorder into the world. The wives, finding themselves rejected by the new Christians who had had several, made such an uproar that the whole kingdom was stirred up over it. The king, who till then had shown us extreme kindness, began to disassociate himself somewhat from the doctrine we were preaching. He often had his ears bent by the argument that it could only be very prejudicial to the whole kingdom, since it forbade having several wives and consequently prevented the country from becoming populated, depriving the king of many subjects.

This offended the prince. The eunuchs whose business it was to guard his wives kept adding fuel to the fire, because they feared that if the king took to this law, which stipulates that a man should be content with only one wife, he might get rid of all those he had, a hundred in number, and that they would be dismissed from court at the same time. This self-interest roused them against us and caused them to contrive a thousand tricks to discredit us in the king's mind.

That wasn't hard for them because they always had his ear and told him a thousand evil things about the law we were preaching, which finally caused the king to publish an edict in which he forbade all his subjects to follow this new doctrine that had been brought from Europe, because it was prejudicial to the state and the basic mores of his kingdom.

We were stunned by this at first, and all the Christians stoutly declared they would obey the king in anything that didn't compromise their consciences; that their faith was much dearer to them than life. But by the grace of God this thunder made only noise, which startled us, but its fire was merely a flash that passed without harming us.

The king still hadn't lost all his partiality for us. After these first impressions had faded somewhat from his mind, he was no longer set on doing us harm. We laid low for a while, then we returned to our former employments as if we had always been at peace, and it was then the number of new Christians grew so large that God palpably demonstrated that He alone ever gives His favors most abundantly in the midst of temptation.

This calm was soon ruffled by another storm, however, caused by the instigators of the former one under a pretext quite different. The new Christians were accused of having smashed some idols. Then the king was told I was a sorcerer and that my breath cast a spell that addled the brains of those I addressed, without possible resistance on anyone's part. At that point the king began finding fault not only with the law I was disseminating but with me personally to boot, and became fearful of seeing me and talking to me, so that when I tried to go to him to clear myself, all avenues were closed to me; and if now and then my friends had sufficient influence to get me into the palace, the king always held himself at a distance from me and granted me only very brief, hurried audiences because of the fear he had of being bewitched by my breath.

I never stopped going about my customary duties until the king finally declared himself openly against us at the beginning of the year 1630. He forbade me to preach my new religion any longer in his land, along with an order to remove myself as soon as possible, either to Macao or perhaps to Cochinchina. The edict was solemnly published in due form and then posted on a big pole at the door of our house.

I leave you to imagine how alarmed our new Christians were at this ugly news, and although I was as distressed as I could be at a misfortune that was no fault of mine, I didn't neglect putting as much heart into them as I could, and retired to their homes, not daring to preach in public any more. Still, I didn't stop making myself available wherever I could be of help to them. I was in one house or another. The Christians would be notified, and they would arrive from various directions so cleverly that although the gatherings were large, the pagans were never aware of them.

I was kept shut up in a house for a while and placed under guard, but I found it easy to win over the master of the house, who let me out every night through a window while my guards were at the door. Thus every night I went into Christian homes, baptizing, preaching, hearing confessions, saying Mass, and then at daybreak I returned to my prison without anyone suspecting.

This lasted two months, after which I was commanded in the name of the king to withdraw to Cochinchina until such time as the Portuguese ship could take me back to China. So I was put on a galley with a company of thirty-six soldiers and one captain to guard me, under orders not to leave me until they set me outside the kingdom of Tonkin. Then it was, completely abandoned by human help, that God let me know with what care He was conducting me.

I related in my history all the adventures on that trip. I was three weeks on that boat, during which twenty-four of my guards became Christians. The captain followed suit a fortnight later after witnessing, during a storm that was about to sink us, an evident miracle that calmed the sea instantly on our throwing a little holy water into it and reciting a *Pater Noster*. This so amazed him he asked to be baptized, which I later did, and called him Augustine, so that I was becoming like a father to them and master of the vessel. They did whatever I wanted, and instead of taking me to Cochinchina they let me go to the province of Bochinh (Ha Tinh), which is the one farthest from the court and where I knew several Christians in whose homes I remained concealed for some time. They gave me a boat in which for four months we sailed about now on various rivers, now on the open sea. We would lie offshore during the day, then we would land at night, going into Christian homes where we rendered all the assistance in our power.

During that time we were reduced to such straits that we were forced to have recourse to the Christians, who generously gave us everything we needed, but at the same time we received word that the long awaited Portuguese ship had arrived safely in Cua Chua harbor, where two of our Fathers had come to fetch us, acting on news they had heard in Macao of our having been banished from Tonkin. The joy we experienced on seeing them and embracing them is beyond telling. We thought we were in Paradise, we four Jesuits finding ourselves together in that kingdom where God had already made Himself so many new citizens.

We went bravely to the court along with the newly arrived Portuguese. The king didn't receive us badly, which gave us the courage to take up our public preaching where we had left off and to do whatever we would have been doing before our exile. We thought we would be left alone after the Portuguese ship had unloaded all its merchandise and headed back to Macao. When we least expected it, we were handed an ironclad order in the king's name to board ship under pain of being declared rebels. We did everything we could to get the order rescinded, but all our trouble and that of our friends proved useless. We were all four forced to leave.

I don't like to recall the acute distress our Christians displayed at this parting, because I can't think of it without giving way. Whatever grief a mother or a father might feel at the death of a child these good people felt in our regard. They streamed in to our lodgings night and day after they heard the news. They wept, they sighed, they wailed, and especially when I bade them my last farewells in church they uttered so piercing a lament that even I was startled by it. Words failed me, but I made up for them in tears. Our two Fathers who had just arrived were amazed at all this, and the pagans themselves were moved to compassion.

For several days running there was an extremely large crowd for confessions. I had to satisfy them all, and I could hardly get to the end of them although I slept neither night nor day, because I was the only one who knew the language. When the last day arrived our house was full from midnight on. When we left to go to the harbor all the streets were jammed with our good Christians. They all followed us, embracing us and drenching us with such floods of tears we didn't know what to do except weep along with them. After boarding the ship I went to wave to them and gave them a little talk into which I put more tears than words, exhorting them to constancy in the love of Christ. They were ashore on their knees, begging my blessing. Many were in the water up to their waists. There wasn't one who wasn't crying.

I saw one good old septuagenarian, one of the foremost doctors in the country, who had come to tell us goodbye and had donned the beautiful official robes in which he meted out justice on high days during the year. He was on the waterfront, a bit removed from the throng, weeping hot tears. He was making us the solemn obeisance one makes the king, kneeling four times and touching his forehead to the ground. Then he went away sobbing. I was told he was so sick at heart that he was never able to eat after that and died eleven days later. Now see whether greater goodness could be found anywhere!

Finally, when we began hoisting sail, tears started afresh on both one side and the other. We kept our eyes on one another as long as we could and our hearts have never parted, for to tell the truth all of mine is in Tonkin, and they show me the honor of remembering me by the many letters they write me and the public prayers they offer in church on all feast days and morning and evening of working days in private homes, where they recite a *Pater* or an *Ave* for this miserable sinner. This is one of the strongest reasons I have for believing God will have mercy on me.

❧27. My Return to China and My Ten Years' Stay There

HAVING THEREFORE been in Tonkin for three years and two months, in other words, from the nineteenth of March of the year 1627 up to May of the year 1630, I returned quite disconsolate to Macao, where I immediately urged our superiors not to leave that wonderful sheepfold without a shepherd. The three Fathers who had borne witness to the great likelihood of entirely converting that flourishing kingdom made the same entreaties as I, and gave the whole college so favorable an impression of what they had seen that every fervent youth and the most sober Fathers were daily at the feet of the superiors begging to be sent to that mission.

Even some who had gone far toward, and were on the point of leaving for Japan, turned their thoughts to Tonkin. Especially Fr. Gaspar Amaral, one of the two who came to rescue me in my need during my exile, thought only of returning, although he had learned the Japanese language and had obtained all the necessary permissions for going to that wonderful island. The superiors gave him permission to go to Tonkin with two other Fathers. They went there in March of the year 1628, where they increased a hundredfold the fine wheat that was beginning to spring up in the Church's field. Several other excellent workers have been laboring there since then with such great success that I learned from the letters written me by Fr. Jerome Majorica—a wonderful and tireless worker in the Church—that there are now 300,000 Chrisitans, 200 churches open to the public, and that every year at least 15,000 unbelievers are baptized; and the good Father writes me that for his own part he has baptized 6,000, has 40,000 Christians and 70 churches under his direction.

With that, now say that a preacher in that country doesn't accomplish as much as fifty of the most fervent in Europe!

After securing this solid help for Tonkin, I began to set myself with all my might to converting the Chinese, but to tell the truth, I didn't find it so easy there as had been my experience in the blessed kingdom I had just left. In my opinion the fault lay principally with me, because although I understood the Chinese language very well, I still didn't know it well enough to make a long speech in it, so that I was forced to preach through an interpreter, which doesn't ordinarily suffice for bringing a soul to make a resolute change in religion and way of life. The other reason might well be the pride of the Chinese, who consider themselves the greatest men on earth. I noticed they came to sermons as long as they had something to argue about, but as soon as they were satisfied they wouldn't be seen again.

Nevertheless, notwithstanding all that, God did us the favor of using us to convert a fairly large number of these pagans, and I certainly baptized at least 1,000 with my own hand. We often ran errands in various towns throughout China, especially in the province of Canton. I frequently went to the capital, which is so large and so beautiful I hardly know one that compares with it; and by God's grace we never came back empty-handed.

I took particularly great pleasure in administering a cure assigned to me in Macao, where I worked very conscientiously. One engaged in ministering to new Chinese converts is called "Father of Christians," instructing them, guiding them, and teaching them whatever is necessary for leading a Christian life. This kept me so busy all day that if I wanted to do some studying to prepare sermons or theology courses, which I taught in our college, it had to be done at night. It was barely daylight before I was busy with my Chinese Christians or with those we were preparing for baptism.

I had the great consolation of meeting an old man 150 years old who had been baptized in the old days by the hand of the great Apostle of the Indies, St. Francis Xavier, when he was in Japan. I was privileged to hear his confession and to have a long talk with him. I was delighted to learn from what he said, and even more from the solid virtues displayed in his manner of living, of the wonderful instruction St. Francis Xavier used to give those he converted to the faith and the method he employed in confirming them in their initial resolve.

I omit many other things that befell me during those ten years, where the time seemed very short to me as a consequence of the endless tasks connected with our building a separate church for the Chinese and establishing a retreat house to which we could take those under instruction to receive holy Baptism.

28. How I Was Sent to Cochinchina a Second Time

AFTER THE time I left Cochinchina, by the year 1639 many important men of our Company had continued to work there with great success and were troubled at various times by many storms that sometimes deprived them of means, but never of the courage to further the glory of God by preaching the Gospel.

The one who worked harder than any and made admirable progress in that kingdom was Fr. Francis Buzomi, a Neapolitan who started this mission, as I said, in the year 1615 and labored in it with incredible assiduity for twenty-four years. He was a saintly man, tireless in his efforts, brave in the face of any danger, firm in all decisions. He spent himself entirely in founding and increasing that Christian community. He succeeded so well that although he found very few Christians on first arriving in Cochinchina, he left at least 12,000 when he went to heaven to receive as many crowns as he had made new Christians.

The other Fathers who ably seconded the labors of this great apostle were Fathers Benedict de Mattos, John Leria, Gaspar, Louis, and other religious of the Company who were sent on various occasions and lived many years in Cochinchina, during which they were persecuted in many ways by the enemies of Jesus Christ and the religion they were proclaiming.

Three times all were expelled from the kingdom by order of the king. The crime they were accused of was the same one so often imputed to Christians of the first centuries: preventing rain and rendering the whole land barren. This false notion so inflamed the minds of the pagans that they were very often on the point of putting these poor Fathers to death, who had no higher design than opening heaven to all of them and letting fall every grace in abundance.

These apostles weren't scared by mere noise and didn't thus desert their family. Some withdrew and remained in hiding among the Christians; others took a little trip to Macao and returned soon after with gifts that appeased the king's ill humor, and had their edict of banishment revoked by this means.

These vicissitudes both good and bad continued until the beginning of the year 1639, which was fatal for that poor Church. A certain governor of the province of Cham, a declared enemy of Christians, gained such ascendancy over the king that he incited him against the Fathers because they made his subjects worship the crucifix instead of worshipping the national gods. A beautiful crucifix that our Fathers held in great veneration was seized by force. It was taken to the king along with a thousand contumelies and prevarications to render it loathsome to him. He peremptorily ordered it to be burned, and any Fathers bringing such nonsense into his country to leave under pain of death.

The Portuguese had sufficient influence to prevent carrying out this sacrilege against the holy crucifix that, thanks to bribery, they rescued from the hands of these impious people, but they were never able to manage to get permission for our Fathers to stay in Cochinchina. They were put on board various vessels and forced to abandon their little flock.

News of our Fathers' utter rout so deeply affected good Father Francis Buzomi, who had gone to Macao to transact some business for the king of Cochinchina, that he fell ill of a sickness that carried him off after a few days. This loss was a calamity far greater for Cochinchina than the banishment of our Fathers. But God's designs are fathomless; they must be reverently adored, and we must submit humbly to His decrees.

At that same time Reverend Father Anthony Ruben, that great light of the Company who was to be extinguished in the pits of Japan* that he might become another star in Paradise, arrived as Visitor to our province of China and Japan. Before going to the scene of his torment and triumph, he wanted to supply all the neighboring kingdoms of China with the workers necessary for establishing the faith. Believing it wasn't enough for a servant of God to serve Him in only one place, he resolved to send his men to as many places as he himself would have liked to have been and there preach the Gospel.

To China he sent Fathers Gabriel de Magalhaëns, Joseph d'Almeida, both Portuguese, Francis Ferrario, an Italian; to Tonkin, only Fr. Thomas Rodriguez, but to tell the truth,

---

* Fr. de Rhodes refers here to the hot springs in which the martyrs were boiled alive. (TR.)

that one alone was worth four; and finally he bestowed on me the grace of being sent back to Cochinchina to restore the mission laid waste by the banishment of all the Fathers.

I went there very gladly at the beginning of February of the year 1640, in hopes of winning over the king and re-establishing Jesus Christ's kingdom in that country. I had so fair a wind I arrived in four days. I was alone as priest and Jesuit, but I had been promised that Reverend Father Peter Albert would come to help me shortly with his zeal and prudence, which two qualities that great man possessed to an eminent degree. He arrived soon after, and we began with one heart to serve our common Master.

᪳᪻ 29. What We Did in Cochinchina the First Year after Our Return

ALTHOUGH I got into Cochinchina quite safely, I still didn't think it advisable at first to be seen in broad daylight. It seemed better to me to hold off a bit and smooth the road before tackling my main objective. I therefore retired to a town called Faifo where much trading is done by the Japanese, who have their headquarters and carry on their business there. I stayed under cover there, and the first thing I did was win over the governor, who was Japanese, a pagan, and a persecutor of our holy faith.

The means I used to achieve my purpose was to offer him gifts that so gratified him—although of no great value—that they changed his heart entirely. From our great enemy he turned into our special protector. He looked for any opportunity of being of service to me regarding both his compatriots and the natives of Cochinchina, to the point of taking me personally to the royal city of Sinoa* where I was leery of going

* This is the city of Hué; it bears no relation to the province of Sinoa, or Thanh-Hôa, previously mentioned. (TR.)

lest the king think I was disdaining his order by which we were banished from all his lands.

The Japanese governor fended for me very adroitly and worked so effectively through his friends that I was quite welcome. I left Fr. Peter Albert with the Japanese, whose hearts he had won completely and among whom he was producing marvelous results, while I went to the king* with the most beautiful presents I could find. It's true that to buy them I had used just about all the money I had brought from Macao to keep me all year, but God provided, for a good Christian called Andrew and his wife sent me all the money needed to reimburse me, saying they wanted the satisfaction of providing the presents destined to win the king's heart.

In truth God so blessed them that they changed that prince's heart entirely, as effectively as the others had changed the governor's of Faifo. He saw me readily and treated me very civilly. It was then I judged the time had come to seize the excellent opportunity God was giving me to work for love of Him. That great lady, but even greater Christian whom as I related above Fr. Francis de Pina had baptized and named Marie, called me immediately to her house, where she had a lovely church that served as refuge for all Christians in that large city.

I began working day and night with our good Christians, who came to receive the sacraments with incredible avidness. I said Mass there every day. The crowd was so large I was obliged to say several Masses every feast day. I spent Holy Week there, and frankly I vow it's there, and not in Europe, that one learns to experience the Passion of our Lord. I stayed thirty-five days in that province, where ninety-four pagans received Baptism, and among others three ladies very closely related to the king whom I solemnly baptized on Easter Day, and a famous idolater priest whom Madame Marie had persuaded to renounce his errors, which he did so wholeheartedly that he has

* Nguyên-phúc-Lan, or Công-thuong-vuong (1635–1640). (TR.)

since been a marvelous help to us in leading many others to embrace the truth.

After covering that whole province I went back to Faifo to my companion, where we remained in hiding for a while to let the Portuguese leave, who were returning to Macao after marketing all their goods. I was convinced that when the authorities saw there was no ship to take us to China, they would be obliged to let us stay in their country, but a certain Onghebo [Ong Nghè Bô], governor of Cham province, seeing we had stayed regardless, was determined to expel us.

He gave us definite orders to leave immediately, by any means whatever, even if we had to walk on the water. We were obliged to give way to force. I bought a little boat that Fr. Albert and I piloted. Necessity taught us to ply this new trade at which we were both apprentices. We succeeded so well the first time, we were able to pass for masters. Never had we coursed so easily over seas so stormy and where so many great ships have considerable trouble making out. I leave you to consider whether two Jesuits and three of my young Christians would have been able to cross the Gulf of Hainan [Tonkin] and that wide expanse of ocean if God hadn't wished to show that He alone was running everything on that little boat, which came alongside safely at Macao on the twentieth of September, 1640.

I think it might be well for me to set down here a wonderful secret that the Christians of Cochinchina imparted to me against the stomach trouble very common among seafarers. It's a fact that I never took ship without being much troubled by this complaint, which lasted with me for the first five or six days. Seeing me thus afflicted, my Christians told me they had with them a remedy that so strengthened the stomach that it was in no way inconvenienced by this complaint, which is caused by the motion of the ship or by sea vapors. One must take one of those fish that have been devoured by, and which are found in the bellies of other fish, then cook it well, adding a little pepper, and take it on boarding ship; this imparts such vigor to the stomach that it can sail the sea without getting upset.

I found this secret very wonderful, but I found it even more agreeable in practice, because I've made use of it ever since, and I have never suffered any attack of that complaint which up till then had been very distressing. I wish with all my heart that it may prove of use to my reader, and especially to those wishing to come work with us beyond the Great Sea, which they will be able to cross without nausea!

⁓ 30. How Reverend Father Anthony Ruben Came to See Us in Cochinchina, and How Distressed He Was to See the Holy Images Burned

ALTHOUGH I was in Macao in the body, my heart never left Cochinchina, remaining always with my good Christians. Furthermore, it wasn't long before I went to see them. As traveling companion I was given Fr. Benedict Mattos, a Portuguese and an excellent worker. We boarded ship the seventeenth of December of that same year 1640 and arrived safely on Christmas Eve, just in time for the great feast. The Christians who knew of our arrival at the port of Kéan ran there from every province in the kingdom, and those who lived farthest away didn't fail to take part in the celebration any more than those who had arrived earlier.

A storm arising at sea at the same time proved very propitious for our mission in Cochinchina. Reverend Father Ruben, Visitor for our province, was aboard a ship headed for the Philippines on his way to a glorious death in Japan. The wind blew so violently it forced the great servant of God and his two companions to put in at the port of Kéan in Cochinchina, where we were privileged to keep them four and a half months, which was a very great blessing to that Church. The tears that saintly man shed continually during Mass watered the vineyard so well we never had a finer harvest. In that short time God granted Fr. de Mattos and me the grace of baptizing 1,937 pagans. We realized we had a powerful intercessor with God, who gave us such propitious help.

But the devil didn't keep still. He tried to disrupt the work of God by his tricks. That great enemy of Jesus Christ called Onghebo, whom I have often mentioned, decided one day when no one was expecting it to dispatch his emissaries into the homes of the leading Christians and remove from them any pictures, crucifixes, or other sacred objects they could find. They unceremoniously entered the house of a long-standing Christian called Andrew who had a lovely chapel where Christians were wont to meet. They seized all the images, took Andrew prisoner along with his two children Louis and Emmanuel, and did likewise in the house of one of the most respected magistrates of the town called Anthony, where they found a beautiful ivory crucifix; but not finding the master of the house, his wife—who was a most honorable lady called Eulalia—gladly took her husband's place and was tied up by the soldiers, who went straight to their governor laden with the spoils of religion.

That impious man set greater store on this plunder than if he had enriched himself by the sack of some enemy town. He immediately assembled a large troop of soldiers whom he sent in pomp to the port of Kéan where our Fathers were, in order to burn all these images before their eyes. He marched at the head of this company of fanatics, and arriving at the door of our house where the Father Visitor and some other Fathers were, insisted they witness the sorry sacrifice he was about to make. He made them come to the town square, ordered Andrew scourged with his children, Eulalia, and the mother of her husband. Then, lighting a huge fire, he had all the images and crucifixes thrown into it.

At this disastrous turn of events Fr. Ruben experienced all the pain possible to a lover of Jesus Christ—as did this faithful servant—seeing an outrage committeed against his Master. He besought that barbarian, dissolved into tears, turned every which way, threatened, tried force, and all that proving useless, he left. Having no other recourse but his own poor heart steeped in grief, he went and prostrated himself before God in his oratory, trying to make amends for the sacrilege of the impious. That same day he wrote me a letter on the subject that I recorded in the book I wrote about his glorious death.* Truly it seems sorrow itself wrote it. When I received it down south where the good Father had sent me, I had my fair share of distress and returned immediately to Kéan, which had been the scene of Onghebo's fury, but I found that good Fr. Ruben had left, not being able to stay longer than one night in that place which that crime rendered more unbearable to him than the most uncomfortable prison in the whole world.

❧ 31. The Things We Did in Cham Province, and the Graces God Accorded Christians There

IT WOULD take rather long to tell, though it wouldn't bore good souls, if I stopped to relate in detail all the blessings God bestowed on this new Church during the six years or so that I had the joy of being there. Still, seeing that I would often be obliged to tell the same things over again, because God never wearied of showering us with His gifts, I shall rest content with relating the outstanding ones and mentioning the others briefly.

* *Histoire de la Vie de la Glorieuse Mort de Cinq Pères de la Compagnie de Jésus Qui ont Souffert dans le Japon avec Trois Séculiers en l'Année 1643*, Paris, Cramoisy, 1653. (TR.)

Having worked a suitable length of time at the port of Kéan, I left there at the beginning of the year 1641 to make a tour of Cham province, which is not the largest in Cochinchina but is nevertheless very rich and very lovely. It is the site of the heaviest trade with the Portuguese, Chinese, and Japanese, who usually come there with all their merchandise because the harbors are accessible, and this province being situated in the center of the kingdom, anything you want can be marketed there.

I covered at leisure all the towns and principal villages of that province, where I found marvelous constancy in the Christians who had already accepted the faith, and a strong disposition to accept it among the pagans. In the town of Halam* I found a virtuous Christian by the name of Emmanuel. The devil had such hatred for him he provided him with a large number of enemies even among his closest relatives, who never left him in peace; but because God put Himself on his side, Emmanuel proved stronger than all his tormenters.

One of his neighbors who badgered him unceasingly, after persecuting him fiercely one whole day, was finally struck dead on a sudden by God late that same day without Emanuel's hearing of it from anyone but the man himself. He appeared to him shortly after his death and made known to him the pitiable condition in which he found himself as a result of the outrages he had perpetrated against him. Emmanuel's mother and youngest brother carried on the same business of mistreating him. They were both horribly tormented by the devil who, after leading them into sin, himself served as punitive agent, so that they finally realized how wrong they had been to persecute Jesus Christ in His servant and resolved to do themselves what they had condemned in Emmanuel. Both were baptized. I called the mother Teresa and the brother Ignatius, confident that these two guarantors would keep the two neophytes safe from the devil who was tormenting them. My expectations were not vain. Never again did they suffer any attacks from that evil

---

* Perhaps the city of Hailang, north of Hué (?) (TR.)

guest after the Holy Spirit came to dwell in them through the grace of holy Baptism.

To prove that the inhabitants of the Torrid Zone aren't so lacking in brains as we sometimes imagine, I must tell what happened to me in this province while teaching catechism to new Christians. I had explained the origin of our souls on the previous day, and I had said that God alone was their author, without our parents having any part in their creation. The next day I expatiated on our first father and the harm he did all his children by communicating to them the infection by which he had sullied himself.

When I had finished my sermon, a pagan with very good sense who had attended both talks got up and told me, "How do you reconcile, Father, what you have just said with what you said yesterday? Our soul, from what you say, has no other principle but the hand of God, and our parents contribute nothing to its vivification. How then can it be infected by the sin of one to whom it doesn't owe its existence? We sometimes see well enough among us that children are declared base born when they have criminal fathers, but here, according to what you say, our soul recognizes no other father but God and still Adam, who is nothing to it, has communicated to it the contagion of his crime."

I was delighted to hear this doubt from the mouth of a Cochinchinese that had once troubled St. Augustine, the greatest of doctors. I took care not to answer him with scholastic subtleties that might have encumbered his mind. I decided to give him a little comparison that satisfied him. "If you have in your hand," I told him, "a beautiful pearl, very white and very clear, which falls by accident into the mud, it becomes all dirty, even though our hands contributed in no way to this filth. But if you wash it, it will take on again all its former beauty. Our soul is like a very precious pearl. It leaves God's hands very clean, but if it falls into a body where it becomes soiled because it is no longer merely a soul, but a man derived from Adam. That's where it becomes soiled, but when it is washed in the waters of

Baptism, all that filth leaves it. It becomes as clear and beautiful as the sun." This comparison satisfied all the attendance listening to me.

In the same place I met a most honorable lady called Agatha who for a long time had been sorely tried by various afflictions that are the usual inheritance of the children of God, but He who gave her the fortitude to endure them wished to let her know that she wouldn't endure them long. Breaking into tears one day on account of the misery she was caused, she saw distinctly in the shadows of her room a beautiful cross all surrounded with light that dispelled all gloom from her spirit and all distress from her heart.

❧ 32. What Transpired on a Visit to the Three Southern Provinces, and Various Events Befalling Us

SEEING WE had a large kingdom composed of six provinces to convert and that there were only the two of us, Reverend Father Benedict de Mattos and I, after keeping together for some time throughout all Cham province, were obliged to part company and divide up our work. He took the two northern provinces, which are Sinoa and Quambin [Quang-Binh], where he worked very profitably. The three southern ones fell to my share, which are Quanglia [Quang-Ngai], Quinhin, and Ranran.* They are all three very beautiful, with plenty of seaports and wide rivers, which are a great convenience to people who travel. The king keeps many galleys on the Ranran side to prevent inroads from Champa, which borders on this province. Besides, that's where the most valuable *calamba* is found, along with the birds' nests that impart so fine a flavor to cooking, as I said before.

* Ranran, or Phu-Yen, was an area just north of modern Phan Rang and Nha Trang.

I spent six months making a tour of these three provinces, sometimes by sea, in which we often nearly drowned, and sometimes on the rivers, where we encountered similar dangers. And overland we had plenty of trouble, but the good Lord was with me and delivered me from all. Seeing I was alone, I arranged to take with me a Christian of long standing called Jerome who was well qualified to assist me in anything possible to a well-instructed Christian who is not a priest, and truly he was such a help to me that during these six months I baptized 1,305 pagans with my own hand.

I started with the province of Quanglia, where I entered first a town called Chaimi,* where all the Christians were waiting for me at the dock and gave me plenty of work and even more consolation the few days I was busy ministering to them. Nothing there made me so happy as seeing a venerable old man named Paul who, together with his wife Monica, had occupied himself ever since his Baptism entirely with the good works worthy of a fervent Christian; but God, whose wisdom is full of unfathomable mystery, willed that he go blind in these holy occupations. When I saw him I thought it was another Tobias. In spite of the handicap of his eyes, that good old man remained unswerving in his service of Jesus Christ.

He was the soul of that whole Church. Every Sunday and holy day he gathered together the Christians in a chapel he had in the enclosure of his house. There he instructed them, preached, and took care to help them in every way necessary to keep them in the faith they had received. His zeal extended to pagans, and he disposed many for Baptism. God had given him so absolute an empire over devils there were none possessed that he didn't deliver. I myself saw and baptized a woman who was tormented by one of these evil guests and who was an object of pity to all who saw her running about the forests and performing a thousand eccentricities. Paul set her at peace and brought her to me to be baptized.

On hearing of my arrival the Christians of the town of Bao-

* Perhaps modern Tra-my. (TR.)

bam* deputed three leading citizens to come beg me to go see them. I did so with a right good heart, but as I was on the point of leaving, Jerome, who had pledged himself to follow me and help me in all these jaunts, changed his mind and came to tell me he found it necessary to return home to see his wife and children. That surprised me, but I nevertheless gave him leave and resolved to stay on by myself, trusting God not to abandon me. He got into a boat at nightfall because there was a good breeze, but when he had gone some distance he heard a terrible voice he had never heard before threatening to destroy him if he didn't return to me. He was so terrified he turned back immediately and came and threw himself at my feet to beg pardon for his infidelity, promising me to work all the more courageously now he saw this was so displeasing to the devil, who had drawn him to commit that cowardly act.

So I went to Baobam, where I can't describe the welcome the Christians gave me, not only those living in town, but those who gathered from the neighboring villages as well. I found a very beautiful large church there, to which I made my way accompanied by that wonderful troop of people. They were so famished for the word of God and the sacraments of which they had been deprived for a long time, they gave me respite neither for eating nor sleeping. It's true that the consolation I got from seeing them surpasses anything I can say, and even now as I write this and recall the sweetness that filled my heart in those days, tears start from my eyes, and it seems to me greater happiness couldn't be known in this world.

I met some who had been divested of the highest offices in the province because they were Christians. They took this loss with the same joy one normally feels on receiving news of some great benefit. Others came to present their children to me, although some had only one and were very rich. I found one who had with him at home a poor wretch all covered with ulcers. He treated him and caressed him as if he were his son.

* Almost certainly the modern town of Quang-Ngai. (TR).

Some months later he had him baptized, and he died in my arms. I seemed to be seeing poor Lazarus, but certainly not the bad rich man. I spent all day hearing the women's confessions and the entire night was often spent in hearing the men's. I often wondered what so many priests could be up to who didn't know what to do with themselves in Europe and who could have found an outlet worthy of their zeal over here.

While I heard confessions, my catechists did their duty by giving instructions, especially to the catechumens. Then I took time out to preach at least twice a day. The pagans came in droves, and God so spoke to their hearts that sometimes the number of those receiving Baptism was too large to be contained in church, even though it was quite capacious. I had to instruct them and baptize them in a large square just outside the door. And with all this work I felt neither weariness nor sickness, and I was so filled with consolation I didn't know whether I was on earth or in Paradise.

What I have just related concerning this Christian community at Baobam, among whom I remained only a fortnight, happened likewise in all the other towns in the provinces of Quanglia, Quinhin, and Ranran that I looked up, so I won't stop now to tell about it. There's plenty here to give an idea of what might be said about all the others.

33. Some Marvels That Happened to the Christians of the Province of Ranran

IN THE great fervor that our Christians showed in the service of their good Master, God didn't fail to reciprocate by giving them proofs of His love for them. I could relate many. I'll limit myself to three of them.

In the city of Ranran, capital of the province bearing the

same name, there was a famous doctor, though an even better Christian, called Emmanuel. He spent his life relieving the bodies and souls of both Christians and pagans, whom he very often converted to the true faith. A short time before my arrival, he was struck down by a serious illness that gave the Christians much ground to fear they might see the torch that was enlightening their whole church extinguished. They were with him day and night, already mourning him as dead.

One day, his bed surrounded by these Christians, he fell into a torpor that led them to fear he had died. It continued several hours, after which he returned to himself, and all present were amazed to learn from his mouth that it had been an ecstasy. He said God had shown him all Paradise, where there were things so beautiful he was incapable of describing them; that among others there were several Christians of his acquaintance who had been shining examples during their lifetime, but he named none in particular. What proved that this hadn't been a reverie was that he got up at the same time, as healthy as if he had never been sick, although he had been in so bad a way shortly before that his life was despaired of. Nevertheless, ever after that time he conceived such loathing for the things of this life, he couldn't keep his mind off the beauties he had seen in heaven. When he was with his relatives and friends, he couldn't carry on any conversation with them other than on what was the object of all his hopes. His eyes were habitually raised on high, and his soul seemed to take no other direction but toward that beautiful palace he had seen.

In fact he could neither eat nor drink nor sleep, and did so only reluctantly, so great was his impatience to be in heaven. This gradually wore him away. He died a few months later in such joy that when he found himself in the last extremity, his face and his whole body could be seen to tremble with happiness such as had never been seen in him, so true is it that those who know heaven's worth could love nothing of all that is called beautiful on earth.

The good Emmanuel was not the only one to experience

these blessings from Paradise. I was even told that, practically at the same time, another fervent Christian, while meditating on the glory of the saints in heaven, heard our Lord's voice clearly calling him to take part in the great feast. He was left so enraptured that he was never able to eat anything afterward, and a short time later he died tasting the delights of heaven, where his place had been prepared.

Among the good works which that so virtuous lady Marie Magdalene, the governor's wife, supported in the province of Ranran, she had founded a fine hospital where all Christians and catechumens were received who were suffering from any incurable illness, and among others there were many lepers who felt inclined to receive Baptism that their souls might be cleansed. Every day someone went to give them the necessary instruction to prepare them for the sacrament designed to confer grace on them. Many Christians of long standing came to help in this good work and receive their share of the good teaching dispensed there.

One of them, a man of great substance and very worthy of credence, told me later that during the whole time of the sermon he saw clearly on the arm of the one preaching a young child beautiful as day with a very joyful countenance, smiling now at the preacher, now at the entire audience, over whom he shed myriad rays of light. The good man came to tell me this with such certainty and such great simplicity that I believed what he hold me practically as if I had seen it myself. This greatly consoled all our catechists and the Christians to whom I related it, assuring them all that He who came to enter our hearts by His grace went before to prepare the dwelling by His light.

The third thing I want to tell about is the deliverance of two possessed women by means of Baptism. This was in that same province of Ranran, where they had been tormented for a long time by the devil, who gave sure signs of his presence, now speaking languages these women could never have learned, now doing things they would never have been able to do if that evil spirit hadn't lent his strength and malice thereto.

The former was delivered by the first exorcism I performed to prepare her for Baptism, as if the rebel had wanted to quit the place at the first news he got that the legitimate prince was preparing to come drive him out. The second gave us much more trouble. Furthermore, she was one of those women called pythonesses, whose stock in trade is making the devil speak through their mouths, especially at funerals, where magicians pretend to call up the souls of the deceased to console the children. They cause the devil to enter these women, who tells very secret things that no one could know. This one had plied this evil trade a long time and had amassed considerable wealth, but she had acquired thereby what she had never meant to: the devil made himself so much at home in her house that he didn't want to leave any more. He tormented her terribly day and night. After remaining seven years in these tortures and making use of every means of deliverance, she and her husband came to realize that there was no other remedy but holy Baptism.

The good woman disposed herself for it as well as she could. Before administering the sacrament to her, I thought the exorcisms would have the same effect as they had had on the first. I continued them for several days, and still the devil always held his ground. When I saw this obtsinacy in the evil spirit, I thought it best to go ahead and confer Baptism that, by making the Holy Spirit present to the soul, would free the body of its enemy. I tell what I saw, and what I can't tell without marveling at the power of the sacraments. The very instant I pronounced the usual words and poured water on her head, that good woman's countenance changed, she lost that horrible look, quit all her eccentricities, and settled into a peacefulness that caused all those present to cry miracle. Never again has she suffered any disquiet of spirit or body. She lives in her house in great tranquillity and is very careful never to give entry again to the evil guest who mistreated her so.

❧ 34. Concerning a Trip I Had to Take to the Philippines, with Some Details on Those Islands

AFTER STAYING six months at my post in the three southern provinces, where God gave me the grace to wage a pretty good fight against His enemies, I began to lie rather low for fear that great persecutor of Christians, the governor of Cham, were he to run across me during the time the Portuguese went to Macao, might force me to board their ship, which bothered me more than death, because I could see that whole Christian body without a single pastor.

But that man, on fire and raging against the servants of Jesus Christ, was watching so closely and was so wary of me that he served me with an ironclad order on the part of the king to leave Cochinchina with the Portuguese. I was betwixt and between for a long time as to whether God wanted me to stay on in spite of the king's order. I didn't want to trust my judgment alone. I called together my leading Christians in the town of Caichan* and asked them what they thought I should do under the circumstances.

The first to speak was one of the town's foremost magistrates called John, who offered to keep me concealed in his house for as long as I liked, saying I needn't fear disturbing him, that he would always be happy to be able to serve Jesus Christ with his substance and at the risk of his life. The other Christians certainly felt the same way, but they weren't of the same opinion. They thought it advisable for me to go away for a little while with a view to returning later rather than endanger both myself and all the Christians by remaining in hiding, in which state I couldn't be of much service to the Church.

* Modern Quang-Tri.

I subscribed to this latter opinion, and because the visitation to my three provinces had kept me so long the Portuguese ship had already left, and Fr. Benedict de Mattos had gone with them, I took a vessel headed for the Philippines, to go from there to Macao and then return to Cochinchina two or three months later. I left July 2, 1641, and after very dangerous sailing due to several storms that nearly wrecked us, we arrived on the twenty-eighth of the same month at a port in the Philippines known as Bolinao, a good 100 leagues away from Manila, where we had hoped to dock, but the storm forced us to put in, otherwise we would have perished.

The Philippines are large islands under the control of the king of Spain. They have since been handed down to Philip II, who gave them his name. They lie almost entirely in the Torrid Zone. The principal city, which is Manila, is situated on the thirteenth parallel. This is considered the outermost limit of the west, although they lie east of China from which they are separated by a mere 150-league strip of ocean, and they are taken for the end of the West Indies, which belong to the Spanish along with the Philippines.

This is what served the malice of two Dutchmen who were the real cause of that bloody persecution that has reduced the Church in Japan, one of the most flourishing in the world, to near nothing. Those two scoundrels, finding themselves at the court of the king of Japan, showed him a map of the world with the Philippines on one side and Macao on the other, which the king of Spain then held in China as king of Portugal, and said to the king, "Do you rightly see, Sire, how far Spanish control has extended? To the east, it has reached Macao; to the west, into the Philippines. See how close you are to these two strongholds. You are the only one left to be taken. It's true that right now he doesn't have enough troops to make himself master of your kingdom, but his ploy is to send here numbers of priests who under the pretext of making Christians are making soldiers allied to the king of Spain.

When their number grows really large, then you will see to your hurt the outcome of his ambition. He will use them to fight you, inciting them against you under the pretext of religion that normally serves him as excuse for pouncing on the estates of all his neighbors, as all four corners of the world have experienced only too well, and which you will soon suffer if you don't begin forestalling their evil design right away."

The king of Japan took the advice these godless men gave him so seriously, that from that moment he declared total war on all Christians, and especially on preachers. In sixteen centuries the Church hasn't beheld a longer or more fanatical persecution than the one that has been bathing every town in that flourishing kingdom in blood for forty years, where the Church was making such great strides. It will be a great honor for the Dutch, who call themselves Christians, to have annihilated that Church to satisfy their passion against other Christians!

There are an archbishop and three bishops in the Philippines. The principal city is called Manila, where there is a large harbor, beautiful churches, and a most devout population. Furthermore, throughout these islands hardly any idolaters are to be found. Jesus Christ is served there almost everywhere. Otherwise the land there is neither beautiful nor very fertile, and the advantages the king of Spain reaps there are so few that he is said to have been sometimes on the point of giving them up. About the greatest benefit is that the gold and silver from Peru is conveniently brought there in exchange for the beautiful silks and other merchandise from China and Japan.

So I arrived, as I said, at Bolinao on July 28, on a Sunday, but I noticed on my arrival that it was still Saturday, July 27th, on that island. We had eaten meat that morning, well knowing it was Sunday, the twenty-eighth of the month, and that evening we saw people abstaining because Sunday the twenty-eighth would come only the next day. After thinking it over a bit, I well saw that both they and we had calculated properly, although the ones were lagging behind the others.

Those who don't know the reason for this difference will find it amazing, but others will only laugh. Here is its true cause. When one leaves Spain to go to the Philippines, inasmuch as one always travels from east to west, it's necessary for the days to be a few minutes longer because the sun—whose course these people follow—rises and sets always later for them. And as each day and night lasts longer for them than for those who live in Spain, they must lose a half day during the trip from Spain to the Philippines.

The Portuguese, on the other hand, who go from Portugal to the West Indies, because they travel against the sun, the twenty-four-hour day shortens a few minutes for them, so that—the sun which they are leaving behind them setting and rising ever earlier—they gain a half day over those who live in Portugal, and at the end of the trip thus find themselves a day ahead of the others.

From which it is easy to conclude that, the first gaining, the others losing a half day, it becomes necessary for the Portuguese and the Spaniards leaving their countries the same day and arriving at the same place from opposite directions, that the Portuguese going eastward should have spent a whole day longer than the Spaniards going westward. And that's the reason why we who were calculating with the Portuguese had come to Sunday the twenty-eighth, whereas in the Philippines they were still at Saturday the twenty-seventh.

So for the same reason, of two priests leaving on the same day, one from Portugal eastward and the other from Portugal westward, saying Mass every day and arriving at the same place at the same time, one would have said Mass more often than the other. And of twins born together, by traveling thus one would have lived a day longer than the other. But enough of that. I guess you won't mind my having mentioned this in passing.

༺ 35. My Stay in the Philippines and My Departure for Cochinchina

AT THE port of Bolinao I made the acquaintance of a fine convent of Reverend Discalced Augustinian Fathers who had the goodness to meet me at the dock and took me to their house, where they received me with extreme charity. I stayed there five days waiting to be able to sail for the capital of the country, which is Manila, but the sea was so rough I had to take the overland route, which is long and very dangerous.

I traveled a good 100 leagues, in many places running across religious of St. Augustine and St. Dominic who showed me a thousand kindnesses, and finally I arrived safely in Manila on the fifteenth of August, dedicated to the Virgin's triumphant entry into heaven. The first to greet me, having come to meet me, was Reverend Father Anthony Ruben, who had left Cochinchina about two months ago and was staying in Manila to take all the necessary steps for the long trip to Japan, where martyrdom awaited him; and God knows with what sweet joy I embraced that holy man. Then Reverend Father Anthony Capèche came and threw himself on my neck, and at the same time our lovable Fr. Francis Marquez, all three my intimate friends; but alas, all three glorious martyrs, and I, ever unfortunate, languishing in this life and uncertain as to my salvation.

I must confess that during the five weeks or so that I stayed in Manila the presence, the friendship, but above all the remarkable courage of these three generous servants of God and aspirants to martyrdom caused me singular struggles about wanting to go to Japan where martyrdom was certain. There lay certainly the object of all my desires, although on the other hand the promise I made my Christians in Cochinchina and the straits in which I had left them weighed heavily on my heart. In my spiritual uncertainty, I wanted God alone to arbitrate the matter. I betook myself to the superiors, by whose mouth He speaks. I opened my heart to them, which felt such attraction for Japan, and I lay before them the considerations holding me in suspense. They judged that the interests of so many Christians outweighed my inclinations and told me that if God wanted me to be a martyr, He would find a way in Cochinchina as easily as in Japan. I acquiesced in this decision and thought only of finding a way back to my Church in Cochinchina. But first I had to veer toward China.

Having made all necessary preparations in Manila for his long journey, Reverend Father Anthony Ruben wanted to go to Macao once more to give final orders to his province, to which he was never to return. I had the good fortune to board ship with that holy man on September 21, feast of St. Matthew. I don't know whether the devils, aware of the shame the triumphs of this great martyr would cause them, might have tried to drown the virtue that was to be their downfall, but I do know that we were beset by a storm so terrible we never thought we would be able to come out of it.

As for me, I thought I had reached the end of all my travels. Our ship had no sails left, we had lowered the mast, and we were rolling with the waves with no other end in view but preparing our souls to meet God. I was watching Fr. Ruben carefully the whole time. He kept his eyes glued to heaven, his countenance cheerful, his demeanor confident. He turned to me and told me in steady tones, "Father Alexander, never fear, we won't be eaten by the fish." He told me this in an accent that led me to believe that God had sent him word of the grace He was intending to accord us.

I then took from my reliquary a hair of the Holy Virgin, which I had had for a long time and which had often been a great help on similar occasions. I put it in a box, then tying a string to it I dropped it into the sea, which was horrible to see.

Wonder of wonders! At that very moment the waves died down, the winds abated and the whole storm ceased to the great astonishment of all aboard, not one of whom didn't consider it a real miracle.

We immediately salvaged all the pieces of sail cloth and rigging we could and patched together some sails, and after having been so ill used by the sea for a fortnight running, we reached land, where our Fathers gave us the best treatment they could afford us.

⚜ 36. My Return to Cochinchina and My Journeyings There During the Course of Two Years

NEVERTHELESS, I confess that this leisure was less agreeable to me than unremitting work and vigils in Cochinchina. I had no greater desire than to return there soon. My main concern was speeding up the departure of the Portuguese ship that was to take me back. I was in this misery for almost four months. Finally we left at the end of January of the year 1642. But I was forced to go alone, having no way of bringing any Father of the Company, for they had been sent out into various kingdoms—so true is it that in those countries one single Jesuit counts as if he were a whole college.

I nevertheless had the good fortune to meet up with a Tonkinese catechist twenty-two years old, full of vim and piety, who came and offered to accompany me on the trip and in all the labors connected with so arduous a mission. I well realized this was a stroke of God's providence in my regard, because I can't say how helpful his company was to me. I had no sooner arrived than all the Christians poured in from several days' journey away. My primary concern was winning over the governor of Cham, who was our greatest persecutor. The gifts I gave him so changed his heart, he left me in peace for two years.

Soon after I made for the king, with every intention of setting him in our favor. I presented him with some new clocks marked with Chinese characters, which pleased him very much, and he kept me at court while the Portuguese returned to their trading. This went on for some time, during which I spent all my days with the king and all my nights with my Christians, who assembled in the houses I designated. I explained certain mathematical secrets to the king, and to the Christians the mysteries of our faith.

That didn't last as long as I would have liked. After some days the king sent me back to the Portuguese and gave me several gifts, but he refused me what I would have liked most of all—to stay longer in that great city where there was so much to be won for Jesus Christ. So I went to the town of Kéan, and I began laying plans to make a tour of the whole kingdom, visiting the Christians, who were many in number, and working for the conversion of the pagans. By God's grace we succeeded well enough in both one and the other.

Never did I feel God's help so near. I was the only priest in a large kingdom, and I can truthfully say my parish stretched over at least 120 leagues; nevertheless, I ministered to it and visited it all within two years, as far as I know neglecting to stay nowhere for as long as necessary to secure the good of souls. I can truthfully say that throughout these two years I lived a continual Holy Week. Everywhere I had to do the same things we do in Europe during that holy time.

When the Portuguese were ready to go, they begged me to accompany them, but seeing the governor gave me no word, I was at no pains to leave. Still I didn't dare show myself in public after their departure. I stayed undercover during the day, and at night I roamed abroad. I often had myself carried according to the native custom in a hammock borne about the neck by two men in such fashion that no one can see who it is, and the sick and the dead are often carried this way. I used this convenience not only to remain concealed, but also to catch a little sleep while traveling, because once arrived at my destination, I had to expect to work night and day.

First I went down south into all the provinces as far as the borders of the kingdom of Champa, then I retraced my course northwards to the boundaries of Tonkin.

The fervor of the Christians was the same as it had been in former years, which is why I won't say anything about it in particular, but I don't wish to remain silent concerning the grace God did me at that time by inspiring ten young men to join in the plans I had for preaching the faith to these peoples. All were from different provinces of the kingdom, but they were one at heart in belonging entirely to God and being completely devoted to the Church. Among these there were three for whom God reserved the glory of being martyrs. The good Andrew came to see me in the province of Ranran [Phu-Yen]. Ignatius, a person of high rank because he had been a magistrate, of high learning because he knew Chinese letters perfectly, but especially of very high virtue because he was a real saint, came from a northern province (Quang-tri) and never wanted to leave me after I had baptized him; and to tell the truth I never had a happier encounter than finding him.

The third one was Vincent, who begged me for a long time to number him among the others. His father, who was a Christian of very long standing in the province of Quanglia, offered him to me with a good heart although he was the white hope of his family and the mainstay of his old age.

The other seven were all just like these first three, and we would all go together throughout all the towns of Cochinchina. God so seconded us by His grace that in a short while the number of Christians had increased by over a thousand.

⇜ 37. Some Miracles God Wrought through
Two Virtuous Christians

IN THE province of Quanglia I met a Christian called Matthew, possessed of wonderful zeal for converting idolaters and helping Christians. He was very good at it, although he was neither learned nor rich; but on the other hand he was very devout and had such a great gift of miracles he cured all sorts of diseases and even raised one who was dead. Here is part of what I learned from persons quite worthy of belief.

A young man of very good family in the town of Baobam was sick unto death. His parents, who loved him as an only child, had made use of all the skill of the doctors and all the superstitious practices of the sorcerers in an effort to cure him. When they saw all that wasn't going to keep their son from dying, they finally had recourse to the remedies of our Christian faith. Matthew, who knew this young man so well versed in Chinese letters and who was in hopes that if the young man recovered he might be of great service in the conversion of others, went to his house with the usual drugs: holy water and one of our *Agnus Dei*. He found the patient practically at the last gasp, but he didn't lose heart. He began praying for the salvation of his soul and then for the cure of his body; and as he seemed to be giving up the ghost Matthew baptized him. At that moment the patient opens his eyes and finds himself so completely cured he gets up on the spot. That threw his family and the whole town into such consternation that many became Christians, and since then the patient has evidenced all the gratitude so manifest a miracle calls for.

Another time this same Matthew was called to see a little sick girl who died before the valiant doctor had time to get there. He found her without any sign of life for some hours, and what bothered him most, he knew she had died without

Baptism. The faithful servant of God immediately betook himself to prayer, asking God to give back to the little creature as much life as might be necessary to receive Baptism and merit heaven. He got what he asked for. The little girl, who had been lying motionless and lifeless for half a day, opened her eyes and kept them open, showing it was possible to baptize her. All present saw it. Beside himself with joy, Matthew baptized her. Hardly was the rite completed than the little girl closed her eyes and quietly died, having received the sure passport to heaven. Finally, not to string out the many other miracles God habitually performed through His servant, certainly He performed so many that many of the most prejudiced pagans were convinced by them and requested Baptism.

In another town of the same province of Quanglia there was yet another Christian called Andrew to whom God had communicated the grace of effecting miraculous cures similar to those I've just recounted. It wasn't only the Christians who profited from them in their illnesses; even pagans were so convinced of them that as soon as they felt sick they ran to Andrew's house as they would to a dispensary. This was so common that no one in the country doubted it any more. You would have said that house was a great hospital where all kinds of patients were well received and soon cured.

38. The Great Results Achieved during My Absence by My Ten Catechists in Various Provinces of Cochinchina Where They Went to Preach

AFTER SPENDING nearly two years following up all the provinces of Cochinchina, although keeping myself always out of sight and practically never appearing except at night, I learned that during my absence the Portuguese had arrived at their regular port on the Cham River, from whence they were ready to leave for Macao. I went to see them before they left, and I found they were all of the opinion that I should sail with them for fear of irritating the king, who would see me far more willingly when I returned after three months, and that I would then serve the Christians in far greater freedom without being forced to hide.

I followed their advice, and before leaving I thought it well to bind my ten catechists by the same oath sworn before me by the ones in Tonkin when I left them. We chose the feast of our glorious patriarch St. Ignatius to hold the ceremony, at which time the ten servants of God appeared publicly in Church, which was filled with Christians. They prostrated themselves before the altar with white tapers in their hands, then swore their oath to serve the Church all their lives without ever marrying and to obey the Fathers of the Company who came to preach in their country, or those they might delegate in their place.

They took the oath with such devotion and with so many tears that the whole congregation was moved by it. As for me, who was at the altar, I was in such transports of joy at seeing these innocent victims consecrating themselves to God so sincerely, that my heart praised God for it and my eyes shed copious tears. After that, I gave them their orders concerning what they should do in my absence. I appointed Ignatius superior over them all, which was quite agreeable to everyone because he was the oldest, the most capable, and truly very virtuous like all the others.

We divided them into two squads. The first was to mind all the provinces to the north as far as Tonkin. Ignatius was to be captain and take Andrew with him. The other was to go through all those to the south up to the borders of Champa.

After I left for Macao in the month of September of the year 1643, they acquitted themselves faithfully of their duties. First, all ten went to stay together for a month in the house we

had in Kéan province; and inasmuch as the pagans had practically destroyed it, they set it up again. During that time some
of them fell sick, among others the good Andrew, who had far
greater zeal than strength. Ignatius, who was their superior,
made himself valet to all and waited on them day and night,
finding nothing too lowly or difficult that would bring relief
to the servants of his one and only master Jesus Christ.

When they had all recovered they divided up as I had told
them. The five who went south did so well that within three
months they baptized 293 pagans whom they judged to be in
circumstances not admitting postponement of Baptism until my
return, and many others they prepared to receive it from my
hand. This caused such an uproar in the province of Ranran
that the pagans, being thoroughly alarmed, complained might-
ily to the governor, who had recently arrived and had a strong
aversion to Christians.

He ordered all these new preachers carefully hunted down
with the intent of punishing them. No respect was had even to
the house of Madame Magdalene,* a relative of the king's and
wife of the former governor, whom the king had appointed a
short time ago to other affairs in his government. Soldiers entered insolently there and went through all the rooms looking
for the catechists, but luckily they weren't at that town any
more. Later they were very sorry to have missed so fine an
opportunity of suffering something for the faith, which they
much preferred to die for than preach, and Madame Magdalene wasn't sorry to suffer this affront—which in any other
circumstances would have been unthinkable.

This same occasion proved the constancy of two Christian
ladies. One, called Angela, was so palpably distressed at seeing

* Also sometimes referred to as "Madame Marie," this lady is not to be
confused with the other Marie Magdalene, the aforementioned widow of
Nguyên Hoàng. Although they were contemporaries and about the same age
this second princess was Ngoc-Liên, granddaughter of Nguyên Hoàng and
daughter of his son the Chúa Sai who was his successor. She became the wife
of General Nguyên-Phuc-Vinh, Governor of Phu-Yen, who built the citadel
of Tran-biên-dihn in 1629. (TR.)

her mother-in-law, called Monica, have a church torn down for fear the governor might ruin her, that she died of grief, not wishing to outlive a crime committed by a Christian, the mother of her husband.

The other was a very good widow who had in her house a church that the enemies of our faith wanted to tear down, seeing this would please the governor. She withstood them so bravely, employing now force, now kindness, and ever zeal for God's honor, that she ended by keeping her church, all the rage of the devils and ill will of the pagans notwithstanding.

While work progressed so well down south, Ignatius with his four companions was no less successful up north. In that short time he conferred Baptism on 303. See if you can call them lazy! They went first to the royal city of Sinoa [Hué], where they were met with a very fine harvest prepared by the care and industry of three valiant Christians who had abandoned their homes and left their country before the fury of unbelievers who had abused them.

It happened that about two years previous, on passing through a town called Kedai,* I had baptized in a space of three days 300 persons whom my catechists had prepared beforehand. The idolaters had been so offended at the affront their false gods had suffered, they swore vengeance against all Christians. First they tortured the one who had instructed the others, called Augustine, whom they left tied up a whole day in a public square exposed to the full glare of the sun, all the while that faithful servant of God was enjoying lights and interior fire far stronger than any burning him exteriorly.

There was another one called Paul, who was one of the most respected men in that same place, but seeing the faith persecuted in his home district, he no longer wished to live there. He left his property, and taking his son named Philip, as good a Christian as his father, he went to find another place to live where his religion wouldn't meet with so much opposi-

* A town just south of Quang-Tri and north of Hué. (TR.)

tion. He chose the royal city the better to lie hidden in that great crowd of people; and at the same time, to produce greater fruit, he became a schoolmaster at one place and his son Philip at another, for both were very skilled in Chinese letters. They did so well in a short time that they prepared many persons for accepting our holy faith whom the catechists later baptized.

But God, who was pleased with the courage of his servants Paul and Philip, wanted to reward them even temporally. Going through the streets one day, the king by chance ran into Paul, whom he had known at one time and thought a great deal of. He showed him much kindness and gave him one of the foremost judicial posts that was then open. Paul was surprised at this good fortune, which he didn't expect at all and well knew that God, for whom he had left everything in his native district, wanted to repay him with interest for all he had lost. This new temporal blessing renewed his courage for doing good both spiritually and temporally to all Christians. He put himself at their service with more fervor than before, and he can be said to have been a true Paul in that huge city.

And so Ignatius, arriving with his troop of elite, continued God's work which these three Christians had so happily begun. He baptized, preached, and confirmed all the Christians in their good resolves. Then going into his own district, which was a town called Hemcum, with a right good will for converting his fellow citizens, he experienced the truth of what our Lord said on profiting nothing by preaching in one's own country. Ignatius passed for a madman in the minds of all those who had looked up to him heretofore. He got nowhere at all except with the two people he was bound to respect most— his mother and his eighty-year-old grandfather. He baptized them both. Then, seeing it was just about the time I had promised to return, he betook himself to the place where I had told them to wait for me. That was the port of Kéan, where they all found one another come back laden with the fine spoils they had wrested from the devils.

❧ 39. My Fifth and Last Voyage to Cochinchina, and the Great Conversions that Took Place at Court

WHILE MY ten catechists covered all the provinces of Cochinchina so profitably, I withdrew to Macao on the advice of the Portuguese. Crossing the great China Sea, we ran into a storm so violent that the sea water, having filled our ship, polluted all the fresh water we had left because the kegs it was in happened not to be well stoppered. That was when we certainly thought ourselves lost beyond help if God didn't stretch out His hand to save us. We were in the middle of a huge ocean, seeing no land whatever where we might put in, and we had no fresh water at all to assuage us.

Despairing of all human help, we had recourse to God's. Everyone aboard got on his knees and made a vow to God that if we escaped this danger we would go on pilgrimage on leaving the ship to a beautiful church of our Lady that sits on a mountain near Macao and that is called Benha de França, i.e., Our Lady of the French Rock, and that we would carry the ship's mainsail on our shoulders. This vow was so pleasing to God that a good breeze arose of a sudden and carried us so well that the next day we began discerning the mountains of China and soon arrived at port, where we immediately discharged our vow. When I arrived before the altar of the Holy Virgin, I fell into a dead faint. Luckily two of our Fathers, Fr. Balthazar Citadelli, a native of Lucca, Italy, and Fr. Paul Calapresio, a Neapolitan, had come to Macao on pilgrimage to this chapel. They were conveniently on hand to help me. They had me carried to our college, where I soon recovered, purely through the joy of seeing my good Fathers after having lived two whole years without the consolation of seeing a priest.

I thought the Portuguese would leave as usual during the month of December, but they weren't ready until the end of January of the year 1644, with the result that I was absent from Cochinchina for about five months, which seemed very long to me as well as to my Christians, especially to my catechists, who were waiting for me at the appointed place. I finally arrived and found them assembled at our house at the harbor of Kéan. There were embraces and tears of joy on one side and the other, as may be imagined. They told me what they had done during my absence, or rather what God alone had done, because no one but Him could have set such great things in motion with instruments so weak.

After thanking the good Lord for all His graces, I left for court with my ten preachers, to all appearances for the purpose of paying my respects to the king and offering him my gifts, but actually to see the Christians both old and new, as well as my doughty Ignatius, whom I dubbed "Master" from that time on to lend him prestige, and made him wear a beautiful surplice when he appeared in public so he would command greater respect.

I saw the king, who showed me great kindness and accepted my gifts with much show of friendship. The next day he took the trouble to come visit me on my ship, where by great good luck he found me. I'm afraid that if he hadn't found me there he might have entertained some suspicion that I had gone to foment intrigue among the Christians; but as luck would have it, having spent the whole night at the home of a captain who wished to receive Baptism along with his wife, where many Christians had gathered to hear Mass and go to confession, I hadn't been able to satisfy them in so short a time. I dismissed them until the following night, where the crowd was such the house couldn't hold so many people, although it was one of the town's great houses. I was forced to ask the regular Christians to leave and make room for the new ones who wished to be baptized. The whole night was spent in

instructing and baptizing 200 new soldiers of Jesus Christ,
most of whom were soldiers by profession who were baptized
along with their wives and children, and among others the good
captain and his wife who were master and mistress of the
house. I named them Joachim and Anne. I leave my reader to
ponder whether it isn't better to spend the night in this good
pious work, baptizing 200 people, than to sleep in some comfortable bed. As for me, I truly declare that on finding myself
so nobly employed, I bore no envy whatever toward all those
having such comfortable beds and sleeping so peacefully. I
leave them that with a right good heart to go to Tonkin or
Cochinchina for such beautiful days and such profitable nights.

40. The Singular Piety of Madame Marie, the King's Aunt, and How I Was Summoned to Her Palace

AMONG THE serious superstitions that are current in the kingdom of Annam, there is one that enjoys great credence in
the minds of those poor blind people, and particularly in those
of princes. They believe infallibly that the good fortune of
their whole family depends on the place they choose to bury
their relatives, and especially their mothers, convinced that if
they can find a really suitable place to bury them, all their
progeny will continue in the royal line; that if the burial place
is unsuitable, their luck will soon leave them and they will
certainly lose their crowns.

In this crazy persuasion they take extreme care and incur
excessive expense in an effort to find a tomb where their relatives will really rest easy. There are many mathematicians
among them who grow rich plying this trade of finding proper

sepulchres for the repose of the dead. There is no important man who doesn't hire them for such research and who doesn't give them very heavy remuneration when they find, or pretend to find, for them what they're looking for.

The king of Cochinchina, who thinks we are very learned mathematicians, is afraid we might find his aunt Madame Marie some tomb so appropriate that the crown would fall to her descendants to the prejudice of all the royal household. This conviction throws him into a fit of jealousy when he hears that we go to her palace and treat with her, as if our purpose were to house her body really well in the earth when it was dead, and not finding her soul a beautiful throne in heaven!

That devout princess had aims far removed from those of the king. She sent word to me many times to ask me to come to her palace and teach her how to live right, and not how to enthrone her posterity. I went there secretly at night, so as not to irritate the king. I found a lady excelling in all Christian virtues, who received me as if I had been an angel. She saw to it that the sacraments were received by her whole family, who were very numerous. She was the first to make her confession and receive Communion. All the other Christians came there to take part in the Sacrament. I spent two days with them, and because there were several who had never seen the Blessing of the Palms, I gathered them all together on Sunday night and performed this beautiful rite of the Church, at which they assisted in such great consolation it seemed to me I was seeing the triumphal procession of the people of Jerusalem who carried palms before our Lord.

They very much wanted me to spend Holy Week with them, but I was afraid of being discovered, and I thought it better to go to the port of Kéan where the Portuguese were and where I would have a greater number of new Christians, who came from very far away to make their Easter duty, because I was the only priest in the whole of Cochinchina.

❧ 41. The Piety of the Christians during Holy Week, and Their Large Concourse from All Parts of the Kingdom

THUS I arrived in Cham province on Holy Wednesday. I found there a large gathering of all Christians in the province who were anxiously awaiting me. If I had had several bodies at the time, or rather if I had had with me several priests, we would have had plenty to keep us busy during these holy days. The Portuguese overlooked nothing that might promote devotion in all the Christians who had come to spend the Feast of the Passion and Resurrection of our Lord with us.

Anything I see in Europe doesn't evoke in me the religious feelings I entertained in that church, where there was indeed cause for praising God, seeing the diligence, the vigils, and the tears of all those Christians. One would have to have had a heart of stone not to have it melt on that occasion. We exposed the Blessed Sacrament on Holy Thursday. Many never left the church all day. In the evening, when they saw me wash the feet of some poor people, their faces were bathed in tears; but the next day, when I exposed the uncovered crucifix for them and had them venerate and kiss it while they chanted some very doleful hymns in their language on the Passion of our Lord, that was when the tears of devotion, flowing from their eyes in minor torrents, provided a laver for their sins and a beverage for all the holy angels. On Easter Day and on holy days and Sundays ever since, more than one Mass had to be said because the church, although quite spacious, couldn't accommodate the people who arrived from all directions.

Those from the more distant provinces couldn't wait for

me to come to their area. They couldn't endure their thirst for Mass and the sacraments that long. They arrived in great troops from the farthest reaches of the kingdom, in other words, from at least eighty leagues' distance, for this purpose alone. I retired to our house in Kéan to satisfy them more at leisure. I stayed a fortnight doing nothing else day and night but hearing the confessions of these good neophytes who, on accomplishing their pious desires, returned to their districts, as pleased as if they had found a treasure on their journey.

But among so many good people, there was one who deserved God's punishment for his malice. A very substantial merchant, but a bad Christian, a native of the province of Quinhin, lived at the port of Kéan and was growing rich by trading. He had left his lawful wife some time ago for another whom he kept to the great scandal of Christians and pagans alike. I had often warned him and on occasion rebuked him sharply for the great crime he was committing, and threatened him with the wrath of God, who wouldn't suffer him to go unpunished.

My warnings and threats were useless. The obstinate man couldn't bring himself to leave that unfortunate woman. God put His hand in by sending him a serious illness, but still he was so stubborn as to resist Him. At the height of his sickness he had me called and told me he wanted to go to confession, of which he had been deprived so long. I insisted that unless he drove out of his house the person who had separated him from God, he could never return to Him nor receive absolution for all his grievous sins.

For so long as he thought death inevitable he promised me he would, but he kept delaying until, finding his sickness relieved, he made mock of God whom he thought he no longer needed. But God certainly made mock of him. A heavy storm arose over the whole sea and land of Cochinchina. It caused such great damage that many ships were sunk at sea and many houses leveled on dry land. There were everywhere many people, some drowned in the waters, some crushed in the ruins of houses. By God's grace not one of our Christians was involved in this misfortune with the exception of that wretch who was still convalescing. Still he thought he had escaped, because he had had himself carried into one of his houses where he thought himself safe.

But God knew where to find him all right. That house, which the storm had loosened in its joints, was completely demolished a few days later by a heavy rain. All others in it were saved. It was only that wretch, whom God's hand pursued after His mercy had long proved futile, who was buried in the ruins whereas his guilty soul was buried in hell—at any rate, he died without the sacraments and in a state of disobedience to God and the Church. This was a powerful lesson to all the others for keeping them in the path of duty for fear of so manifest a judgment of God.

42. The Wonderful Conversion of Certain Noteworthy Persons

AT THE time this distressing accident occurred in Kéan, I had gone secretly to the royal city to assist several devout persons who were expecting me. I made the palace of Madame Marie, the king's aunt, my retreat where I heard confessions and distributed Communion without the slightest respite for a fortnight, and even so I was obliged to send many away whom I judged still not sufficiently prepared.

We even baptized several from the king's palace, and among others an excellent goldsmith whom the king loved dearly, who was converted so completely he himself became a preacher and produced much fruit, especially in the town where he was born. He prepared many pagans for Baptism. He built them a beautiful church at his own expense and then begged me to go complete God's work that he had so happily begun. I went gladly and found a very beautiful house ready there. I did all that was necessary on my part in instructing and baptizing these new Christians.

Going farther north I found a fervent Christian called Dominic, baptized by Fr. Benedict de Mattos hardly three years before. He was a real apostle in his district. He had already caused many pagans to decide to quit their superstitions. He had instructed them very well concerning all our mysteries and had even persuaded them to observe Christian fasts and feast days. I found thirty of the lot quite ready to receive Baptism, which I conferred on them after further instruction. This increase continued so happily day by day that in a short time a fine Christian community existed that the fervent Dominic cultivated with incredible care, and he even built them a beautiful church.

After covering the whole core of the kingdom, I finally reached the province of Quambin, which is on the Tonkinese border where that strong wall that separates the two kingdoms is situated. The Tonkinese have often made efforts to gain control of it, but this has always proved futile. I went immediately to the chief city of the province and presented my gifts to the governor, who showed me much kindness, and he spoke to me so pertinently about our mysteries that I had reason for believing he had once been a Christian, which nevertheless he would never admit.

It's there I met an excellent Christian, a soldier by profession who was called Francis and lived at home with his wife Teresa in the practice of all the most beautiful virtues. The good man had begun honoring the holy Virgin even before becoming a Christian. He found a beautiful picture of Our Lady of the Rosary in the hands of some pagans. He bought it quite dearly and from that time he placed it in a shrine within the enclosure of his house where he honored it day and night. It wasn't long before he was repaid for his trouble. That benign guest soon obtained the grace of Baptism for him and then that of a holy life, both for him and his wife as well.

Francis was an example to all the Christians, and Teresa had a special gift for driving away devils, for whom she had once served as pythoness, but she became their great scourge. Both one and the other had no other occupation beyond bringing unbelievers to knowledge of the true God. I found a large number of them already prepared for receiving Baptism. I gathered them all together in Francis' house, which had been converted into a church, but the chapel where he kept the picture of his good patroness was very well appointed. He had such great reverence for her he never dared set foot there without purifying his soul beforehand, performing some bodily mortification, as he himself admitted to me; and certainly the holy Virgin gave him a hundredfold in exchange, because besides exterior graces he had a wonderful gift for performing all kinds of miracles.

43. How My Former Christians in Tonkin Sent a Distinguished Delegation to Invite Me to Go Visit Them

THE TONKINESE Christians living in Bochinh province heard tell I was at the Cochinchinese border and thought they could easily persuade me to push on a bit farther to go comfort them. They immediately wrote me a beautiful letter in the name of all the Christians in general and of each in particular, in which they implored me not to refuse them the favor of going to see them. The letter was written in such obliging terms that it really touched me. I would have liked to accede to their wishes with all my heart, and I think I certainly desired to take them the sacraments as passionately as they wished to receive them.

But I was nonetheless reminded that I couldn't cross over into Tonkin without going through the great wall separating the two kingdoms; that the guards watching it for the king of Cochinchina wouldn't fail to report my leaving his kingdom to enter his enemy's; that this would make him suspicious of me and angry with the Christians, with possible dire consequences for both. These reasons seemed to me so sound that I chose the peace of the Cochinchinese over the desires of the Tonkinese. I limited myself to writing them a letter of regret and sent them my excellent catechist Ignatius, who went to preach to them and strengthen them in the Christian faith, whereby he brought them such blessings that those devout Christians couldn't bear to have him leave after doing them so much good.

But, the better to accomplish their purpose in drawing me to their country, they thought a delegation would be more forceful than just a letter in bringing me to such a decision. They delegated ten leading Christians of the province of Bochinh, who came to see me in Cochinchina. I admit that when I saw them I experienced in my heart every emotion of love, joy, and yearning that a mother can feel for her beloved children.

Foremost among them was an excellent Christian called Simon, whom I had baptized in Tonkin when he was sixteen. At this first meeting we embraced each other with so many tears on both sides we couldn't part. The good fellow related to me the wonderful things God had done through his instrumentality over the whole district where his home was. In the town where he lived there was not one pagan. All the devils had been driven out. There were at least a thousand Christians who were living very holy lives although they had never seen a priest.

One who was a marvelous help to Simon in this loving work of piety was another Christian called Francis, one of the ten who had taken the trouble to come see me. He had a singular gift for performing miracles. A very large number of them were described to me.

You can imagine how I longed to go see this new fold of Jesus Christ and bring it the spiritual nourishment of the sacraments, which till now they had never received, but I told them out loud the same things I had written them. They stayed with us a few days, made their confessions, and received Communion with an exterior devotion mirroring that in their hearts, and after a thousand embracings they returned to their country, filled with zeal for working harder than ever to establish the kingdom of Jesus Christ.

⤳ 44. About Three Leading Magistrates Who Took a Fancy to the Christian Doctrine, Which They Would Not Embrace through Human Respect

HAVING SPENT sufficient time in this last province of Cochinchina, I returned to the royal city to visit with the Christians in passing, without staying long. At court there was a leading magistrate who stood very much in the king's good graces, and he had even been employed to instruct him and to teach him to write Chinese. Since first coming to Cochinchina some twenty years or so ago, I had the good fortune to be known to him, and I had seen all along that he was partial to Christians, although human respect proved more powerful in his soul than the truth he had come up against.

In the year 1644 I made up my mind to see him and speak to him more fully about our mysteries, which I had not done in the past when I lacked fluency in speaking the native tongue. He received me with very great kindness and listened to me gladly. I also presented him with some books written in Chinese characters that our Fathers had put together, in which they explain the Christian truths. He accepted them with great reverence and promised me certainly to read them at leisure, and furthermore, after reading them carefully and assimilating them, to speak seriously to the king about the Christian religion. I thereupon importuned him to embrace it himself that he might persuade the king all the better. He didn't dare take the step, but he gladly permitted his wife to, and all those of his servants who wanted to become Christians. I baptized the good lady and several other persons in the family, hoping God would move their master's heart more profoundly.

Another magistrate very influential at court, on hearing me spoken of to his friend and neighbor Onghebo, invited me to come see him and tell him something about our mysteries. I don't know his motive in summoning me, but on entering I found a room filled with pagans, among whom were many idolatrous priests whom they call *sais*.

I began my talk by describing the justice of God, who is the supreme King of the world. I showed how rigorous He is toward those who refuse to obey Him, to the point of punishing them with eternal fire, and on the other hand how gentle and gracious toward those who live right and the care He has for them both in this life and the next—which I explained by means of the story of the three children God saved in the furnace in Babylon.

Several of those listening to me were beginning to savor my words, but the more obstinate ones sometimes interrupted me and put forward some nonsense from their idols and their books, so I besought my Ignatius, who was present, to refute them, because he was very well versed in all their books and possessed special grace for disproving all the errors of these idolaters. He did so with such vigor and enlightenment that all these gentlemen remained at a loss, though not disposed for conversion.

The embarrassment they suffered on this occasion turned to rage against the valiant preacher. They swore to destroy him on the spot, and to accomplish their purpose they betook themselves to a lady* whom the king maintained as his wife, al-

* Tông-thi-Toai. (TR.)

though she had formerly belonged to his brother—which the laws of the kingdom forbid, but impurity knows no law.

The lord who had asked me to his house was considerably better humored. It's true the talk didn't convert him, but he nevertheless remained so satisfied with it that he was partial to Christians ever after. As I left his palace he presented me with a goodly sum of money for the trouble I had taken in coming to see him, but I declined, telling him that I had anticipated no temporal wages in coming to teach him the way to eternal life. After that he spoke to the king so effectively in our behalf that he permitted me to come and go freely at court. He even gave evidence of entertaining a kindly feeling toward our holy faith, and we enjoyed the effects for some time.

45. The Zeal of a Devout Christian Called John in Converting Unbelievers

WHEN I saw the king so favorably disposed toward me, I tried discreetly to see to it that our holy faith should reap the benefits we desired. At Madame Marie's palace the manager of her son's affairs, the king's uncle, backed me up marvelously in my purpose. He skillfully seized every opportunity he ran across to lead those involved in error into the way of truth.

Among others whom he challenged with a mind to conversion, he had very much at heart the salvation of an old octogenarian who had served idols very conscientiously all his life and had acquired a great reputation at court and throughout that large province. First he set about showing him the stupid errors to which idol worshipers subscribed, ever proving his statements by their most authoritative books. Then he led him to realize the importance of putting to good use the few years of life remaining to him in order to make satisfaction for his whole past life, during which he had contracted such heavy debts—that there was no better way than bringing one's whole mind and heart to the knowledge and love of the true God and His only begotten Son Jesus Christ.

The good old man listened attentively to all these wonderful words, which made such a strong impression on him that then and there he turned over all these excellent admonitions in his mind and finally consented to whatever John might prescribe for his salvation. He wasn't content with receiving Baptism but wanted his whole family to receive it. At the first session I baptized thirty of them, of whom he was first, and he continued to secure for many others the same happiness he had himself obtained at the end of his life.

John didn't succeed so well with another great lord who was a captain and commanded part of the king's troops. He had already grasped the truth of our holy faith so well, and especially how it accords with reason, that he was entirely resolved to embrace it. He had already renounced idol worship. He was reading our books and giving them to others to read. He had our pictures and was venerating them.

When it was a question of going into battle, he didn't care to perform any of those profane ceremonies that pagans are foolishly convinced are necessary for succeeding at it. The good captain laughed at all that and much preferred to direct his petitions to the true God who was both able and willing to lend him His aid.

His piety gave scandal to the unbelievers, who complained about it to the king, who was very annoyed. Feeling his military future was at stake, he summoned the captain and berated him sharply, ordering him to quit all Christian superstitions and remain true to the native religion. The poor man found himself too weak to withstand the king's anger. He preferred to obey him rather than God, who had made the truth known to him.

A quite similar circumstance prevented the conversion of

one of the greatest lords of the kingdom, which pained me
very deeply. I have often spoken of the devotion of Madame
Magdalene. Her husband was governor of the province of
Ranran [Phun-rang, Phu-Yen] and held all the most important
posts at court. His wife, as much by her good example as by her
words, had given him great respect and love for all Christians,
but it had never been possible to persuade him to surrender to
the light that was showing him the way to heaven.

Taking my leave of him one day, I said in the presence of
his wife that I was extremely unhappy to see him resist God so
long, that he must make up his mind if he didn't want to lose
his soul forever, that he was already over eighty and that his
life couldn't last long. I advised him to think on eternal things.
He was touched by these words, which his wife seconded and
enlivened by her own exhortations filled with the spirit of God.

He surrendered completely and told me he was ready to do
whatever I told him, that he wanted to become a Christian
and was very sorry he had delayed so long. At these words
Madame Marie and I were transported with joy. We blessed
God for it with a right good heart, and so as not to defer a
thing we had so long hoped for, I began instructing him immediately to prepare him for Baptism. Already everything was
in readiness for performing the ceremony. I had the surplice
on, the candles were lit, the holy water ready.

I explained all the duties of a Christian to him, and among
others that of never offering homage to any idol whatsoever.
Thereupon he told me that as far as he was concerned he was
quite resolved never to put any faith in the cult of all those
devils, but he could nevertheless not dispense with showing
some exterior deference to a certain idol that all captains com-
manding the king's armies are obliged to honor; that in his
heart he would always be far from it, but if he took it upon
himself not to make at least this show, he would ruin his fortunes and might even endanger his life; that he wasn't going
to gamble on losing either one or the other.

Never was I more surprised. His wife and I exerted all the

pressure and made all the remonstrances we could think of to help him overcome this trifling difficulty that would be an obstacle to his whole salvation. He would never give in, so great is the power of self-interest over a heart enslaved to its passions. We had to lay aside everything we had started to do. Still, he wanted me to give him on paper the sacred names of Jesus and Mary written in my hand, and he promised me he would always keep them on him. I trust this devotion and the constant prayers of his most virtuous wife will obtain him more generous resolves from God before his death.

❧ 46. About a Famous Doctor Who Remained Obdurate in Paganism

BEFORE RELATING another instance, wherein I proved to be not so good a doctor to souls as another was a good doctor to bodies, perhaps you won't mind my saying something about the doctors of Cochinchina, their skill, and the methods they use in practicing medicine.

In all these countries where there is such great strictness and so much ritual is used in graduating doctors, I was especially surprised never to hear of doctors of medicine. These people will become objects of ridicule if I say anybody who wants to can set himself up as a doctor, and it would seem a bad idea to entrust oneself to people who must certainly make sport of the sick; still, I who have found myself in their hands and who am witness to what they can do, can state that they are not inferior to our doctors and that in some things they even surpass them.

It's true that with them there is no university where one studies medicine, but it is a science taught from father to son. They have their private books that never leave the family, containing the secrets of the art, which they communicate to no one. They excel particularly in knowledge of the pulse, by which they are supposed to recognize all the particulars of an illness. As soon as the doctor calls on the patient, he takes his pulse and spends over a quarter of an hour contemplating it. Then he is supposed to tell the patient in what part of his body he is ailing and all the symptoms he has had since he fell sick.

This is the way the doctor's ability is judged. The patient never tells him his trouble, but the doctor must tell him, along with all he has suffered. If he doesn't hit it right he is dismissed as an ignoramus. If he can say what the patient has experienced, he is to be trusted. They divide the pulse into three parts and say the first corresponds to the head, the next to the stomach, and the third to the belly. Also, they always feel it with three fingers, and to tell the truth, they read it very well.

All physicians in this country are apothecaries. They never call on a patient without being accompanied by a valet carrying a bag filled with all the simples they use in their remedies. They prescribe them and have them made for the patients themselves, so there can never be that *quid pro quo* on the part of apothecaries so often complained of in Europe. I don't know how they do it, but their medicines are never hard to take like ours, and what's more they aren't expensive, for the highest priced don't cost over five cents.

They never purge intermittent fevers, but only give certain medications that correct the character of the humors without purging. It has been my experience that they get rid of a fever that way at least as often as we do in Europe with so much purging, enemas, and bloodletting. Cupping-glasses are much used by them, and as the weather is never cold there, I often saw them applied in the middle of the street.

When a doctor begins seeing a patient, the fee to be paid is agreed on with him, but it is paid only after the patient is cured. If he dies the poor doctor gets paid nothing. They figure, perhaps quite rightly, that the fear of wasting his time makes the doctor more solicitous in treating the patient. One of my companions came down with a very troublesome ailment that was like a kind of canker. I called the doctor, and following the native custom I bargained with him about what I would pay him if he cured him. He told me that if the patient were younger he wouldn't cure him for less than 100 crowns, but that he would be satisfied with 20 because he was already old and the life he would give him couldn't last long. I gladly promised him the twenty crowns, and he cured my sick man very well in a short time. That's what I know about the doctors of the country I'm now speaking of.

In June of the year 1644 I was beset by a fever so violent I thought it would carry me off. I called a very famous doctor who, after feeling my pulse in a most leisurely manner, told me with a smile, "Don't worry, Father, your sickness is in no way mortal. Whether you take my medicine or whether you leave it, you'll surely recover, but you'll recover much sooner if you take it."

"I want to take it," I told him, "and pay well for it!"

Thereupon he took certain simples from his bag, made various packets of them, and then told me how to prepare and take the medicine in two doses. I took it the next two days and on the third I was feverless. Soon after I was completely restored.

I felt an obligation to my doctor not only to pay him the money I had promised him, but far more to cure his soul by making him forsake idols and acknowledge Jesus Christ. I spoke to him so often and God worked so well in his soul that he promised me to become a convert. I began instructing him in our mysteries and, explaining God's commandments to him, I told him the obligation we were under to keep no idol nor any altar dedicated to one. He told me to stop there, that all the doctors in the country had great reverence for a certain ancient doctor who had first taught medicine, that every doctor had a little altar dedicated to him in his house.

As for himself, from then on he would be careful to pay him no homage at that altar, but that if he was obliged to tear it down, he couldn't obey me, because on seeing that, his servants would immediately broadcast it and nothing more was needed to discredit all his prescriptions and even render him liable to punishment as a traitor to one of the most beautiful customs of the kingdom. With that I had to desist. My prayers and remonstrances proved useless. He had cured me so well, and he couldn't cure his own poor soul. I learned with great sorrow that he died a pagan for not having availed himself properly of the remedy God was supplying him by my ministry.

47. First Triumphs of This New Church in the Glorious Death of Andrew, Catechist and Proto-Martyr

UNTIL NOW the Church in Cochinchina had pretty well enjoyed peace and quiet, although at times it had been attacked rudely enough, but she still hadn't shed blood in support of her Master's cause and couldn't appear before the throne of the Lamb clad in purple, bearing the crown on her head and the palm in her hands, because she still possessed no martyr willing to lose his life rather than lose his faith. God reserved this honor for a young man nineteen years old whom I had baptized three years before and whom I had in my company about two years helping me teach catechism.

I don't want to take long in telling this beautiful story, which I wrote up in a separate volume and that I made available in French and Italian. With all my heart I would like to make this admirable servant of God known to as many nations as there are on earth in order to excite them to the knowledge and love of the One this young man died for. I will relate here very briefly the circumstances of the story, referring my reader to the book I wrote on it.*

* *La Glorieuse Mort d'André, Catéchiste de la Cochinchina, qui a le*

It was then in July of the year 1644 that the governor of Cham province returned from court with an order—not from the king, who had manifested great friendship for me—but from that queen who as I said bore such hatred toward Christians and who had sworn especially to destroy Ignatius. The governor willingly undertook the commission because it was consistent with the ill will he had shown us for some time. He began with a good old man called Andrew, whom he took prisoner. Then he sent a company of soldiers to our house to get Ignatius, whom he was determined to put to death.

As luck would have it, I happened to be out with Ignatius and my catechists, except for a young man called Andrew, who had asked me to let him stay to nurse four of his companions who were sick. I had gone to pay my respects to the governor not knowing what he was contriving against us. I was apprised of it only at the door of his palace, where a Portuguese lord came to tell me what was afoot. He advised me to leave as soon as possible and take my catechists to some safe place.

I dismissed all the young men immediately, who asked for nothing better than to die. I went on to the governor as though completely unaware of what he had done, but he spoke to me very insolently, and I well saw I would have trouble changing his mind. I went on to the prison to see the good old man, whom I found loaded with a ladder according to the native custom, but nonetheless so cheerful you would have thought he was in a palace. I wanted to stay with him all night, but the jailer wouldn't let me. I retired to a boat where all my little band lay waiting.

Meanwhile the soldiers were doing a lot of damage at our house. They had entered by main force. They had made a careful search for Ignatius, but on Andrew's telling them they were all guilty of the same crimes they held against his comrade,

premier versé son sang pour la querelle de Jésus-Christ en cete nouvelle Eglise, par le R. P. Alex. de Rhodes, S.J., qui a toujours été présent á toute cette histoire (Paris: Cramoisy, 1653). The Italian translation was Corbelletti's (Rome, 1652).

they were ashamed to return without having carried out any part of their commission. They took Andrew and led him off securely bound, after ransacking the place and stealing all the holy images, along with all our church furnishings. Andrew very blithely followed them, and he preached constantly the whole way to those taking him to prison on how to avoid hell and go to heaven.

This rather served to irritate them than convert them. They passed by the boat where we were hiding and asked whether we had seen Ignatius. The dark of night saved us. Young Andrew was taken to the governor and indicted as a Christian and a preacher. He was straightway taken to the prison where the other confessor of Jesus Christ, whose name was also Andrew, was to be found already. Together they spent the rest of the night, which they were convinced would be the last of their lives, and bolstered each other's courage by hopes of being both in heaven the next day.

When morning came the governor, desirous of putting a good face on his crime, got some sort of trial together. The two innocents were made to appear together and immediately condemned without so much as a hearing. They were then led back to prison with execution of sentence due to take place the same day. I got there as soon as I could, but the sentence had already been formulated and pronounced. The Portuguese all went with me to the governor and to whoever had any influence over him. We pleaded many times with him, going so far as to badger and threaten him. He remained unshakable in his evil resolve. He told me that as far as the old man was concerned, he would grant his life because he felt sorry for his children, but as for that young prig who said he was a Christian and that death itself couldn't make him relinquish the title, he would die as he said, in order to teach everyone the obedience they owed the king.

When I saw it was beyond my power to save my good Andrew's life, I determined to prepare him to lose it like a true Christian and martyr. I won't dwell on what I did with him in prison; it would take too long to tell. When he saw me after his death sentence had been pronounced, he fell into wonderful transports of joy. He told all the Christians, who came to see him in droves, everything a St. Lawrence ready for grilling might have told them. He made his confession, betook himself to prayer, bade farewell to all, and blithely followed a company of forty soldiers into a field a half league outside town.

I was at his side the whole time, and I could hardly keep up with him he was going so fast, despite being burdened with a very heavy ladder. When he arrived at the scene appointed for his triumph, he immediately got on his knees so as to do battle more courageously. The soldiers surrounded him. They had me put out of their circle, but the captain allowed me to come in and stay near him. He was therefore kneeling on the ground, his eyes raised to heaven, his mouth ever open pronouncing the name of Jesus.

A soldier coming up behind him pierced him with his lance, which emerged at least two palms' length at the front. At that the good Andrew looked at me very lovingly as if bidding me adieu. I told him to look to heaven where he was going and where our Lord Jesus Christ was waiting for him. He raised his eyes and shifted his glance no more. The same soldier, having pulled out his lance, drove it a second time with redoubled force as if seeking his heart.

That didn't even shake the poor innocent, which seemed utterly amazing to me. Finally another soldier, seeing that three blows from the lance hadn't brought him down, gave him his scimitar across the neck, but accomplishing nothing, he struck another blow that so severed his throat that his head fell to the right, held on only by a bit of skin. But at the moment his head was separated from his neck I heard very distinctly the sacred name of Jesus—which could no longer come from his mouth—issue from the wound, and the instant his soul flew to heaven, his body fell to earth.

The soldiers withdrew, leaving us this precious relic. We took it up in our arms, placed it in a beautiful chest, collected all his blood, and gave the holy martyr burial—not very sumptuous, but certainly devout. I carried the precious remains into my boat where all my companions were waiting. When they saw me with the remains of their dear comrade who had gone straight to heaven, you would have thought they were out of their wits, they experienced such sorrow and happiness at once. I sent the holy body to Macao, where it was received with great magnificence at our college. Later I had the verbal testimony of twenty-three witnesses who had seen this great steadfastness, but I kept the head for myself, and God granted me the grace of taking it to Rome.*

I don't wish to relate here in detail the great wonders God wrought after this holy death. In the book I wrote about it I told how fire, sea, and earth testified to the glory of this faithful friend of God. Three days after his death fire broke out in the town where Andrew had been condemned. It burned down the prison where he had been locked up, the whole street he had passed through, and several temples dedicated to idols. I'll tell later what happened to me at sea, and since I've been in Paris four different people who were very sick, on commending themselves to the prayers of the glorious martyr, have recovered their health in ways each considered to be entirely miraculous, as can be seen in the book.

ᵔᵔ 4 8 . The Constancy of Another Christian Called Andrew, and Many Others

ALTHOUGH THE junior Andrew carried off the martyr's crown over the elder, the fact is the latter won that of a glorious confessor of Jesus Christ. He was the Christian of longest

* The head of Andrew, whose cause is now (1965) before the Holy See, is today in the Jesuit Curia in Rome. His body was taken to the Jesuit Church in Macao and enshrined there with those of numerous Vietnamese and Chinese martyrs, but the Church was later destroyed by fire. All their ashes were gathered together and are now kept in one small box. (TR.)

standing not only in the town of Caichan where he was born, but in all Cochinchina. He had the honor of having been the first to be persecuted for the honor of Jesus Christ, not only once, but four times, and he always upheld his Master's cause so bravely he always came out ahead over all enemies of the faith.

He was the first to be taken prisoner in the religious struggle and was the first to sport as Christian soldier and knight that beautiful yoke of honor we call the "cross of Cochinchina." He was delivered from all his encounters, and although it's true martyrdom missed him, he didn't run out on martyrdom. He had a wife called Ignatia and two children, Emmanuel and Louis, faithful replicas of his own virtue. His house was the great refuge for all Christians in both calm and storm. He had built a quite capacious church there where many pagans were baptized, instructed, and strengthened by the sacraments. This is why he was so often attacked in his person, his children, and his goods, but none of it could tear Christ from his heart. He was the most respected magistrate in the whole town of Caichan, but he always preferred the opprobrium of the cross to all the honors of Egypt. Eventually Onghebo tired of harassing him before he tired of suffering. Thereafter he lived peacefully at home. In the latest letters I received from that country, dated in the year 1648, I learned that he died a holy death in his house, ever steadfast in the faith and covered with glory for the many insults he endured for its sake.

After the glorious death of Andrew I was given a very express order to leave Cochinchina when the Portuguese ships went; nevertheless I thought it would be extremely cowardly to abandon the flock of Jesus Christ while wolves were attacking it and then leave it without a pastor. I thought it better to risk my life than the salvation of so many souls the Son of God so loves. I decided to remain in hiding in a boat in order to go visit the Christians by night and dispense the sacraments to them.

The better to disguise my purpose, I boarded the Portuguese

ship in plain sight of the whole city of Cham when they left for China, but I had sent word to my catechists, who were hiding in a sampan, to go wait for me three leagues out of the harbor. There I left the Portuguese ship, where I put my martyr's body to be taken to Macao, and I boarded my sampan, happier than if I had been in a gilded mansion. We spent our days in all the pious devotions we could, and to tell the truth those nine young men lived there like angels. When night fell it wasn't a time of rest for us, but when our work began, for we always had to be out in the field.

In the meantime the persecution continued on the increase, and the zeal of our good Christians, also on the increase, braved the fury of all tyrants. Onghebo was carrying on a very thorough search for all holy images and was dispatching soldiers into all Christian homes to cart them off. A good matron called Magdalene, although very old, showed remarkable strength of spirit in the encounter. The pagans knew she kept a beautiful picture of our Lord in her house that had heretofore been in the church. They were determined to get it, but she said she'd die rather than give it up.

They tormented her all night long, putting her feet to the torture, but she laughed at them and all their tortures, assuring them they were taking trouble for nothing, that even if they cut off her feet, her tongue would never betray her heart, which was all Christ's. In fact the persecutors, getting nowhere, were obliged to leave, taking with them only their embarrassment.

Many other Christians manifested a like constancy in the horrible tortures they withstood to make them surrender their images, but God finally took matters into His own hands. One of the soldiers, who had been among the more insolent in the search for holy images, was suddenly seized with a pain in the neck so violent that he died of it within two days as though mad. The governor was not punished in his person, but in his goods. Cattle are very highly valued in that country because they are used to cultivate the land. The governor lost fifty of them in a few days. These two accidents occurring at the same time softened the persecutors a bit.

I couldn't keep silent about the generosity of a Christian called Anthony Té, who was the richest and most powerful man in a large town where he lived with his family. He had done so well that there wasn't a pagan left in that town. When he saw the horrible persecution, he was afraid many of his recent converts would be shaken by it. He got them all together, and after exhorting them strongly to constancy, he asked them for all the pictures and holy objects they kept in their houses so he could put them in a safe place, and told them not to worry if fines were imposed because he would pay them all. Which he did with so light a heart that through Anthony's liberality that whole fine church grew rich in merit and remained firm in the faith.

49. The Great Confession of Faith Made by Thirty-five Christians during a Heavy Persecution

WHEN THE Christians of the Province of Quinhin heard of the glorious martyrdom of Andrew, far from wanting to give ground when attacked, they rather took fresh courage in resisting tyrants one and all. I had entrusted the administration of this church to a very virtuous Christian called Anthony Ngu who, fired by the desire of winning a crown like Andrew's, took to the road immediately to come get advice on what he should do in such an eventuality. I sent him back right away with orders to encourage all Christians in the struggle in which they might find themselves involved in the threatening persecution.

He set to at just the right time and acquitted himself so well of what I had told him that all the Christians found themselves marvelously prepared to meet their enemies when they came to attack them. Only a few days later a criminal judge sent by the governor came to the province, and on entering the first town immediately ordered all Christians to step forward and declare themselves, under pain of severe punishment should they be discovered.

He thought this would terrify the soldiers of Christ and that no one would dare declare himself for fear of being penalized, but he was quite astonished to see Christians arriving in droves to get their names entered. In less than a day there were 700 of them, and more appeared by the minute. The judge didn't want to press matters further, well aware that pursuing this course would serve only to increase his embarrassment.

He would have liked to retract his statement, but finding himself honor bound, he selected thirty-six out of the large number, whom he ordered heavily shackled, and took them to Cham province where our great enemy Onghebo was waiting for them. But he was no less astonished than his deputy when he saw the squad of thirty-six Christians standing before him determined to give way neither to his threats nor his insults.

He didn't even have the nerve to question them, but handed the job over to another, who began by asking them whether they desired to live or whether they had really made up their minds to die. "We want to live," they all said, "but live the life eternal that Jesus Christ promised to all who believe in him," and that in order to possess this life, they considered it a favor to be allowed to die. He subjoined various queries, but such courageous replies were always given to him, they only led him to despair of changing their minds.

Nevertheless, among the three times twelve disciples of the Son of God, there was a Judas who like a coward abandoned Him. He was an old man who was exceedingly rich and powerful within his clan. He proved to be far less brave than his thirty-five comrades, who felt lively sorrow at seeing their brother and dear friend thus take leave of their Master and Captain because he was afraid of death and the loss of his goods, which he loved inordinately. The poor wretch renounced his faith. I tried to see him later to bring him back to his duty, but I never got a chance to see him, since the pagans watched him so closely for fear he might escape them on a second occasion.

The cowardice of this deserter increased the courage of all the others, who remained steadfast in the solid confession of faith they had so well begun and for which they hoped to be able to reap death, which would make martyrs of them for Jesus Christ. But the governor, who well knew that the force he was using exceeded the powers he had from the king, who would take it ill if he put all these Christians to death, limited himself to intimidating them all by his threats. He selected six out of the whole thirty-five for a public flogging in the main square of Caichan, thinking this would be enough to frighten all the others. But before making the selection the next day, he had them locked up to spend all night in prison.

When I was apprised of what was going on, I found a way of winning over the guards, who let me into the prison, which seemed a paradise to me. As soon as my thirty-five confessors of Jesus Christ saw me come in, we all knelt on the floor to thank the Father of lights for granting us such wonderful brightness in the dark night of prison. Then after a thousand embraces, I began instructing them on all they should do in the circumstances, when they might either win or lose all.

They all made their confessions to me, heard the Mass I said for them, and then received Communion from my hands. The delights felt on such occasions are ineffable, because they are akin in nature to the delights of heaven. They are furthermore foretastes of them. After thus comforting them, I left at daybreak.

A few hours later the judge delegated by the governor came to the prison to choose six out of the thirty-five to be loaded with those uncomfortable ladders we call the cross of Cochinchina, and then cruelly beaten before the eyes of the whole town. Then was seen the finest battle ever beheld in

Cochinchina: thirty-five Christians who all loved one another like brothers and were all of one heart and mind, began a holy fight among themselves, as if only the love of Jesus that united them were capable of spreading dissension among them.

All wanted to be among the chosen six, and none wanted to be out of that number, because he wouldn't have the honor of suffering. This was the sole cause of their loving dissension, because no one wanted to be let off from torture. One alleged as his reason that he was the Christian of longest standing; another that he possessed greater endurance for suffering; another that he was less necessary to the Church; finally each conceded his comrade's greater merits in order to excel him in glory by suffering.

Under the circumstances the judge didn't know whether he should get angry or laugh, whether he should satisfy them all by making them all suffer, or whether he should punish them all by dismissing them all without chastising any of them. But when he saw a father and a son engaged in this gracious struggle, that was when he realized the wisdom of Christians has laws he never heard of. The father was lovingly telling his son that he was surprised that he would dispute precedence with his father, that he had much less strength than he, but no less courage than he. The son respectfully replied that he was far less necessary to the world than his father, who had a large family to feed; that in this alone he could dispute with his father and disobey him without sin. They both wanted to have that ladder put on their necks, and both came forward to receive it; but the judge, enchanted by such warfare, made peace between them by acceding to the wishes of neither. He dismissed them both, quite astonished at the generosity Christian faith imparts.

He chose six others, first among whom was Anthony Ngu, of whom I spoke at the beginning of this chapter. Ladders were put on the necks of all of them. Then, the other twenty-nine having been dismissed, the six were led to the square to be chastised. You would have noted a very different mien among them. The twenty-nine who were leaving without receiving the slightest injury had melancholy faces and were walking very quietly. The others, whose shoulders were laden with a heavy load, were going along gaily as if they had wings. When they arrived before the judges, they expected to be condemned to death, and that was the great grace they hoped for.

They were very surprised to be condemned only to a sound thrashing and flogging in the main square of Caichan, and they were even less happy when they saw that the soldiers supposed to execute the sentence felt sorry for them and would carry it out only very gently. They were satisfied with giving each one four or five blows of a stick and then dismissed them all.

The six of them came together to find me, complaining loudly of the excessive gentleness of those judges and their deputies. I consoled them by telling them that before God good will supplies for its effects, that maybe this first encounter was a little rehearsal for some major assault when they would be able to prove their faithfulness fully.

50. The Last Runs I Made While Hiding in a Boat around the Southern Provinces

THE FURY of our sworn enemy Onghebo didn't abate on thus harassing the Christians. It extended even to the churches where they were wont to pray. He had three very beautiful ones torn down in Quinhin province, but the fervor of the faithful didn't cool at that. It rather grew more ardent for its enemies' outrages. I remained in hiding for a few days in the town that had been the scene of the courageous stand of those thirty-five generous soldiers, and I was delighted at the time that several pagans wished to be baptized in the hope of being able to die in defense of the religion they were embracing.

This went on until the fifteenth of September of that same year 1644. Meanwhile I sent my wonderful catechist Ignatius to the north, and I took off for the southern provinces to console the Christians for the loss of their churches that they had sustained. A worthy Christian called Peter Lao, one of the latter six confessors of Jesus Christ in the town of Caichan, bravely offered to accompany me everywhere and to pilot my boat wherever I wanted to go, even offering me his house to rest in and get the Christians together there whenever I liked.

A few days before we made our appearance on the coast, robbers had committed a heavy theft in the town of Quinhin. When our boat was discovered, which was kept at a distance in very out-of-the-way places, we were believed to have pulled off the job. Suddenly we were surrounded on all sides while I was vesting to say Mass. The boat was immediately boarded. All my companions were bound and soundly beaten in the belief that they were the sports who had committed the theft.

We all thought we were being mistreated this way for being Christians and not brigands. I handed myself over to the soldiers to be tied up like my companions, but no one dared touch me with baneful intent. We were taken to the judge, who began laughing as soon as he saw us and dismissed us after apologizing to us, ordering his soldiers to restore to us any trinkets of ours they might have. We then realized the reason for this harassment and praised God who had sent it to us.

After this incident there was no longer any way of concealing my arrival. All the Christians who were informed of it arrived from every direction. That fervent Christian called Anthony who was the catechist for this sector had recently baptized 140 pagans, children, or others who had been in no condition to defer this salutary remedy. He brought me a huge troop who had had the time to wait. We had the consolation of finding more still, all of whom we baptized.

After a few days the Christians decided that if I remained thus in full sight of all the enemies of our holy faith, I was

risking doing them great harm and incurring the same for myself. They started a rumor that I was leaving and found me the
house of a Christian lady of long standing called Paula, widow
of a worthy servant of God called Basil. I remained concealed
in this retreat where it was very convenient for me to minister
to the pious needs of all the Christians, who came without fear
to hear Mass and receive whatever consolation I could give
them.

Here in passing I must relate an incident that occurred in
the family of the widow who was harboring me. She had a
daughter named Secunda who for a long time had been asking
God for a child who would be consecrated to Him in the
service of the Church. God soon gave her a child, but only to
install him immediately in heaven. The good mother wasn't
left behind her child on earth for long, but she didn't get to
heaven as easily as the little innocent who had had nothing to
pay for on the way. A person entirely worthy of belief told me
that while in the middle of a field she saw on a nearby mountain a huge ball of fire in the midst of which Secunda stood
moaning and accusing all her relatives of extreme cruelty because they didn't bother in the least to help her in her misfortune. The person was very alarmed at this vision. When she
came to tell me I immediately said Mass for the deceased
woman, and never again was she seen in the deplorable state in
which she had appeared.

After staying a month at Paula's house, the Christians
thought it best for me to go to another out-of-the-way spot six
leagues from there where many Christians worked making salt.
I went there by night and found a house well suited to my purpose for converting pagans and maintaining the Christians in
their duties. The man who put me up was a Christian of long
standing called Jerome Giap, who spent his whole life in good
works together with his wife Lucy, as virtuous as her husband.

They had an only son called Eugene who for three years
had been urging me to admit him into the number of catechists
who comprised my band. But he had gotten nowhere with his

entreaties to me because until now he hadn't been able to budge his parents, who found it painful to give up the one who was the sum total of the little consolation they had. But after I had stayed at their house a few days they finally made up their minds to make this noble sacrifice to God. They did so with very good grace. Publicly in church one Sunday morning they gave their dear child to God, bedewing him with many tears, which increased the flame of charity in which they consumed the victim they offered God.

Two other young men as virtuous as Eugene followed his example and consecrated themselves to God for their entire lives. They had a great deal of trouble securing their parents' permission, without which I never received anyone into the service of the Church, but finally supernatural love overcame the parents' natural inclinations. They consented to let their children leave them in order to belong more completely to God. When they had solemnly dedicated themselves by the usual oath, I took them into my band, and thus I found myself with twelve catechists who I can truthfully say possessed the spirit of the Apostles.

51. The Trouble We Were in at Christmas Time

ALL THE Christians were eagerly awaiting this beautiful feast and were preparing to spend it devoutly, but their enemies, being informed that this was really the time to take them by surprise during their gatherings, were on the lookout so as not to miss this opportunity of catching them.

The town where the saltbeds were had been chosen as our meetingplace for these holydays that Christians the world over celebrate so devoutly. The house of one of the Christians of longest standing called Nicholas Hao was readied for the purpose because it was very fine and very large. I don't know how the pagans got wind of it, but they arrived there armed two days before the feast, thinking to catch me red-handed.

But as it happened I was in a neighboring house at the time saying Mass. When we heard the noise I stopped, not wanting to go further because I hadn't reached the Consecration yet, and I was afraid that the pagans on rushing in might desecrate the Sacred Body of our Lord. The Christians who were present told me there was nothing to worry about. I finished as promptly as I could, and then we all braced ourselves to suffer the onslaught of the insolent crew who were making a great racket in the house next door.

They had run across none of our Christians there except for a blind man called Joseph, together with two of his cousins whom he was sponsoring for Baptism. He was immediately set upon in an effort to learn where I was hiding, but he kept making fun of them, telling them he hadn't bothered to notice me, being blind. They put him to the torture to make him tell where I was, but still they couldn't get anywhere. We were so close to the people looking for me, we could hear their every word, and the screams of that innocent man suffering on my account broke my heart. I wanted to dash out and give myself up to rescue him. The Christians prevented me from doing it because I would have placed them all in great danger. By God's will the sky soon cleared. Finding nothing of what they were after, the soldiers were obliged to leave.

I stayed the whole next day, which was the Vigil of Christmas, until evening in that house, where I baptized twenty-two catechumens and heard without let-up the confessions of those who had been unable to go on the preceding days. At nightfall I went into the house of Nicholas Hao, where I found all in readiness. Seven or eight hundred Christians were gathered there whom I found kneeling with heads bowed, and most of them with tears in their eyes.

It's in places like that that one really learns to spend the Christmas vigil devoutly. In the night silence I seemed to see all the lights of heaven. I won't tell all the consolations I received then, but I certainly will say that in the fine churches and ravishing music of Europe I had never seen or experienced anything like it. Only one who has tasted it could know it. At daybreak I ordered everyone to leave, well suspecting what would happen as soon as we left.

That same company of soldiers who had come two days before didn't fail to return, considering our capture a foregone conclusion. They weren't in the least mistaken. Five of our Christians had fallen asleep by morning after watching all night. They were immediately tied up, and Ignatius in particular, who had drowsed off after teaching catechism a large part of the night. He was bound so securely he would have died of it if he hadn't been loosened a little.

But all those shackles couldn't deprive him of the freedom to proclaim the glory of his master Jesus Christ. He preached so well to his persecutors that he changed their hearts. They were forced to yield to the invincible power of the Holy Spirit speaking through his mouth. They retired utterly nonplussed, leaving their captive in his bonds.

Ignatius, who hadn't used his eloquence with a view to being untied but with the intention of breaking the chains which held those unbelievers captive, wouldn't allow the Christians to undo his fetters, but I sent word advising him to save himself for a better occasion. He allowed them to remove the ropes from him and thereupon immediately came looking for me.

52. Ignatius and I Taken Prisoner and Later Remanded by Order of the King

WE SPENT the rest of Christmas Day in our customary spiritual exercises in no dread of our enemies' wrath, but when night fell we got into our boat to retire to a safer place. The next day, the Feast of Stephen, we thought ourselves safely hidden four leagues away from our headquarters. The Christians came there to make their confessions, but a short time after a sergeant dispatched by the local judge arrived who ordered me to follow him along with Ignatius to the place where the judge was waiting for me.

This news on the feast of the Church's proto-martyr didn't displease us. We obeyed the order we had been given. We accompanied the soldier to the judge who sent us the summons. He was in the house of the Nicholas Hao where we had spent Christmas night. Far from mistreating us, he was so well-mannered he wouldn't even sit while speaking to me.

He nevertheless summoned the pagan leaders of the place and ordered them to guard me closely until the next morning. I figured God was offering me a very fine opportunity of disclosing the great light of the faith to all these pagans during the course of the night. We spent it entirely in this endeavor, which was a thousand times more agreeable to me than resting. I showed them how much more reasonable Christian faith is than pagan superstitions, and they grasped my reasoning so well there wasn't one who didn't admit I was speaking truly.

Still, although convinced in their minds, their hearts didn't follow the light they had been given. Some told me the religion I was preaching to them seemed pretty good to them but that they had trouble believing what I said because the king didn't subscribe to it.

I answered them that this has always been the course God has taken in spreading the glory of His Church, that He always began with the littlest ones and eventually ended by reaching the greatest monarchs, that His plan was to glorify His friends only after testing their fidelity in trials and persecutions, that He always began that way, finding His glory in conquering princes in such wise that all their wrath proved incapable of overcoming it, that the same thing would happen in Cochinchina where the Christians, after being objects of the king's anger, would eventually find him their comrade in the faith.

Another said that nothing surprised him more in our religion than the great ease with which we forgive sins of any kind at all. But especially did he see no shade of logic in that we forgave them not three or four times, but as often as the malefactor liked.

I answered them that such ease in pardoning offenses was proper to God alone, who draws His glory mainly from the goodness by which He surpasses all the princes of the earth by as much as He surpasses them in His power for vengeance, but for all that His mercy never infringed on His justice, that in this life the former seemed excessive for not inflicting eternal punishment, but that justice would be seen in all its rigor in the next life, where there would never be any respite from punishment nor pardon for offenses.

They all admitted I was right, and they showed me such courtesy that I took the liberty of asking their permission to say Mass. They gladly let me. I had a fine altar set up, and I then celebrated Holy Mass in their presence, which pleased them no end. Several yearned for our holy religion, but not one had the nerve to do what he wanted to do.

Meanwhile it was quite late in the day and the judge didn't appear. The people guarding me thought it best to take me to his house, six leagues from there. Ignatius and I went along quite lightheartedly, hoping not to get off without winning some nice crown. When we arrived, the judge didn't dare try the case. He preferred to refer it to another court having greater authority and wider jurisdiction. I was taken there immediately.

I found six magistrates who questioned me on the new doctrine I was preaching and why I was making so many converts despite the king's interdiction. I answered that I was obeying God in so doing, who was above the king, that we were all equally bound to obey Him fearlessly. Then I was asked who my companions were and why I had taken them on. With that Ignatius started talking and spoke so well and to the point that all the gentlemen, finding no reply, said they didn't want to pass judgment on me or on my companions because we weren't within their jurisdiction, that the king would regulate the matter as he pleased, but that the three Christians who had concealed me in their house to say Mass would go to jail.

At that I said it would be an injustice to punish the innocent and let the guilty go; that I was the one who had done all the harm, if indeed there had been any in such disobedience; that I would go to jail quite gladly but asked that those three Christians go free. We spent a long time arguing, but we finally came out so well they were satisfied with a stiff fine, which I had those Christians pay whose means were larger than the others'. Thus my three hosts were released, and even Ignatius was set free.

Only I was still detained awaiting the king's orders. One of the leading magistrates in those parts—but an even more devout Christian—named Ignatius, asked to put me up at his house until the king made his wishes known, and said he would see to it that I appeared when they wanted. He was granted his request. I stayed at his house twelve days, during which I was kept busy continually administering the sacraments to many pagans desiring Baptism and to Christians coming for confession.

When the head judge of the province learned what was going on he ordered me to leave Ignatius' house and keep to my boat to await the king's orders there. I had to comply without argument, although my host was very sorry to see me go. I went to my usual retreat aboard my little sampan, where the magistrates often had their guards call on me, which obliged me to stay there all day. At night I carried on as usual, being free to go here and there. This routine lasted two months, during which rumor often ran that all my catechists would be jailed and that I would be driven off in my boat to go wherever I pleased outside the kingdom. This forced me to send my catechists back to some private homes belonging to Christians who kept them out of sight. I lived alone on the river with a little boy who did my marketing for me so that if any danger arose I would bear the whole brunt of whatever might threaten us.

Nevertheless all these fears proved groundless. The king was better disposed toward me than we had ever hoped. He ordered me set free. Our enemies were surprised at the news, and the governor, who had understood that I would be treated far worse, ordered me to leave his province. I said I would obey him, but that I asked for a slight delay in order to repair my boat, which was in no condition to carry me over the high seas without obvious danger to my life.

He granted my request, to the satisfaction of the Christians, who were delighted to keep me. I retired to the house of the magistrate called Ignatius who had put me up before. I spent a few weeks there, where we were very busy, especially at the beginning of Lent when our new Christians were delighted to witness the beautiful ritual of the ashes that they all attended, and during all that time they gave me wonderful proofs of their faith.

53. How Ignatius Was Imprisoned with Some Other Christians, and the Fortitude They Displayed

AT THE beginning of Lent the Christians came every day to the house where I was staying and were very seldom out of it. As luck would have it, it happened that a certain fiscal judge was sent by Onghebo in connection with an important matter that was Ignatius' responsibility because he was the chief magistrate of the area. The notary was put up at our house, but he was downstairs and we were upstairs. Thirty Christians had spent the night with us in order to receive the sacraments, and in the morning they were saying their prayers as usual. The noise they made intoning them awoke the notary's valet who, suspecting what it was, informed his master who immediately ran up, and catching the crew of Christians red-handed, raised a loud uproar all through the house. Ignatius, who was putting us up, was very surprised to learn that the judge was under orders from the governor to arrest any Christians he ran across practicing their religion.

I was in an adjoining room where I was praying to God in private. I ran immediately and got all the images for fear our enemies might desecrate them. While I was hiding them three of my companions, Ignatius, Joseph, and Maurus, were taken to prison and loaded with those heavy ladders made in the native style. They all took off as if to a feast, and especially Ignatius, who led the way not like a prisoner, but like an apostle, preaching the glory of his master Jesus Christ to all.

At the prison door a lovely thing befell them that comforted them wonderfully. In the dark of night several of the pagan prisoners saw a handsome man full of majesty enter the cell where Ignatius and his companions were. They were enraptured with the beauty of his face and began saying that it was certainly the Lord of heaven they had heard tell of who was coming to console the Christians because they were truly His servants. And to prove the vision was no dream, they remained so impressed they all decided to embrace the faith for which Christians were so fortunate as to receive such noble visitations in prison. And a short time later they put their resolve into practice by receiving Baptism.

The three magnanimous prisoners didn't see their Captain's presence with their bodily eyes, but they certainly felt its effects in their hearts by the consolation they received in their affliction. They were ever more zealous in preaching Jesus Christ in that prison, and when they were allowed to go out during the day as is the usual custom in that country, they went to the public

squares bearing their ladders, which were glorious badges of
their courage, and in this condition they preached by word and
example the veracity of their religion with such great success
that many became convinced of it and requested Baptism.

I wasn't exempt from the disturbances raised by this tempest. The magistrate had me summoned and ordered me to
hand over the images I had made off with; that if I refused to
obey him, he surely had ways of making me regret my obstinacy. In reply I suggested that he go right ahead and try out
all the worst of his tortures on me, that I hoped to show him
that the hearts of Christians were tougher than the anger of
all their persecutors, that Jesus Christ was my good master who
had always been so good to me that I could never be so
cowardly as to deal Him an insult He never deserved. On seeing me thus determined he didn't press matters further, well
aware he would reap only shame from it.

At the same time I well knew that the Christians in the
town where I had been caught would be molested. I advised
them to flee before the storm and run into the woods with their
entire families. When the hoodlums found nobody in the
houses where they expected to catch their prey, they became so
highly enraged they unleashed several big dogs and sent them
into the forests where they knew the servants of God had retreated, thinking they would especially tear to bits any children
they came across.

But it was God's will that those dogs harm not one Christian as they ran through the woods. With holy simplicity the
children themselves later told me how often they had run up to
devour them only to leave them always unharmed. Finding no
Christians in the town, the company of soldiers went through
all the neighboring hamlets searching for whatever they might
find there. First they ferreted out the well-known Christian
Anthony, whom they knew to be as it were the mind and soul
of that whole fine Church. He was at home with one of his
relatives whom he had converted not many days before. They

both permitted themselves to be taken, and they were immediately dealt the bastinado.

Anthony suffered it with a cheerful countenance and with
such generous courage that the soldiers were amazed at it. His
companion Matthew showed by his face that the rough treatment distressed him. Noting it, Anthony spoke to him words
so full of the holy ardor he had in his own heart that Matthew
was ashamed of the cowardice he had displayed and imitated
the fortitude of his friend Anthony. After these first caresses
they were both laden with the usual crosses commonly put on
all thieves. Then they were dragged off to prison, which they
entered with greater joy than if it had been a banquet hall.

As soon as I was informed of it I went there, not to console
them, but rather to rejoice with them over the honor God was
doing them. When they saw me come in they both threw their
arms around my neck. It was an unbelievable consolation both
for them and for me to be able to embrace one another so. After
mutually congratulating ourselves, Anthony wanted to go laden
as he was into all the town squares preaching to all who knew
him that Jesus Christ, his good Master, was the reason for his
suffering, saying everywhere that the king had nothing in his
whole treasury that seemed so precious to him as that ladder,
which he would use to go to heaven on.

The Cochinchinese have a custom permitting prisoners to
go into the town squares to beg a living provided they keep
that ladder around their necks and have a soldier who stays
with them and takes them back to jail. But they don't give
Christians any soldiers to lead them because they are quite
certain they won't fail to return to prison, which they love too
much to escape from.

Two other virtuous Christians, Philip and Sylvanus, received
the same badges of honor in that hamlet. They were locked up
in the same cell and loaded with similar crosses, all four of
them dwelling in the darkness of the prison house in greater
consolation than if they had been in their own homes.

❧ 54. The Noble Fortitude of Four
Christian Ladies

O UR ENEMIES' fury didn't spare even the sex whose weak-
ness ordinarily draws pity from the most fanatical. There
were four Christian ladies who proved that faith animated by
love of God and hope of heaven imparts even to the weakest
the courage to triumph over all trials. The first was a noble
matron called Paula who when taken and put to the torture
suffered the pain and infamy with unshakable fortitude, betraying neither fear nor displeasure to the point that her persecutors dismissed her with praise for her steadfastness, which
they were forced to admire, not being able to overcome it.

This virtuous lady had never had any children, but she had
adopted two young ladies whom she kept at home, and after
making Christians of them, she provided them with every pre-
cept and good example possible for drawing them to the practice of the highest virtues. Their names were Lucy and Ruffina.
Both were arrested with their good mother and displayed no
less courage than she.

A very heavy thick bar was fastened to their necks by a rope
joining the young ladies as if they were dogs on a leash. This
is the way the Cochinchinese punish their worst women criminals, who hold this kind of punishment in great horror, but
Lucy and Ruffina only laughed at it. In this beautiful adorn-
ment they were led before the tribunal of a judge called
Ondelin [Ong Dê Linh?], who overlooked no threat or cajolery
in an effort to bend the two girls' wills, but they possessed more
courage than the judge possessed cruelty or finesse. They were
put to the torture, and they were exposed to the sun at high
noon, a time when the heat in the torrid zone seems unbearable.
The pagans, seeing those angelic faces beneath the rays of the
burning sun, couldn't help betraying by their tears the com-

passion they felt for them, and now and then they even covered them with great big hats.

Even the judge, who was present, was moved at the sight. He stated that if they wanted to be shaded by those hats they must renounce Jesus Christ. As soon as they heard these words, they threw away all the hats and told the judge that if he didn't have any better means than the heat of the sun for making them forsake their faith, he could never hope to conquer them, and that even if fire seemed hotter to him, he could carry out an experiment on them to see whether the flames of Jesus Christ weren't more powerful than any tyrant's furnace. The judge was put to shame and the whole crowd amazed at the strength Christian faith imparts to the weakest persons.

There was nevertheless in this same place a Christian lady who to begin with wasn't so magnanimous as the three former ones. She was so horror-stricken at the kind of fetter they wanted to fasten on her neck, with its heavy wooden stock, that she preferred to relinquish her faith rather than bear it. But when she learned what Lucy and Ruffina had done, she was so ashamed of her cowardice that she sent to ask me whether there weren't some way she could repair her fault and make amends to Jesus Christ whom she had so outraged.

I sent word and then told her personally that we had so good a Master we could always restore ourselves to His good graces provided we really wanted to, that truly her fault had been serious, but there was a way of making real reparation if she had the courage to go look up the same judge she had been afraid of and declare in his presence that she was ready to undergo anything he pleased for love of the One to whom she had been unfaithful.

She didn't have to be told twice. She left right away and spoke to Onghebo so resolutely that she put him out of countenance. He threatened her, he gave her sweet talk, and finally, unable to get anywhere and with no hope of changing her mind, he drove her out of his house with as much credit to her as she had deserved blame the first time.

⌘ 55. The Wonderful Courage of Nine
Generous Christians

SEEING THEMSELVES thus worsted by women, the judges
didn't dare attack them further, but they didn't leave our
poor Christians in peace, persecuting them outrageously. Nevertheless I was among them all the while, and I passed up no
opportunity of assisting them with sacramental remedies and
Christian instruction. The king had given me permission to go
as I pleased, but the governor of Quinhin couldn't stand having me in his province. The Christians were of the opinion that
I should leave and go work in some other one in greater
security and with greater profit.

As I was making plans to leave I saw nine of my Christians
arriving from the farthest northern provinces, which means
they had traveled a good 100 leagues at a very inconvenient
time of year due to the deep mud. They had heard that I was a
prisoner and my life in danger. Their sole purpose was to come
offer me their services and to help me in the plight to which
they thought I was reduced.

I leave you to imagine how such goodness touched my heart.
I thanked them as well as I could and wouldn't accept any of
the presents they wanted to give me, always telling them that
by God's grace I was in need of nothing. When they saw I
refused all their services they wanted to spend their means and
even their lives in helping other Christians who were being
mistreated for the faith.

They overlooked nothing within their power in succoring
them, and their zealousness went so far that they even went
boldly in search of the governor, told him how wrong he was
to persecute innocent people, and adjured him to cease exercis-
ing such cruelty. The governor was surprised at this Christian

liberty. He seethed with anger but didn't dare vent his spleen by punishing them because they weren't within his jurisdiction. He drove them out of his province, from which they were forced to remove themselves a few days later.

The main reason that had brought Bartholomew, one of the nine, was to satisfy the great desire he had of entering my company to assist the catechists, and the principal object he had in mind was acquiring a fortune like Andrew's. He was a man forty years old, strong, healthy, and quite rich in his own country. I would willingly have done as he wished, but he was married and even had a little girl he had to bring up.

He replied that his wife was a pagan, and so obdurate in her error that he had never been able to win her over to Christianity, that inasmuch as she wouldn't recognize the true God, he no longer wanted to keep her as his wife. As far as his daughter was concerned, he would direct a good Christian from among his friends to provide her with all the instruction proper to a Christian woman.

Still, I told him to go back home and once more do whatever he could to win his wife's soul to God for which Jesus Christ had died, that if she remained obdurate in her error after that, I would allow him to leave her and would open the doors of our house to him so he might serve God more perfectly. He dutifully did as he was told, as I shall relate later.

56. How Some Spanish Nuns on Their Way to the Philippines Passed through Cochinchina

IT WAS February 15 of the year 1645 that I left Quinhin province, leaving the Christians well prepared to meet all attacks from their enemies. I put out to sea with the intention of going to Cham to spend Holy Week, but the wind was so

contrary, we were forced to land on a deserted shore to perform the Blessing of the Palms, which we were to distribute
among the Christians later. That done, we continued on our
way in palpable danger of shipwreck, because our rudder had
been smashed by a heavy sea. Nevertheless God miraculously
helped us, bringing us to an island where we repaired our loss,
and after spending the night there and saying Mass on Holy
Thursday morning, we reached around midnight a well-known
port called Faifo, which I mentioned before.

I found myself just in time to preach the Passion and perform the services on Good Friday morning. There it was a
great comfort to me to see two Portuguese vessels newly arrived from Macao that brought me various letters from our
Fathers, but I was greatly surprised to see none of them come
to accompany me as I had been promised. It had been a whole
year since I had seen a priest, and consequently had no way of
going to confession.

I learned most opportunely that two Fathers of St. Francis
had arrived at the harbor of Cham quite near Faifo, in a
Spanish ship on its way from Macao to the Philippines. The
ship had been forced to put in in Cochinchina on account of
the storm and had been stopped at Cham several weeks. I went
there by sea and arrived at nightfall. Those good Fathers were
extraordinarily kind to me and showed me such charity I was
made to feel ashamed. I had arrived in the nick of time, because
the ship was due to sail the following morning and the first
thing I wanted to do was make my confession, having been a
whole year without receiving the sacrament I had administered
to thousands. I then spent the rest of the night in the company
of the good Fathers and the Spanish gentlemen, who told me
all they had done at the court of the king of Cochinchina concerning a matter I shall relate.

When the Spanish in the Philippines learned that the
Portuguese in Macao were shaking off the yoke of Spain to take
sides with the king of Portugal, they sent a large ship, very
well manned, with a captain and soldiery to reinforce those in

Macao who wished to subscribe to the rule of the Spanish king. But after defeating them the Portuguese took them prisoner and then sent them back in their own ship without harming them in the least, and because there were four Spanish nuns in Macao come from the Philippines some time before to found a convent of St. Clare, the Portuguese—in order to eschew all entanglements with this nation, which they have never cared for much—thought it well to put the four young women aboard their country's ship under escort of two properly authorized Fathers of their own Order.

They left Macao at the beginning of February of the year 1645, but a very violent storm driving them off course for the Philippines brought them to the harbor of Cham in Cochinchina. On hearing I had been a prisoner in the province of Quinhin and that Christians were being severely persecuted there, the two Fathers wrote three very excellent letters for me which I still keep, wherein with very great kindness they show compassion for my sufferings, offer me their services, and inform me of all that happened to them at the court of the king of Cochinchina.

For, when the four nuns arrived the news spread immediately throughout the kingdom and especially at court, where the king and queen, on hearing the kind of life these young women led, wanted to see them. They held them off for quite a while, saying they were indisposed, but finally the king had to be obeyed, who insisted that the Spanish captain together with a company of his soldiers escort the nuns to the court.

Before going there they had been installed very comfortably in a little house we had at the port of Cham, which they found very convenient as a retreat. All the ladies in the neighborhood used to come to see the young women, who they were told were very holy, living perpetually enclosed and veiled. But they wouldn't believe it when they were told they cut their hair, which is highly unusual among these people where the women especially are extremely solicitous about keeping their hair well, which you might say they love as much as their heads.

Above all other ladies in the land Madame Marie Magdalene, the governor's wife, showed extraordinary kindness to the saintly young women. (That's what they called them.) Every day she sent them some new gift, saw them every day, and even gave them her only daughter to stay with them a few days. This young lady, about thirteen years old, took such a liking to the nuns and conceived such regard for their virtue that she was determined to follow them, and it took considerable trouble to make her change her mind about going to the Philippines in their company.

ꙮ 57 . The Honor the King of Cochinchina Paid the Nuns

MEANWHILE THE ladies were compelled to go to court by the king's command. He sent a fine galley for them that conveyed them very comfortably. On arrival they found their way to the house of one of the leading magistrates where they were magnificently entertained by his wife and daughter until the king summoned them to his palace.

It was around two o'clock in the afternoon when they went there, always heavily veiled, accompanied by two Fathers religious, the Spanish captain, and about fifty soldiers from his guard who were all very well got up and never wanting in that grave demeanor that is characteristic of their nation. The king was waiting for them, leaning out a window overlooking the palace's huge courtyard. The queen was at another near the king. A nook had been prepared in the great hall, hung with tapestries and very nicely appointed, where the nuns could stay out of sight without being exposed to the gaze of the whole court.

The king and queen were magnificently appareled. The leaders of the kingdom who constituted their court were present. The guard for the occasion numbered 4,000 men, divided into 4 companies of 1,000 men each, so adroitly stationed in various spots they blocked in no direction the view of the king's seat, the queen's, or the place allocated to the nuns. The companies that were nearest the king were clad in long purple damask robes with golden breastplates. The two others wore long, very dark jackets, and each soldier had a huge scimitar heavily wrought with silver. They all stood in formation, and not one moved or said a word.

When the nuns entered the hall they were led to the covered place at the king's left. The Spanish captain, the two leading lords of his retinue, and the two religious went up to the king and paid him their respects in the Spanish manner, heads uncovered and omitting none of their solemn ritual. The king didn't fail to accord them generously at least as much in return, together with many fine words of esteem and courtesy, then had them all sit on raised seats that had been set up for them and ordered all the soldiers to sit cross-legged on the floor, which they did instantly and noiselessly.

The ceremony began with a fine collation that was set on various round tables, lacquered and gilded. Each one had his own. They were laden with very tasty dishes, royal in sumptuousness. The king invited them to eat and entreated the nuns from a distance to eat their fill. During the collation the young ladies of the court danced a beautiful ballet, and the Spanish gentlemen vowed it wasn't better done in their own country, nor perhaps even so well.

The collation ended, the king desired the nuns to emerge from their enclosure and go to the window where the queen was. They came out, always heavily veiled, passed before the king, and saluted him. Then they went over to the queen, where they sat down. The first thing that princess asked them was to lay aside their veils, because she wanted to see whether it was really true that they shaved off their hair, which nobody at court would believe. The nuns said they couldn't remove their veils, especially under the eyes of so many men, but they raised them before the queen and let her see their faces. The king was somewhat offended and said that inasmuch as he showed them his face, he didn't see why they refused to uncover theirs.

The queen, who was a great idol-lover, asked them what their rule was and what kind of prayers they sang. The good nuns always answered as they ought, but the woman who was their interpreter didn't transmit their answers accurately. Then the queen ordered one of the ladies to put her hand on the nuns' heads and see whether they were shaved as alleged. The lady touched the head of the oldest one, and finding no hair on it exclaimed loudly that it was certainly true. This was considered a very great wonder.

The party lasted several hours, during which various games were played in accordance with native custom, with truly royal magnificence. When night fell the king had a great number of torches lit throughout the palace, and when everything was over he provided an escort from his own men for the nuns and the Spaniards, who after thanking the king for his kindness left to spend the night in their galleys where they thought they could rest more at their ease.

The next morning the king sent various presents to the whole company, especially all kinds of exceedingly dainty preserves, then he permitted the Spaniards to choose whatever lodging they pleased in the city. One of the leading magistrates housed the Spanish captain and his two first officers at his palace and gave the rest of the soldiers a quite roomy house where they lodged very comfortably. The nuns and the two Fathers went to a magistrate who was a good Christian. I mentioned him before. He was called Joachim and his wife Anne. Both of them welcomed these servants of God with intense joy into their house, where a church that was very convenient for these good young ladies' spiritual exercises was located.

Day and night the house was filled with people coming to

worship. The ladies of the court ordinarily came there along with all the high society of this large city. Everyone was charmed to see the young ladies' modesty and saintliness of life as they sang the Office. All those good Christians, who had never seen the like, dissolved into tears. The good Fathers were kept busy day and night hearing the Christians' confessions, and within ten days they baptized fifty-four pagans, among whom were some of very high rank.

The fruit would have been even greater if their stay had been longer. All the enemies of the faith didn't dare say a word. Mass was said publicly, and all our mysteries were preached without fear of edicts from the king, who permitted this without taking offense.

58. The Fine Show the King Put on for the Spanish, and Their Return by Boat

ALL THE while the presence of the good nuns was being very helpful to the Christians, the king wanted to show these strangers, who have such a high opinion of their own country, that Cochinchina was no nation of barbarians.

The first thing he showed them was a wonderful mock combat between twenty golden galleys executing a thousand maneuvers on the city's wide river. The king himself was aboard a very magnificent galley in which he took part in the games along with several lords of his court. At the same time his son and his brother, mounted on richly caparisoned horses, were in a large adjoining field where they were putting on a magnificent tournament, so that the Spaniards watched two exhibitions at once, one on land and the other on the water, and they frankly admitted they had never seen anything grander.

The next day the king put on another show for them involving fifteen galleys performing on the river. Some were gold, others painted in fiery colors. The king was seated on a throne on the riverbank and had 2,000 men at his side, all clad in matching livery and armed. The galleys were proceeding three abreast with such nice precision that one never passed another by so much as a finger's breadth. They moved at the same speed and in the various turns they made they kept perfect pace.

The third day the king wanted the Spaniards to see a ceremony he held in honor of his departed ancestors. It took place in a large courtyard before the palace. All the soldiers entered in perfect order, numbering about 6,000. They were all clad in crimson, with gold helmets and highly polished muskets. The captains were at the head of their companies. Each kept his place in line as though at battle station.

When everything was set and the king present, there came one of the native priests who performed certain rites around some tables prepared for the purpose, and after saying some words nobody could hear, he set fire to some paper horses, then fired some cannons. At the same time all the soldiers discharged their muskets and then began target shooting. The king gave very fine prizes to those who hit the bulls-eye properly, but those who shot wide of the mark lost a month's pay.

This took place in the morning. The king wanted to show the Spaniards a naval battle between eighteen beautiful galleys, larger still than those they had seen the previous days. The whole afternoon was spent in these exercises, after which the gentlemen took leave of the king with a thousand thanks for his kindness and with incredible esteem for the magnificence of his court.

After the ten days thus pleasantly spent at that court, the nuns and their company embarked for the port of Cham to return to their ship. One couldn't begin to tell the regret all the Christians evinced at seeing them leave. The high society ladies and all the others came to bid them adieu with many tears.

Some insisted on accompanying them a considerable distance. Others followed them with eyes and hearts.

But above all Madame Marie, the king's aunt, came to meet them in a galley quite far from the harbor where she gave them a thousand tokens of affection and many gifts. She manifested such devotion for their holy habit that they gave her one of their rope cinctures and promised to send her one of their robes later, which they faithfully did after they reached the Philippines.

That's what I learned, partly by letter, partly by the recital of the religious who, after affording us consolation for one night, departed on Holy Saturday morning and once more left me the sole priest in a huge kingdom.

59. How I Was Taken Prisoner Together with Eight Companions

AFTER THE departure of the Spanish vessel I spent the Easter holidays in the city of Cham, where we had a crowd of Christians coming to make their Easter duty during the holydays. From there I returned to the Japanese town called Faifo, where Ignatius labored very successfully in converting several pagan women married to Japanese Christians, who until then had been unable to make any headway in getting them to forsake their superstitions. Ignatius put an end to it within a few days, and truly he had so extraordinary a gift from God for preaching that it happened very often that he delivered sermons that lasted all night long without anyone finding them too long. There wasn't one of his listeners who wouldn't have wanted him to go on longer. I realize that those who will read this will have trouble believing what I say, but I certainly do attest to what I saw.

From Faifo I thought it right to go comfort the Christians who were in the royal city, where they had suffered a great affliction, especially the great servant of God Madame Marie, the king's aunt, because her son, as the result of a little joke the king made against Christians, had a large church torn down that his mother had built on her palace grounds. The good lady was so beside herself with grief at her son's crime that for a week she ran hither and yon, hardly knowing what she was doing.

So I went to console her, but not daring to show myself in the big city in the daytime, I stayed undercover in a small neighboring town. As soon as the lady learned of it she slipped away from her palace to come see me. A large number of Christians followed her, whereupon God blessed our labors.

But an accident occurred that caused us very grave concern. The king came to relax in the same town where I was hiding and was lodging in a house near ours. When a fire broke out in our neighborhood, everything was thrown into confusion. I didn't dare leave because the king couldn't have helped seeing me if I tried to save myself. What's more, the fire was coming our way and the wind was blowing the flames onto the roof of our lodgings.

We would have been done for if God hadn't obviously helped us. We had recourse to prayer, and as a result of our Lord's wonderful kindness, the wind changed and blew the flames in the opposite direction so opportunely that we had nothing more to fear. Imagine doubting that God helps His servants!

I stayed shut up in the same house for some days, always discovering more to be done there. Nevertheless I decided to leave my post and go to the other end of the kingdom to the north, where I hadn't visited my flock for some time. I boarded my sampan with eight catechists just three days before the feast of Pentecost, but as we were enjoying a very fair wind that drove us nicely down the wide river, we were discovered by three of the king's galleys that were patrolling all rivers and the sea for fear the new king of Tonkin might have designs on Cochinchina.

They immediately rushed to seize us, thinking we had been sent by the king of Tonkin. News of it was dispatched to the court of Cochinchina. Nevertheless, when we informed all these soldiers, who were treating us very roughly, that we possessed no weapons of any kind, they began to soften, and the captain himself, who undertook to hold us pending the king's orders, was such a good fellow that he put us up at his house and set up a very nice chapel to which he invited the Christians. He used to prepare the altar for Mass. I enjoyed all the same freedom in his home that I would have had in our own house. In the course of seven days I baptized seventy pagans there who according to what they told me became Christians with the hope of accompanying me to prison and martyrdom.

I never saw such a crowd. Christians who learned that we were prisoners gathered from all directions to follow us and help us out. In one day I saw arrive five large shiploads of these generous servants of God come to find us. I appeased them as well as possible by administering all the sacraments to them and imparting whatever instruction I could give. One must admit that the goodness of these people is without parallel in those European countries outside which we are convinced everything is barbarous.

60. How We Were Taken to the King and Put in Prison

MEANWHILE THE king's order stipulated that we be brought to the court. The good captain who had given us such courteous treatment at his house bade us adieu with many tears.

We had done all we could to induce him to receive Baptism, but we couldn't elicit this favor from him although we had received so many others. He commended himself to the prayers of all the Christians, he embraced us and did all he could for us, but he would never gratify us in what we wanted most.

So we boarded our sampan. Only one man was charged with taking us to the king. We were nine, and he was alone. You can imagine how these people must have feared we would run off. This soldier was so kind he let us go into all the Christian homes along the way. We would see large troops of them come to take us to their homes, where they received the sacraments and looked on us as martyrs already.

The fervent Christian called Bartholomew whom I spoke of above came to meet us and immediately brought up the promise I had made him to accept him into my company if his wife refused to be converted, that he had made every effort to overcome her obstinacy and that he had gotten nowhere, that inasmuch as he had done what I had told him to do, it was only right that I should do as I had promised him.

"How can you suggest such a thing?" I told him. "Don't you see, my dear friend, that I am a prisoner? This would be a good time to leave my company, not join it!"

"What are you saying, Father?" this valiant Christian rejoined. "This is the reason I want to join more than ever. It's because you're heading for prison and martyrdom that I want to follow you. Do as you like, but you can't break your promise, and I'm not budging from you." And with that he jumps into our boat, mixes in with my other companions, and despite anything I could say he came along with us to the court and to prison.

We reached port at nightfall, and our soldiers made no difficulty about letting us spend it entirely with our Christians. The next morning, Feast of the Holy Trinity, I said Mass believing it would be my last. I cheered up my good Christians, who filled the house and were weeping as if they had lost their father. I bade them adieu and then we went blithely to the place where we hoped to meet a death we considered a thousand times more desirable than life.

We were immediately taken to the place of honor, in other words, into a very gloomy prison. We went in quite cheerfully although we were very displeased that the magistrate who took us prisoner in the king's name took our entire wardrobe and the church vessels I used for saying Mass. Leaving us not one penny to help ourselves, he sent everything to the king, who returned nothing to us except the Mass vestments, because he was told that we used these to offer sacrifice to the great king of heaven and earth.

In this dire poverty, in this dark and foul prison, my catechists and I never ceased finding a real paradise. In the meantime ladders were being prepared for us, which we eagerly awaited as sure pledges of the martyrdom that was our fondest hope.

61. How I Was Condemned to Death and Then Released

A FEW DAYS after our arrest my case came up before the council. With his own mouth the king condemned me to having my head chopped off and ordered it done without delay that very day. Alas, here is what I had certainly desired with all my heart for such a long time, but so great a sinner as I doesn't deserve such a grace, which our Lord usually accords only to His favorites.

Preparations were already being made to carry out the king's order by decapitating me, when by extreme misfortune one of my friends, desiring to do me a good turn, rendered me the worst service I could expect from my greatest enemy.

A certain magistrate highly thought of by the king and very influential in his cabinet for having once taught the king Chinese characters and given him the highest education in the country, got up and spoke so well on my behalf that he softened the king, telling him it would be a crime to stain his sword with the blood of an innocent man, that it wasn't a crime worthy of death to preach the Christian faith, which advocates nothing evil, that if I were condemned for some other crime, he wouldn't ask that my death sentence be revoked, but that if I were guilty of nothing else, depriving me of life wouldn't be an act of justice, but cruelty.

This good person wasn't a Christian, nevertheless as I said before, I had stayed a while at his house, and I had often spoken to him about our holy faith. He had wavered a long time over accepting it, but finally human respect had triumphed in him to the detriment of his conscience. I had nevertheless baptized his wife and several of his servants, and he himself had retained a certain affection for me in his heart.

But he put it to very bad use on this occasion. On hearing his words the king regretted having condemned me. "Very well," said he, "inasmuch as I've been spoken to on behalf of this Portuguese priest, I'm satisfied to retract my word and spare his life, but on condition that he leave my kingdom as soon as possible and never come back. It's under pain of death that I order him to stay away."

When they came and gave me these two pieces of news in prison I could have died of misery, and I never think of it without blaming—not so much the magistrate, who wanted to do me a good turn—but my own guilty life, on account of which God judged me unworthy of dying when so splendid an opportunity offered.

❧ 62. How My Nine Catechists Were Loaded with the Cross, and What We Suffered in Prison

At the same time that I was notified of the stay of execution, ladders were brought to set around my companions' necks; but alas, when I saw there were only nine I was doubly grieved to see these innocents so mistreated and that only I was to have no share in their glory.

Of these nine servants of God there wasn't one who didn't accept that ladder as joyously as if he had received the most desirable thing in the world. For some time now a young fifteen-year-old whom I kept with my other companions had been entrusted to me so he could learn to lead a Christian life. He went to prison like us, and when the ladders were carried in he was among the first to offer his small neck to be laden with the yoke. The judge, who saw that the yoke was four times heavier than the one carrying it, felt sorry for him and ordered it replaced by a lighter one.

Ignatius (which is what the young innocent was called) was immediately opposed to the relief they wanted to give him and said that he had sufficient courage and strength to carry our Lord's yoke, which was always light because the One for whom it is worn always helps us bear it. He pleaded so eloquently in favor of his cross that he won his case and made his appearance in this splendid livery of God's children along with his eight other comrades who were all happily bearing the ladder by which they hoped to climb to heaven.

I, poor wretch, was the only one to be shamed by not bearing this mark of honor. We languished in that prison with only the consolations heaven could give us, because beyond that we were without any help whatever. We slept flat on the ground.

We had so little to eat we had trouble to keep going, because what money we had had been taken away from us, and the soldiers, who wanted us to give them some, treated my companions very cruelly, beating them almost every day, and in spite of anything I could say nothing would satisfy them.

Finally I found a way of procuring a sizeable alms from the Christians that proved sufficient to quiet the misers and relieve the dire necessity in which we found ourselves. God even willed that a young Christian very learned in Chinese letters should join us and help Jesus Christ's captives. He even wanted to act as our cook, and he performed in that prison all the acts of charity we could have expected from a very competent valet, so ingenious is God's grace in succoring those who suffer for His love.

63. How I Was Banished from Cochinchina by the King's Order

AFTER STAYING there a few days I was quite convinced I wouldn't be allowed the benefit of such good company for long. When I thought they were going to make me leave, I let my companions sleep a couple of hours and then woke them all up and prepared myself to bid them adieu and instruct them concerning everything they must do in prison. They made their confessions and all received Communion at the Mass I said for them before dawn. God knows with what tears and endearments I spoke to them and embraced them all. The mere memory melts my heart.

The following day the magistrate who had condemned Andrew to death came to find me on the king's behalf and ordered me to follow him to the town of Faifo to sail with the Portuguese when they returned to Macao, and never to return to Cochinchina under pain of death. The king had confided this duty to this governor because he knew he was an avowed enemy of Christians, and actually he treated me so cruelly he didn't even give me time to embrace my dear companions.

He ordered his soldiers to remove me from prison, and without giving me time to speak to anyone, to take me to the ship that would convey me to the Portuguese. They dragged me through all the streets of town to the great distress of the Christians, who followed me as far as the ship, and even after I was aboard some followed me along the strand and others got into sampans to meet up with me some leagues out of the harbor, where they were able to stop me and hear me speak once more. I bade them a last farewell, mingling their tears with mine. I gave them a few prayerbooks in their language, along with some blessed medals I still had. Then, duly leaving them responsible for the nine prisoners, we headed out for Faifo and the good Christians returned to their homes.

Hardly had we gone four leagues or so down the river after the Christians from Sinoa had left, when two other Christians reached the riverside and very insistently requested permission to speak with me in private. Seeing these people had run a long way to see me, our guards took pity on them. They let them enter my sampan and allowed them to speak to me.

They drew me aside and told me sobbing that they had it on good authority that the king, not having dared put me to death in sight of the whole town, where he feared a disturbance, had given orders to the soldiers who were escorting me to throw me overboard once I was out of sight of all my friends, and that the order was certain to be carried out that night. They shed so many tears in the telling they could hardly speak. I thanked them for their kind warning. I embraced them never expecting to see them again, and I sent them away assuring them they couldn't have brought me more welcome news.

After they left I began to recollect myself and think seriously of eternity, considering myself as good as at the gates. I thought the thing they told me quite likely, because the soldiers did seem to me capable of carrying out some evil design. I no longer doubted that I was to lay down my life for God that night and appear before His judgment seat.

To prepare myself to accept this welcome death properly I retired by myself into a corner of the boat on my knees, holding in my hand the crucifix Reverend Father Mutius Vitelleschi had given me on leaving Rome. I begged forgiveness for my ingratitude and kissed it lovingly, placing my trust wholly in the infinite sweetness of His mercy. For dinner I took a few lumps of rice and drank one glass of water, expecting soon to be surfeited with it. Then I began praying again, crucifix in hand, not wanting to sleep at all for fear of being surprised in my sleep, and well aware of how the Venerable Fr. Gonzales Sylveira had acted on a similar occasion.* At the slightest sound I thought they were coming to throw me overboard. I kept wondering when the happy moment would arrive. Never did time seem to drag more, because I wanted them to come right away and send me off to eternity.

I saw the soldiers all sleeping very peacefully, which led me to doubt the warning I had been given, but when daylight came I knew for sure that it was false, to my very great misfortune, I who, alas, had been so rash as to believe I would win that splendid crown when I deserved it so little.

🎴 64. My Stay in the Town of Faifo, Where I Was Held Prisoner Twenty-two Days

WITHIN TWO days I arrived at the town of Faifo, where I was to board ship and leave Cochinchina. The Portuguese, who had heard of my imprisonment and were very

---

* First apostle and martyr of South Africa. Made aware of his approaching death by private revelation, he spent his last day baptizing fifty catechumens, then awaited his hour prostrate before his crucifix. At midnight eight executioners fell on him and strangled him. (TR.)

grieved over it, were very happy to see me, but the captain who had brought me was under orders not to let me move freely for fear I would escape. He handed me over to a very good Japanese Christian to guard until such time as the Portuguese would leave for Macao.

I went to this house very gladly, well knowing I would be entirely free to attend to all my regular duties. I wasn't disappointed in my hopes. This honest fellow, called Francis, together with his wife whom I had recently baptized, received me so courteously that instead of finding a prison at their house I discovered a place very convenient for the Christians.

It's true the king had expressly ordered that I be prevented from dealing with them. At the door of my lodgings I had a soldier who stirred neither day nor night, as much to see to it that I didn't leave as to send away anyone who might want to come see me.

Nevertheless my host was so good and so well disposed he supplied me a way of tricking the soldier and satisfying the spiritual needs of our good Christians. The virtuous Japanese who put me up at his house discovered an expedient to deliver me from the inconvenience of the guard. He had another house on the bank of the river quite close to the one I was in. He got it ready, then sent word to all the Christians to meet there every night, with the assurance that I wouldn't fail to be there, prisoner that I was.

When our guard was fast asleep Francis would set a ladder under the window of my room. I would go down very quietly and betake myself to the house, which I always found filled with Christians. I would spend the whole night there hearing confessions, preaching, catechizing, conferring Baptism on many new converts. Two hours after midnight I would say Mass, at which there were always many communicants. I would take leave of them before daybreak, and climbing up my ladder, would stay locked up all day without the soldier or anyone else suspecting a thing.

This schedule continued twenty-two days, in the course of

which ninety-two pagans forsook the idols and received Baptism from my hands. During that time we had the opportunity of greatly comforting and strengthening the Christians; but inasmuch as my nine prisoners were the principal objects of my solicitude, I had them visited several times on my behalf and sent them a sizeable sum of money that the Portuguese lent me.

Ignatius, who had carried into prison the zeal that always kept him living the life of an apostle, preached Jesus Christ continually, and amid the horrors of darkness in which he was shut up, shone with the most splendid lights of paradise, setting many free who burst the chains of their sins. He sent me word saying he wanted only rosaries, pictures, and medals to give those who profited from his sermons, that he held me discharged of any further obligation. I sent him all of these spiritual weapons I could find, which this generous soldier of Jesus Christ wielded so skillfully.

This wonderful servant of God had a brother called Peter who was also very zealous, but he had been unable to become a catechist like Ignatius because he was married before becoming a Christian. When he learned his brother was a prisoner he came to find him immediately and give him all the assistance he could.

The king of Cochinchina had recently passed an edict whereby anyone at all was forbidden to spend the night outside the area where he maintained residence. This regulation was being strictly enforced, but the brother of Ignatius of whom I was just speaking and another Christian whose name was Stephen, knowing nothing of this prohibition, stopped for the night at the home of another Christian to whose charity I had strongly commended the prisoners.

Having no fears at that house, Peter and Stephen wanted to say their prayers together before retiring in accordance with praiseworthy Christian practice, and they said them so loud that a pagan neighbor, suspecting what it was, turned them over to a neighboring judge who immediately took them into custody and brought them before the king the next day, informing him that they were Christians. The king asked them whether this was true. They answered yes and that they hoped to be so till death.

The king ordered them to be given 100 lashes on the spot. The order was carried out without delay and with such rigor that it was thought these two generous Christians would surely die of it, they were so lacerated from head to foot; but by a very great marvel, they found themselves so completely healed a day later that not one mark from all their wounds remained on them, which made them desirous of suffering even greater things.

〜 65. My Banishment from Cochinchina, and How God Saved Us Miraculously on the Way through the Prayers of Our Glorious Andrew

BESIDES THE nine companions I had left in prison I still had five others whom I had sent to the southern provinces to preach the Gospel while I went north with the others. Hearing what had happened to us, the others didn't fail to come to me, and when they saw me on the point of leaving wanted to follow me, but I took care not to accede to their wishes. I pointed out to them the need all the Church in Cochinchina had for their services at that time, and especially their brothers who were likely to leave prison only to meet death. I gave them orders in writing for everything they should do, appointing one of them superior over the others. Then embracing them in a final farewell, I gave them my blessing and promised them that inasmuch as I couldn't return, I would do everything in my power to provide them with other Fathers as soon as possible who would do far more than I.

I couldn't describe the laments and tears of the Christians who gathered at the dock when I had to leave with the Portuguese. Some threw themselves to the ground as though half dead. Others wailed so lugubriously my heart was breaking with grief. Seeing the goodness of these good people I spoke to them only by motions of my head, my arms, and even more with my eyes.

When I boarded the vessel the magistrates of the town wanted to be present and accompanied me until I left the harbor. In the presence of the Portuguese they had the edict of my banishment read aloud, in which the king forbade me ever to return to his country under pain of death, and that the Portuguese captain who brought me back would surely lose his head.

It was on the third of July of the year 1645 that I left Cochinchina in the body, but certainly not in the heart, any more than Tonkin. In truth it dwells wholly in both, and I don't think it can ever leave. As soon as we were on the great China Sea we ran into a storm so violent the ship was practically wrecked. In this evident, or rather general, danger for all on board, I took the head of my good Andrew and set it in a good spot in the middle of the deck. I had all the people who were on the ship come up, then I began to recite the litanies of the Blessed Virgin out loud, imploring my protector's help. Before I had finished them the storm ceased so abruptly that everyone cried, "Miracle! Miracle!" The wind blew so fair it carried us quite safely into the port of Macao exactly twenty days after our departure from Cochinchina.

God knows the thanksgiving each one offered the great martyr, but our astonishment was even greater when we learned a few days after our arrival that two other big ships, one coming from India, the other leaving Cochinchina at the same time as we, had unfortunately sunk off that very coast where we had been happily saved. Some of those who had escaped—very few in number—gave us a report, and we learned they had suffered shipwreck at the very time in which we had been in such great danger. But we had an advantage on our ship that the others didn't have—a head severed for Jesus Christ that was worthy to command the winds and rule storms.

The vessel that had carried the body of the holy martyr to Macao the previous year had been accorded a quite similar miracle through his intercession. The pilot manning the tiller was doing all he could to hold a course that to him seemed quite proper for bringing the ship speedily to port, but despite making every effort to turn the ship in that direction, he kept feeling a contrary force making him go another way. This went on so long he was obliged to allow himself to be taken where he didn't want to go, and stoutly said as much to everyone on board.

But when he reached port four days later he well realized that the secret force which had resisted him was the loving hand of the martyr he was carrying, because they learned that on the course he wanted to take there were Dutch pirates who at that very time had captured and taken some ships going to Macao— which was so commonly known all over town that it was discussed with admiration everywhere to the glory of the great servant of God. Which obliged everyone to accord extraordinary honor to the sacred body, as I related elsewhere.

☙ 66. The Glorious Confession of Faith of My Nine Imprisoned Companions after My Departure for Macao

I HAD BARELY left Cochinchina when my nine glorious soldiers of Christ whom I had left in the lists to fight against their Master's enemies were shortly attacked, and they behaved with such fortitude they all carried off glorious crowns.

It happened the twenty-sixth of July of the year 1645, just one year after the glorious death of their comrade Andrew and three days after my arrival in Macao. The king had them summoned in an effort to change their minds. All nine went, sporting those heavy ladders about their necks and angelic modesty on their countenances. They appeared at the great court and in the king's presence with so confident a mien that everyone was astonished and felt sorry to see them so mistreated when they had committed no crime, and even so, if they had committed one, they were only asked to deny it.

The king himself questioned them, thinking to confound them. He asked them whether it was true that they were Christians, and that if they had been so till now, he ordered them to be so no more. Ignatius spoke for all of them and said they all were, and that given God's grace they would be so till death; let him test as soon as possible the truth of what he was saying.

This boldness of speech angered the king. He retorted that if they were so ill advised as to oppose his will, it remained to be seen whether their ability to suffer exceeded his own to torture them. Ignatius replied that they were indeed weak, but that the grace of Jesus Christ was more powerful than all the kings of the earth, that this wasn't the first time it had triumphed through very feeble instruments over the highest powers of the world.

The battle of words went on for some time. Ignatius spoke almost the whole time. Vincent couldn't keep himself from speaking out in turn. The others all approved what their captains were saying by motions of their heads and smiling. Several lords of the court took it upon themselves to advise them to obey the king if they didn't want to wind up miserable wretches.

"Wretches!" replied Ignatius. "Never was a true Christian a wretch. Whoever sees heaven opened doesn't bother to run from death, and whoever holds death in contempt has nothing left to fear."

The king, unable to endure this boldness, ordered Ignatius

and Vincent, who had spoken for the others, to have their heads chopped off that very day, and the seven others each to have a finger cut off. At this sentence Ignatius and Vincent began embracing each other in transports of joy before the assembled company. The other seven evidenced great displeasure at their being satisfied with merely one of their fingers instead of chopping off their heads.

They were taken off without further delay. A company of 200 soldiers conducted them to a field outside town. All nine proceeded joyously in their ladders and walked as fast as if they had had wings on their shoulders. An untold number of Christians followed them, not to lend them courage, but to acquire it themselves by their example.

The field where the executions were to take place was overrun with people. The nine glorious victims finally arrived and held the attention of the great crowd marveling at their courage. But it was especially noticeable that the faces of Ignatius and Vincent, who were doomed to death, displayed a joy quite different from that of the seven others who were to have only a finger cut off.

Meanwhile Ignatius' mother would have the courage of those brave mothers of the ancient martyrs who without grief had watched their children die, and would imitate somehow the courage of the glorious Mother of the King of Martyrs. When she learned her son had been condemned to death because he was a Christian, she wanted to go see him die and lend him courage by mingling her tears with his blood.

She broke through the crowd, advancing generously toward her son. She kissed him and didn't speak tender words to him, but spoke to him like a mother of the Machabees. Ignatius begged her prayers and couldn't hold back his tears as he bade her adieu, but later he spoke to her in such fashion that he proved these had flowed from natural necessity and were no effect of fear. They said goodbye several times in the presence of all the people, none of whom knew what to say, but there were very few who weren't weeping very heavily.

I'm sure his brave brother of whom I spoke above took care not to be absent, in order to complete the entire resemblance to our good Savior who at His death had His mother and St. John present. Nevertheless I can't be positive, because it wasn't noted in the circumstances of his death, but I think it quite likely.

Be that as it may, Ignatius, brave as ever, prayed to God, raising his hands and eyes to heaven, bade farewell to all present, and then his head was severed with one blow. Those who stood near have testified under oath and have protested to us with all possible assurance that the holy head pronounced the sacred name of Jesus three times as it fell to earth. When I said in connection with my very dear martyr Andrew that he pronounced Jesus' name through the wound in his neck after his head was cut, I related what I had heard quite distinctly, but what I have just said about Ignatius I don't say as having heard it, because I had been in Macao three days; but the people who say they heard it are very many and entirely worthy of belief, and besides that the wonderful virtue, zeal, and charity of that tireless preacher makes the marvel quite believable to me because I can say after observing and directing Ignatius for more than four years that hardly in my whole life have I seen a servant of God more faithful, a preacher more filled with His spirit whom we can truly call a real apostle of this new Church.

After Ignatius, Vincent was dealt with in the same fashion, and he displayed a courage entirely like that of his comrade. All this took place under the eyes of the other seven glorious prisoners who on seeing their comrades' fortitude were dying of desire to die. Each had a finger cut off, and there wasn't a one of them who didn't say he would have felt far less pain if they had cut his neck.

That was the glorious end of my companions. Three suffered martyrdom in Cochinchina, without counting those in the other kingdoms. Many magnanimously confessed their faith there before tyrants, and being unable to give their lives, they gave their limbs. I alone am left without receiving some mark of Christ on my body. I pray with all my heart that He make me worthy of repairing this loss and soon following those who used to call themselves my children and who are now my good masters and protectors.

Part 3. The Return

Foreword

WHEN OUR superiors saw I had been thus banished from Cochinchina, they wisely decided that it would be foolhardy to send me back so soon, inasmuch as that would only serve to embitter the ruler and inflame him against the Christians. With the thought of waiting until his anger cooled a bit, they decided to send me to Europe to fetch spiritual and temporal help. They believed me sufficiently acquainted with all the great needs of the country where I had spent so many years, and that I would lay before the Holy Father the extreme need of these Christian communities for bishops; before Christian princes the dire poverty of all our Fathers laboring in these fine missions; and before our Reverend Father General the great hopes for converting all these kingdoms if we had preachers to proclaim the Gospel to them. They charged me with these three commissions, which I very willingly undertook, and I made preparations from July 23, when I arrived in Macao, until December 20 of the same year 1645, during which time I occupied myself mostly in thoroughly instructing two Fathers of our Company in the Cochinchinese tongue. The first was Fr. Metellus Sacano, a Sicilian; the second, Fr. Charles de Roca from Turin, who were to take my place in that fair kingdom at the time I was to board ship for Europe.

❦ 67. From Macao to Malacca

WHEN IT became known in Macao that I was to leave for Rome, several of my friends offered themselves, and others offered me their children to keep me company on the long dangerous voyage. I had settled on a Chinese, a Tonkinese, and a Cochinchinese to take along with me to show Europe a sample of these three new Christian communities, but our superiors thought it would be quite enough to bring one Chinese, whom I took with me. And I left as I said on December 20 of the year 1645, in a beautiful fleet of eight large Portuguese ships that were leaving for India and then for Lisbon.

We ran into heavy storms at the beginning of our trip, but when we had gone a bit further south to this side the sea was very calm. A quite distressing accident saddened us: a Portuguese lord, among the most important in our whole fleet, was traveling to Goa with his wife for the sole purpose of gratifying the wishes of his only son, fifteen or sixteen years old, who desired to consecrate himself to God in the holy order of the Augustinian Fathers.

At nightfall the young man wanted to try to climb a rope ladder the sailors regularly used, but not being strong enough, he fell into the sea before the eyes of his parents, who wanted to plunge in themselves to rescue him. They promised a large reward to anyone who would jump into the sea to save him, but no one had the courage to do it because the wind was good and the ship was sailing very fast. So the child met a watery death, leaving his parents with this regrettable loss following them to their graves.

After twenty-five days at sea we arrived safely at Malacca January 14 of the year 1646. I must admit that when I entered the city tears came to my eyes. It was the day on which the

Dutch celebrated the anniversary of the taking of the city just six years before. We were told that when the Dutch attacked it there were only twenty-five Portuguese in it, who resisted for a long time; but when they saw no help was forthcoming from Goa, being half dead with hunger, they were forced to abandon this beautiful place to its besiegers, who attacked it fiercely and caused great havoc among so many good Catholics who died gloriously in defense of their country.

Certainly this holiday was very sad for us as we went through all the streets from which I saw every mark of the true faith completely obliterated. I admit I was struck palpably to the heart noting the great change from what I had seen twenty-three years before in this beautiful city during the nine months I stayed there at our college, which was built on a very lovely hill. Alas, our church dedicated to the glorious Mother of God, where the great St. Xavier had so often preached and where he had performed such great miracles, was then being used for the preaching of heretics and for vomiting forth a thousand blasphemies against the Virgin and the saints.

I had left there a large number of other churches magnificently built and exceedingly well endowed. I saw them now either torn down or wretchedly desecrated. Never was I so affected as when I heard our college's old bell ringing for the detestable practices of the heretics, and above all did I note one thing especially unworthy of people who call themselves Christians: the Catholics of the country weren't allowed the smallest chapel, whereas idolaters were permitted to have a temple at the city gates where they offered their infamous sacrifices. Now tell me that these heretical gentlemen possess Jesus Christ in their hearts!

The only consolation I found in that city was meeting two of our Fathers who lived outside town and kept themselves strenuously occupied in assisting the poor Catholics who remained in the country. The first was Fr. Stanislaus Torrente, an Italian who was destined for our China province, and Fr. Diego Oliveira, a Portuguese, both great men who labored very hard in the devastated vineyard. I joined them to share in their good works while awaiting the opportunity of sailing to Europe and continuing on my way.

ৰ🙾 68. My Forty-Day Stay in Malacca and the Courtesy Extended Me by the Governor

OUR SUPERIORS had ordered me to go to Europe by way of the Dutch rather than the Portuguese, who stop a long time in Goa before sailing on to Portugal. And to be sure I thereby had proof of God's providence in my regard, for if I had left with the Portuguese I would have taken the ship of our good friend Don Sebastian Lobo de Sylveira who sadly lost his life on the way.

His ship ran onto a large reef against which it was entirely shattered. Many escaped to land and he foremost, but inasmuch as the whole coast where they landed was deserted, he soon found himself so exhausted he could go no farther, for he was very corpulent and little accustomed to walking. Being very rich he begged his men to carry him and promised them a very large reward, but on so long a journey the burden seemed too heavy to them. After carrying him a while they wearied of it. He was forced to throw himself down under a tree with a Chinese valet who was so faithful to his master he would never leave him and elected to lay down his life with him. Such fidelity certainly seems to me remarkable.

During the forty days I tarried in Malacca I was not without employment among the Catholics of the country and the Dutch heretics as well. In particular I ran across many French soldiers who were delighted to learn they could make their confessions to a French-speaking priest. I heard all their confessions and gave them Communion, which was a comfort to them because they had been a long time without an opportunity of doing so and hardly ever hoped to have it as long as they served masters who were not servants of God.

Nevertheless the governor who was then in Malacca was a very upright lord to whom I must acknowledge a serious life-long obligation. He was kind enough to invite me often to his table and passed up no opportunity of doing me every favor in his power. I had a great desire to return his friendship by being of service to him where his salvation was concerned, which was the thing that mattered most for him. I lost no opportunity of acquainting him with the error of his false religion, and three or four times he certainly gave proof of being completely shaken.

One day I was strolling through a long gallery in his house where there were many beautiful paintings, and among others those of St. Ignatius and St. Francis Xavier. He asked me to tell him something of their lives. When I had done so he took my hand and, rapt in consolation, told me, "I assure you, Father, that if I were a Catholic I would join your Order, because in Japan I saw with my own eyes the great courage shown by your Fathers in the horrible tortures they are made to undergo for the faith."

Another time when I was at table with him I pointed out to him the certain danger his salvation was in as long as he remained in that sect, and the assurance of salvation the Catholics have, even in the opinion of their enemies. I tried to make him realize that, and he was so affected by it that a good Catholic who as his servitor assured me he didn't sleep all night as a result, walking up and down in his room and repeating a hundred times the words, "Is it true I can't be saved in my religion? That Father says not. Is it really true? I would never have thought it, I would never have thought it."

Thereafter he was so partial to me he refused me nothing I asked of him. He allowed us to say Mass in public for our

Catholics, to preach to them on our mysteries, and even to hold processions at a chapel two leagues from town where the image of the Virgin was located that they say shed tears before the fall of Malacca to the Dutch.

He furthermore promised me he would endeavor to recover for us the chalices and other sacred vessels that had been taken from the churches during the sack of the city, and which were then being used by the heretics at their banquets and in all their profane services, promising us he would see to it that we could buy them back for money as we desired to do.

Eventually he so favored us that the minister accused him of showing too much partiality to Catholics, which shortly caused him to be removed from the governorship of the city and to be given that of the Moluccas, where they thought he wouldn't see priests so often. At my departure he showed me a thousand kindnesses and promised me to return soon to Holland and think seriously about the state of his soul.

⁀ 69. My Trip from Malacca to Java, Site of the City of Djakarta Built by the Dutch

AFTER staying forty days in Malacca, I could see no hope of finding any ship bound for Holland. I decided to go to Java, where the Dutch maintain their center of trade and a harbor filled with vessels controlling all these waters. So we left on February 22, 1646, on a big Dutch ship that brought us safely to port after eleven days' sailing.

But it was on the third day of our trip that the great marvel occurred that I described in the book of the martyrdom of my dear Andrew, the proto-martyr of Cochinchina. On February 22, around two o'clock in the afternoon, inasmuch as the heavens looked auspicious to us and the wind very good, our sailors were so little on their guard they didn't notice a huge rock practically at water level against which our ship rammed so forcibly it made a noise like thunder. The blow was so violent the ship foundered and stuck fast on the reef.

With that we considered ourselves gone beyond recall. I went up on deck, and seeing a huge plank from our ship floating in the water I warned our people to prepare themselves to die and then have recourse to the help of the Lord. We all made our confessions, for I had with me the two Fathers I had found in Malacca. Then we all got on our knees and prayed to our good Andrew. I had his precious head with me, and I told him lovingly, "My dear Andrew, if I'm to be buried at sea, I won't be taking your head to Rome!" At the very time we were at prayer the ship pulled from the reef and we began to move forward.

But we certainly thought we would sink to the bottom immediately, because we were sure our ship was breached, having seen the planks in the water. As we were waiting, some sailors told us the boat wasn't shipping any more water than before the shock, and that it was no wonder because as it was old, it had been boarded over in several places and the planks we had seen were only from the outside. The rest of it remained whole.

In this conviction we continued merrily on our way, thanking God who had so graciously delivered us. We continued at sea quite safely for another seven days, but when we reached port we found that God had done far more for us than we had thought. They wanted to repair the vessel immediately, and when it had been put in drydock marvelous evidence of God's providence was revealed. There was a large hole in the bottom of the ship, but in breaking through, the rock itself had broken off and plugged the opening it had made with a big stone. People ran from all over town to see this wonder, but we in whose favor it had been wrought had greater cause to marvel at it and to thank God and His servant Andrew who had so lovingly used his influence to save us.

So we arrived at the harbor of Djakarta the fifth of March.
The Dutch made some difficulty about admitting us there with
the Portuguese, because they had got news a few days before of
the bad treatment meted out to them in Brazil. They ordered
the Fathers to leave, but they let me enter because I was
French.

The Dutch founded this city only recently, which they
called New Holland. It is well built and fortified according to
modern standards, very much in accordance with regulations.
The streets are long and very well laid out. There is a wide
river that courses through the entire town and affords unbelievable convenience. There is a large number of bridges and
hardly a street not lined with big palm trees that provide shade
all day. It's a very practical and beautiful sight to see. It's true
the houses aren't high there for fear of earthquakes, which are
common on that island. There is a good fort and a large,
commodious harbor because it can be approached at all seasons
of the year, which is unusual with these Indian ports, as I noted
above.

It is the main military center and the richest trade outlet of
the Dutch in all the Indies. It is situated four degrees off the
equator on the side of the Tropic of Capricorn, almost at
the same location as Malacca, which is on the other side of the
Equator. We find there the same fruit, the same high temperatures, and the same providential wonders to temper them.

Greater Java, where this city is built, is a large island in
the Torrid Zone ruled by two kings—of Mataram and Bantam
—who are constantly at war trying to gain control of the whole
island. Djakarta is in the section held by the king of Mataram.
I'll speak later of the English who are under the king of Bantam. All I can add here is that neither one nor the other put
themselves to any trouble to convert the pagans, so little love
do they have for making Jesus Christ known. What's more, to
tell the truth, they themselves only half know Him.

70. How the Dutch Imprisoned Me in Djakarta

As I was in that city waiting for a chance to ship out, my main concern was helping the many French Catholics who were serving under the Dutch and were being treated so badly by them that I was struck with pity for the great misery they labored under, both spiritual and temporal, but they were obliged to put a good face on it because they were too far from their country to think of escaping.

I also had the pleasure of often dealing with many heretics who little by little came to see their errors, and by God's grace I was easily able to say Mass every day at the home of a Portuguese lord called Innocent Viera de Campos, who boarded me most charitably and wanted to take me to Europe. We nevertheless did so with a minimum of noise and always behind closed doors so as not to give any cause for complaint.

Still the gathering was very large, especially on feast days. All the Catholics in the country, of whom there were a fair number, came there to receive the sacraments. The fruit was so abundant that a Portuguese lord, Anthony d'Almeida Borges, told me he didn't think I could hope for greater success in my work even in Japan, where he had lived a while, so many were those changing their manner of life, renouncing either sin or heresy.

But every worthwhile success in religion is always opposed by its chief enemy, who is the devil. I had continued five whole months in these noble pursuits, wherein I was delighted to find success beyond anything I could ever have expected. Even less did I realize the grace God intended to grant me in affording me an opportunity of confessing His holy name in prison for about three months.

On a Sunday, the twenty-ninth of July, 1646, the Catholics had come to our house in very great numbers to receive the sacraments. I was saying Mass for them as usual. Shortly after the Consecration we heard a loud noise and were told it was the judge of the criminal court arriving with constables to surprise the Catholics in the practice of their faith.

I was very much alarmed for fear of seeing the sacred Body and precious Blood of our Lord desecrated. I cared very little about any outrages that might be perpetrated on me, provided my most adorable Lord didn't fall into the hands of His enemies. I communicated immediately, consuming all I had consecrated for the Communion of many of those attending Mass, then hearing no further noise I decided to say the prayers after Communion.

Turning around as usual I saw the judge before me, who ordered three officers to seize me and drag me off to prison. They immediately fell on me and wanted to lead me off wearing the priestly vestments through the whole town up to the prison. They would no doubt have done so if seven Portuguese gentlemen putting their hands to their swords hadn't opposed it. I was afraid some greater disaster might befall, and I begged the gentlemen to let me go to prison, that making me suffer for Jesus Christ was the greatest honor one could do me.

At that the judge ordered them to let me take off all the vestments, and at the same time he seized all the sacred appurtenances and some pictures, and had the whole house searched for anything belonging to me. He even carried off my Breviary and my diurnal, leaving me neither books nor papers, nor anything whatever that might be of use to me in saying the Divine Office or afford me some consolation.

He escorted me to prison personally. The Portuguese who were following me begged him to take me straight to the governor, but he wouldn't hear of it and allowed none of these gentlemen to come in with me, expressly forbidding me to hold any communication with them, which was very stringently enforced. The names of all those who had attended Mass were taken down so a fine could be imposed on them. They were satisfied with imprisoning two Catholic soldiers, one French, the other Portuguese, because they had caught them in this great crime.

When I had been locked up in jail I fell to my knees, thanking God for the honor He was doing me in making me worthy of suffering for Him, and at that moment I noticed there was a big hole through which the other prisoners could see me and speak with me. And sure enough all of a sudden I saw a Dutch Catholic come and kneel before the aperture and ask me to hear his confession. I did so with a right good heart, but those gentlemen, noticing the hole, decided to remove even this small consolation from me.

Two days later, in other words on the actual Feast of the glorious St. Ignatius, they made me go to another jail that was very dark, where they were wont to lock up criminals who couldn't avoid the death penalty. Those who saw me going there said out loud that I was done for, that I must surely have committed some serious crime inasmuch as I was condemned to the prison no one ever left save to meet death.

When I found myself all alone in that darkness, which eliminated any possibility of reading even if I had had books, I decided to deal wholly with the Father of lights and ask Him for the spiritual enlightenment necessary to establish me in a state proper for glorifying Him. I performed my spiritual exercises in complete solitude, for I saw no one except the man who brought my food once a day, and he would leave me immediately after, but I certainly learned by experience that God never gives Himself so generously to us as when all creatures abandon us.

I remained ten days in this retreat, where in truth I was never so consoled. I was very sorry when they took me out on the Feast of St. Lawrence to return to the former prison, where they had stopped up the aperture through which I could communicate with the other prisoners. I certainly begged the jailor to leave me alone in that cell where nobody bothered me. He

was astonished that this dreary abode should please me, but he
didn't know the blessings God was conferring on me there.

⚜ 71. How I Was Twice Questioned before My Judges

S o i was taken to that other prison, where there was a lone
Dutchman, a very bad heretic who had squandered in de-
bauchery 12,000 crowns set aside for feeding the poor. I tried
to win his heart first by doing him several favors, then I spoke
to him at length about his bad religion. He gave proof of all
the friendliness I could wish for, but he would never take my
advice where his salvation was concerned.

The two Catholic soldiers I mentioned were soon released
from prison with a small fine, as a result of which they were
sentenced to losing two months' pay. This was quite hard on
them because it was all they had to live on. As for me, who
was far more culpable, I didn't get off so cheaply. I was left in
prison a whole fortnight without being spoken to by anyone,
after which I was finally called to answer before the judge of
the criminal court and two assistants, along with a notary who
took everything down.

They were all seated and I remained standing like a criminal before them. First I was asked why I had said Mass in their
city where it was so expressly forbidden. I answered that I had
said it because I was a priest, that the prohibition was unknown
to me inasmuch as it had never been intimated to me, that considering the permission I had been given to enter their city and
remain there in priestly garb, I had assumed I would be permitted to live there also as a priest and to discharge the duties
proper to my calling.

This answer embarrassed them, and they couldn't say anything except that Mass was forbidden in their territory. I added

further that being French I should enjoy at least as much freedom in Holland as the Dutch enjoy in France, where they are never punished for practicing their religion.

The next thing they asked me was whether it was true that I had thrown into the fire several books of their sect that had been brought to me by those making profession of the Roman faith at my hands. I replied that I hadn't burned any because I never had any, which was very true, although I didn't consider it a crime to toss into the fire books which prevented Christians from going to heaven.

They made a special point of the fact that it must be true that the governor of Malacca had been converted to papism and had made his confession to me. I replied that I had in truth received many tokens of his kindness, but that I had never had the good fortune to be able to repay him in kind and prevail on him to be converted.

After spending all of two hours making these replies I was returned to prison, from which I was taken once more a fortnight later to appear before a panel for the prosecution composed of seven judges before whom I had to remain standing a long time bareheaded, which I gladly suffered, reminding myself of the insults our good master Jesus Christ had endured. Finally the judge of the criminal court pulled out a long document listing the indictment against me on nineteen counts, which were reducible to the three I just mentioned, concerning the Mass I said, the burned books, and the converted governor of Malacca. The remainder were mere quibbles, but he finally ended by sentencing me to four things: to such corporal punishment as the lord judges pleased, to perpetual exile under pain of death from all lands subject to the sway of Holland, to the overall confiscation of all my goods. The fourth was the most unbearable of all: to have to stand beneath a gibbet while all the holy images were burned by the hand of the executioner. The presiding judge gave me the paper in hand with an order to make answer on all these points within three days.

I won't set down my replies here, which I made so clear no

rejoinder was possible, but concerning the fourth point of the punishment imposed on me I said that corporal punishment was the greatest favor one could do me, that it would be a very great honor for me to bear on my body the marks of Jesus Christ, that for thirty years I had sought the glory of martyrdom among the Chinese, the Tonkinese, and the Cochinchinese, that I had never been worthy of suffering any outrage to my person, that if the Dutch gentlemen wished to accord me this grace which idolaters had never accorded me, I would consider it the greatest I had received in my whole life. As for the other point, that of banishment from all their territories, I accepted it wholeheartedly inasmuch as I had come to this one only on the very civil invitation extended me by the governor general, the said Cornelius Vanderlin who, on learning that I had through my own efforts saved six Dutchmen from death in Cochinchina, had thanked me most civilly and had invited me to pass through Djakarta, and whose letters I still possessed, that the confiscation of my goods would hardly enrich anyone to whom they were given, that I had kept them safe for thirty-five years by giving everything I had to the poor in order to follow Jesus Christ naked on the cross.

But on the last point, which was an insult to my Lord Jesus Christ whose images they wished to burn, I begged these gentlemen rather to tear me into a thousand pieces and reduce me to ashes, poor miserable sinner that I am, that I couldn't believe that people who called themselves Christians would want to commit so horrible a sacrilege that would draw down God's wrath on them all and eternal disgrace before men, who would know that servants of Jesus Christ had shamefully burned representations of their Master by an executioner's hand.

This is pretty much what I replied to these gentlemen in writing, who on receiving my answer decided to think it over at leisure while I remained in prison unable to say Mass or read the Breviary and unable to enjoy the consolation of any of my friends. The Portuguese lord had the goodness to send me something to eat once a day and would have liked to send it twice a day if I hadn't prevented him. For the rest, the jailor inspected everything scrupulously, and the Dutch gentlemen of their charity never presented me with so much as a glass of water.

⚜ 72. The Sentence Pronounced on Me and How the Sacred Images Were Burned

THROUGHOUT ALL these reverses God comforted me in a way I could never have expected. One of the men running the prison had a slave who was blind, but a very good Catholic, an Indian by nationality, a former convert of the Fathers of St. Francis who had been taken by the Dutch and enslaved at the fall of Malacca. He had preserved his love for the true faith most tenderly, and he comforted all Catholics as much as he could, especially when he learned they were in prison.

He came to me one night when he saw my heretic companion was sound asleep and called to me through an iron grating. I was greatly surprised to be spoken to at that hour. I drew near him. He told me his life story and asked me to hear his confession and then lent me for the night an image of our Lady beautifully carved in ivory. Every Saturday the good man assembled a few Catholics of his acquaintance to honor the Blessed Virgin before this image, which he entrusted to me on condition that I return it to him the following morning. This delighted me exceedingly. It was the night before the Feast of the glorious Assumption of the Blessed Virgin, which the good blind man didn't know. I considered this a special mark of affection that the most benign Mother of love wished to give me on the solemnity of her feast. Bonaventure (which was the name of the blind man) came to see me almost every night with his image after that. I tried to return his charity by rendering him all the spiritual help I could from the wretchedness of my prison.

They soon finished trying all the cases of all those who had attended my Mass, who were all sentenced to fines. On top of a heavy fine the Portuguese gentleman who had lent me his house to say it in was sentenced never to set foot again on Dutch soil in the Indies, but he showed such generosity he even insisted on paying personally the fines imposed on all the others, which cost him a lot, but he wanted to show how noble a crime he considered having Mass said at his house, to such a point that he wanted to bear alone the punishment of all those who had heard it.

I was still waiting for sentence to be pronounced on me, having already been two months in such strict confinement that no foreigner was able to see me or write to me, but by God's grace I wasn't alone in such harsh solitude. Finally, on September 22 I learned my sentence had been decided on, but they put off pronouncing it for three days because the lord judges obstinately insisted that I stand under the gibbet while the images were burned, which the governor never wanted to allow for fear, said he, that the Catholics would rise up on seeing me so abused.

So it was on the twenty-fifth of September of the year 1646 that I was taken to the prosecutor's court where my judges were waiting for me in their official robes, seated with becoming solemnity. As I stood bareheaded, at the end of the hall an officer led me up so I could hear my sentence more clearly. The clerk advanced to the center of the room and read the entire sentence for a solid hour, all in the Dutch language.

I replied that inasmuch as that language was unknown to me I hadn't understood anything of what had been said. Thereupon one of the judges who spoke French very well said that I had been sentenced to three things: to leave the country, to pay a fine of 400 gold crowns, and that the images would be burned in the public square beneath a gallows on which a criminal would be hanged at the same time.

I replied that I considered the exile a favor. As for the money, I was quite sure none would be got from me because I owned nothing, but concerning the horrible sacrilege they wished to commit against the sacred image of Jesus Christ, I began raising my voice, and weeping profusely I told them I appealed their unjust verdict and that if there were no one on earth to heed my appeal I would summon them before the tribunal of Jesus Christ, who would be their judge and would in His wrath avenge the sacrilege they committed against His honor, and He would deal with them as guilty of the greatest crime that could be perpetrated.

I was prevented from saying more and taken back to prison shouting and even begging them to burn me, but not to take it out on Jesus Christ. I gained nothing by either my tears or my entreaties. Those infamous scoundrels had erected two gallows on which two thieves were to be executed, and a huge bonfire where the crucifix was to be burned, which was immediately carried out with unparalleled impiety. The Catholics all shook with rage, and even the heretics said they seemed to be witnessing the whole bloody tragedy of the Jewish crime at the crucifixion of the Savior between two thieves.

And it really was a true reproduction of it, if not a much more atrocious crime in that it was committed by Christians. Alas, two robbers were hanged, and at the same time, being unable to crucify Jesus Christ in His person, they put Him to death as well as they could by destroying His image by the fire they all took part in lighting, making a thousand jokes about the holy crucifix.

There was only one poor Catholic slave who would never obey his master the presiding officer, refusing absolutely to pick up the images or light the profane fire to burn them with, but all he did was weep in the sight of that huge crowd of people who were present and countenancing the just sorrow of the poor wretch who will one day condemn all those impious persons.

It's true God didn't delay long in showing some signs of

His anger. A man of honor, a very good Catholic, assured me
he saw at the time three balls of fire in the air that were no
doubt threatening the wretches with the eternal fire which
would punish their sacrilege. The presiding officer and the
fiscal judge who had engineered the whole crime lost their jobs
within less than a month by an order come from Holland.
Everyone considered this the first manifestation of the vengeance God was preparing for these two judges who had perpetrated so horrible an injustice.

⚜ 73. I Leave Prison and the City of Djakarta

AFTER I was sentenced everyone was free to come see me in
prison, where I remained another month, and I was urged
to pay quickly the sum necessary for deliverance from this
bondage. I continued to protest that I would never give a
penny, even if I had to stay in prison all my life. I couldn't
find a sweeter death than the one that would be my lot in a
prison where I was detained for saying Mass.

In mid-October ships coming from Holland brought orders
that Sir Cornelius Vanderlin was to be governor general of all
the Indies under the sway of Holland. Until then he had been so
only by warrant since the death of the other general, Anthony
Vendima, who had held the post for nine years and had made
himself feared throughout all the Indies, especially after he
took and sacked Malacca over the Portuguese.

Many public festivities were held for the arrival of the new
governor. Among other benefits he released all prisoners, no
matter what their crime. My fiscal judge, who was expecting to
get 400 crowns out of me, was greatly astonished to see the
governor release me from this penalty and let me out of prison
in spite of him.

But he suffered greater vexation still when he had to give up a small coffer in which I had a few papers and a little money that the Portuguese had lent me. The good fellow already had his eye on the money and thought to make it his booty. I went and complained to the governor, who very kindly made him return it all to me. I was told that he gave the judge a good tongue lashing and even a few blows for having used too much severity toward me and the Portuguese who had lent me his house.

The judge was too proud to boast about that. He saw no more of me, but he assigned me a constable who never left my side. I went to thank the governor for the courtesy he had extended me in regard to my entry into Djakarta, and when he released me from prison he showed me much kindness and apologized for his countrymen. I left in a skiff to find the Portuguese who were waiting for me on their ship to go to the kingdom of Macassar.

They welcomed me with unbelievable kindness, especially my distinguished benefactor Lord Anthony d'Almeida Borges, whom I embraced with many tears. He it was who fed me so charitably during three months of imprisonment. I advised him to wind up his affairs soon and to leave this hateful country where God was so ill served.

We boarded ship on the Feast of St. Ursula, the twenty-first day of October, after a stay of eight months in Djakarta, three months of which I had spent in prison. The Portuguese wanted to head straight for Macassar. I begged them to give me time to go to Bantam,* also in Java, ten leagues from Djakarta, because that's where the English keep their main stores for the Indies. I very much wanted to see whether I couldn't get to Europe aboard one of their ships.

I arrived in that city the same day and found treatment there very different from that meted out to me by the Dutch. Sir Aaron Becket, English governor for the Indies, received me with all the kindness I could have expected from a very zealous

* A port no longer extant. (TR.)

Catholic. He invited me to his table, where he treated me so civilly that I was of the opinion that he was a Catholic, until one day at table he let me know well enough by his conversation that he was enmeshed in the common misfortune of that poor country which, once the delight of true piety, shortly lost the thing that had caused her to be held in reverence by all other nations for so many centuries.

So this lord offered me protection and courtesy of every kind, but he told me that considering the trouble there was in England over religion at the time, he couldn't allow me to take any of the ships that would be leaving soon, that if I wanted to wait a year he promised to take me there himself with the assurance that he would defend my life at the risk of everything he held dearest in the world.

I thanked him, saying that having lost eight months already among the Dutch, I was in a hurry to get on with my trip. He gave me very liberal passes for entering any locality where there was English traffic. I have used them very often since with all the happy results I could hope for. Thereupon I took leave of him and, returning to the Portuguese ship, we set out for Macassar.

14. How We Went to the Kingdom of Macassar and Our Stay There

WE BEGAN our trip on October 25, 1646, and spent two months and five days at sea, which was unusual, because when the winds are favorable the trip is much shorter. Over three months had elapsed since I had celebrated Holy Mass, and I would have remained in this predicament much longer if the Portuguese hadn't taken the trouble to find me some consecrated vessels to say it with, because the Dutch had taken all I had.

I began saying Mass in the most suitable spot on shipboard on October 28, a Sunday and the Feast of the Apostles Sts. Simon and Jude, and by God's grace I didn't spend one single day on the whole trip without this consolation. It was thus God willed to let me repair the loss I had sustained while among the Dutch, and as I had no Breviary, luckily a Father of St. Dominic happened to be aboard who every day lent me the one he had brought for his own use.

To tell the truth, I couldn't omit mentioning here the exceeding piety of the Portuguese captain who commanded the vessel. He was a lord of the high nobility and very rich, but he was full of virtue and charity. He always attended not only the Mass I said but also the catechetical instruction I gave every day after dinner. He summoned everyone on board to it. He received Communion frequently and had his valets receive. In a word, he neglected nothing that a Christian lord might do.

God let him feel the effects of His protection, for the trip turning out to be longer than we had anticipated, there was nothing left for us to eat or drink. God alone provided us with both one and the other. He sent a heavy rain that furnished us plenty of water and by casting nets into the sea we had fish for many days.

With these provisions we arrived safely at the port of Macassar on the Feast of St. Thomas, December 21. Informed of my arrival, our Fathers, who had a very lovely house in town, came immediately to fetch me and take me there. I went as if I were going to paradise, so pleased was I to see my good Fathers just one year after my departure from Macao.

Macassar is a very large and very well-known island that our maps call Celebes. Its main harbor is four degrees off the Equator on the south side. The island is extremely rich in rice, and all the fruits of the Indies grow there very well, especially those beautiful palms bearing coconuts. There are cattle, chickens, and squabs in great numbers, but no hogs at all because the natives, who are Mohammedans, have exterminated them entirely from the country.

The temperature there is very equable and very healthful. The heat isn't oppressive for the reason I mentioned in speaking of Malacca, because the sun makes a fine parasol for itself when it would burn everything up, and draws up so many mists and vapors because of its great power that the dead of winter is the time we call here the height of summer. The main staple of all these people is fish, which is very cheap because of the great abundance there is of it, and to my mind it's so good Europe has nothing like it.

Because the climate is so mild it's never really cold, the men go naked from the waist up, but the women are entirely covered from head to foot, in such fashion that not even their faces can be seen.

I can't even think of their religion without feeling intense regret. A very few years ago they were all idolaters, but so well did they realize the vanity of the idols being worshiped in their country that they decided by common consent of everyone great and small to change their religion; however, not knowing whether they should subscribe to the religion of the Christians or to the Mohammedan sect, instead of inquiring into the truth of the one and the falsity of the other, they used a quite irrational means of finding out about them.

They sent ambassadors to Malacca, asking the Christians to send them some priests capable of instructing them in their faith, and at the same time they sent a delegation to the king of Achin, a Mohammedan, entreating him to send them some *caciz* who would explain the superstitions of Mohammed to them, with the intention of adopting the religion of whoever arrived first.

I don't know whom I should blame in this instance, the poor reasoning of these people or the lack of zeal on the part of the Christians at the time who delayed so in a matter of such great consequence that they allowed themselves to be forestalled by the Mohammedans, who got there first and were so welcome they established their evil sect there. The Christians who arrived there later were thrown out, and the wound bleeds till now

without any likely remedy for an evil that may possibly continue for centuries.

✲ 15. About the High Governor of
Macassar and the Conversations
I Had with Him

ON ARRIVAL I made the acquaintance of the high governor
of the whole kingdom, who is called Carim Patingaloa,
whom I found exceedingly wise and sensible, and apart from
his bad religion, a very honest man. He knew all our mysteries
very well, had read with curiosity all the chronicles of our
European kings. He always had books of ours in hand, especially those treating with mathematics, in which he was quite
well versed. Indeed he had such a passion for all branches of
this science that he worked at it day and night.

But he was a man so virtuous that all the people and no-
tables of the kingdom, seeing that the king was a very small
child and aware on the other hand of the great capacity for
leadership to be found in him, offered him the crown, but he
would never hear of it. He preferred to be subject to his legitimate sovereign than to wear a diadem on a guilty head.

He governed the kingdom all the while the king was a
minor. When he saw he had reached an age capable of ruling,
he divested himself voluntarily of all the royal authority, but
the king felt so indebted to him that he left him with all the
influence that had been his, doing nothing without his advice.
He was in fact the prime minister, without whom nothing of
importance was effected anywhere in the kingdom. He it was
who had brought our Fathers into this country and maintained
them there when serious efforts were made to drive them out.
It was he who housed us in a very beautiful spot and per-

mitted us free exercise of all our ministry. Indeed he usually attends all the sermons personally, especially on the principal feasts of the year, and brings his whole court. He follows our processions, particularly during Holy Week, with such modesty and devotion one would take him for a very zealous Catholic.

I have often heard him speak of our mysteries with great respect. He always called the Pope the high pontiff of the Christians. He never pronounces the names of the saints without adding praises in their honor. To hear him speak without seeing him one would take him for a native Portuguese, for he spoke the language as fluently as people from Lisbon itself.

He was so well informed on all points of our religion that he often argued them against heretics and routed them completely. He attacked the Dutch particularly on the authority of the Pope and ridiculed them for trying to create a body without a head, proving to them clearly that it could only be a monster.

As soon as I arrived our Fathers thought I should go pay my respects to him in my capacity as Procurator for the Japan province, which the good governor had favored with so many benefits. He received me with great civility, assuring me he loved our Fathers and would protect them against any enemies who might try to drive them out of Macassar. Seeing that he was pleased to talk of mathematics, I began conversing with him on the subject, and God willed him to take such pleasure in it that he wanted to have me at his palace as a matter of course thereafter.

It happened that I predicted an eclipse of the moon to him a few days before it took place. I described it all to him exactly as he saw it later. This so won him over he wanted me to teach him all the secrets of the science. I, who had in mind teaching him the science of going to heaven rather than the courses of the stars, never saw him without always throwing in many things that might move him to conversion, and even when he sometimes changed the subject I never failed to return to my objective.

He always listened to me without emotion, but he made little answer to all I laid before him. Sometimes he spoke to me of St. Francis Xavier in terms of great esteem. I tried to tell him he had had free access to Macassar, where he had baptized 25,000 people in the kingdom of Tolo alone. He brought me up short and told me that the kingdom of Tolo where the Apostle had labored so successfully was not in Macassar but surely in the Moluccas. I replied that this was probable but not entirely certain, which he had trouble allowing.

I neglected nothing that might win for Christ this man on whom the conversion of the entire kingdom depended. He never held it against me, but he didn't thereby change for the better. I was never able to discover what this came from, because from all appearances his life wasn't bad. He had no entanglements with women. I simply came to the conclusion that I was too big a sinner to bring so excellent a project to fruition.

When I was on the point of leaving I went to tackle him one last time on the subject of his salvation. As I took leave of him I spoke with many tears and proposed to him reasons quite sufficient to touch his heart; but after my talk, which was rather long, he replied to it all with nothing more than these few words, "Well done, Father, you have discharged your duty very well." With that he bowed to me many times and kissed me several times, but on the most important subject he said not a word.

On my return to our house he sent me a Portuguese who was his great confidant, who made me a thousand protestations of friendship on his part and brought me various gifts along with a memorandum of curious articles he wanted me to bring him back from Europe, adding finally that he very much wanted to see me return and that he implored me to pass through his territory again, where I would always find proof of the high regard in which he held me. I had to be satisfied with these compliments and make him a return in kind.

76. My Departure from Macassar with the English, and the Good Treatment They Showed Me in Bantam

AFTER STAYING exactly five months in Macassar, I left on June 15, 1647, with the English, who willingly accommodated me aboard their ship and gave me one of the most comfortable berths on it, with such deference that they never neglected inviting me to their table, where even there they always gave me the place of honor. Because of me they even received two Catholics, a Frenchman and a Spaniard, who afforded me much consolation the whole trip.

Along the way we came across a very beautiful seaport of Java called Djapara where the king, albeit a Mohammedan, was nevertheless very partial to the Portuguese and hated all Dutchmen so much he had often bent every effort to drive them out of the island. He saw us gladly, and as luck would have it a Portuguese ship was in the harbor. As soon as they learned of my arrival on the English ship, the captain came immediately at the head of his entire company to visit me and offer their services.

I was delighted to see them because it was the Vigil of Corpus Christi, and I wanted with all my heart to be able to say Mass the next day, which I would not have been able to do among the English. They took me to their ship, which they had adorned very richly. I spent the whole night there, hearing the confessions of all who were making the voyage. In the morning we said Mass, held a fine procession, spent the day in prayer, and at nightfall these gentlemen insisted on taking me to my English ship, where they gave me so many excellent foodstuffs we had enough for the whole remainder of the journey.

We left the next day to return to Bantam and go from there to Europe, or at least to India. We arrived on June 30 at this port, which is very near a very famous strait called Sunda, between Java and the island of Sumatra. There I saw the English captain again, Sir Aaron Becket, who showed me all possible courtesy with such candor and goodness that I was embarrassed and amazed at it. He wouldn't have me stay anywhere but at his house, where he entertained me most royally at his table, never hearing of taking anything from me.

Once again he urged me to stay with him for a year and promised me that afterward he would take me as far as England at his own expense, guaranteeing that I would meet with no unpleasantness there, although I was known to be a priest and a Jesuit. Still, after giving him to understand how sorry I was not to be able to avail myself of the honor he offered me, I told him that the importance of my business wouldn't admit of my tarrying. He stated that he didn't want to coerce me, that I should choose whatever route I wanted, and that he offered me anything lying within his power.

Besides that he allowed me to take into my company a very worthy Portuguese called Francis Secpa, whom he gave me most courteously, even after having refused him to another Portuguese who had made the same request. But in every respect he showed very special partiality for the Fathers of our Company, loudly proclaiming that it was our Fathers in Goa who had mediated the settlement between the Portuguese and the English, for which he felt under great obligation to them.

At that house I waited one whole month for accommodations on the ship going to India. Every day I went to say Mass at a place removed from any establishments occupied by the English, because I didn't want to offend them in view of the extreme courtesy they were showing me. All the Catholics in the place and all the slaves of the English hardly missed a day coming there. I heard all their confessions and gave them what other consolations they might expect from me. I found there besides a few Chinese Christians who traded at that port. They were most happy to find a priest to satisfy their pious needs.

Hardly a meal was got through without some point of controversy being brought up before me. It's true I always let them begin, so as not to annoy them to no purpose, but later I confounded them in such fashion that they were usually left without rejoinder. The minister was the first to attack me on the real presence in the Blessed Sacrament, which I proved to him so clearly through Scripture that he lost face greatly over it, although I always spoke very respectfully so as to give no cause for offense. The good man had read our Father Maldonat on the Gospels, and he made much of him, whereby it was easy for me to confound him with the words *supersubstantial bread** contained in the Lord's Prayer.

Another time we spoke of abstinence from meat at certain times of the year, concerning which the president himself, who was very well educated and understood Latin, Greek, French, and Portuguese, put various questions to me, at which he always showed himself well satisfied with my answers. This same man got around to discussing the celibacy of the clergy, Communion under one species and traditions, about which I always tried to show the Catholic truth so clearly that several in particular admitted to me that they were shaken. But alas, human respect prevailed over the reproaches of conscience, and fear of losing goods or life caused the fear they should have had of losing their souls to evaporate.

---

* Found in some English versions of the Lord's Prayer for the words usually translated "daily bread." (TR.)

☙ *11*. The Trip from Bantam to the Mogul's Lands

THE MONTH of July over, the ship was ready to sail for India. I took leave of the English captain, to whom I was so deeply indebted, telling him with many tears that I would beg God all my life for the eternal salvation of his soul, which he was losing in his bad religion.

We boarded ship at nightfall before the Feast of our glorious patriarch St. Ignatius, whom I took as my special protector for this long and hazardous sailing, during which I could never say Mass or receive any spiritual consolation except for my Portuguese Catholic (and even so he was snatched from me by a serious illness that carried him off in a matter of days), so heretical were all my shipmates, who nonetheless continued throughout the entire trip to render me every courtesy that good Catholics could have.

The wind was so favorable from the very beginning that we very easily got through the Sunda Strait, which is usually very difficult because of the heavy storms encountered there. It wasn't possible for us to hold a straight course for India because of the gales and dangerous channels that the pilot, who knew his business well, prudently wished to avoid.

This was the cause of our going very far afield, and instead of heading straight from the fifth parallel where Sunda Strait lies to the north where all India lies, we went to catch the winds around the island of St. Lawrence, which is called Madagascar, which we didn't reach because we turned toward Africa as though heading for the Red Sea.

During the whole trip the English gentlemen continued to treat me most civilly. The captain would never allow me to eat away from his table, where he always gave me the place of honor, although I declined it as well as I could. They didn't fail to attack me fairly often on points of our holy doctrine, but I gladly treated of these matters, endeavoring to show them the Catholic verities in the light of reason. I nevertheless didn't see them give any evidence of desiring to follow them.

We remained a month on the high seas, always enjoying so fair a wind that our pilot, afraid of arriving in India before the proper time, struck all his sails except for one small one that provided us with breeze sufficient to get us to the port of Surat right at the beginning of October when the winds are good and approach to the harbor easy.

We therefore spent two whole months on this journey, during which we certainly covered at least 2,000 leagues. I entered the harbor of Surat on September 30, 1647, and the next day I went into the town four leagues distant from the port, where the English gentlemen continued to do me a thousand favors. Sir Francis Breton, their mayor in this town, came to meet me and received me royally on the recommendation given him by Sir Aaron Becket. He insisted at all costs on putting me up at his house and feeding me at his table free of any charge to me.

I nevertheless declined, because by good luck I ran across Fr. Francis Zénon, a French Capuchin, native of Anjou, who on hearing of my arrival came immediately to offer me his house, where I found things far more to my liking than in the magnificent home of the English lord, well knowing that I would have greater opportunity to live in a religious manner and be of service to my neighbor. I asked Lord Breton please to be so kind as to send me some furnishings and provide me with whatever might be necessary for my board. I leave you to imagine the sentiments of gratitude I bore him.

I therefore withdrew to the little house of this virtuous religious, where I thought myself in a paradise. The good Father was a great servant of God, very austere as far as he was concerned and wonderfully filled with compassion toward others. Also he endeared himself to all who knew him. He preached with great profit every feastday and Sunday, and ministered to all Catholics coming to trade at this beautiful port. I spent four months in his most agreeable company, and I can say I consider myself fortunate to have met a person so saintly and charitable.

Six weeks after my arrival I had the good fortune to entertain my great charitable benefactor Lord Almeida Borges, who came to Surat with his entire lovely family. I was so deeply indebted to his charity I showed him all the gratitude I possibly could. Some days later we suffered a very heavy misfortune through the misconduct of one of his valets who, in what desperation I know not, went and threw himself into the arms of the Mohammedans and made profession of their evil faith.

God nevertheless gave us grace to snatch him from the hands of these infidels and bring him back to his duty, but this wasn't without receiving many blows of sticks and stones, one of which knocked me down. For all that we didn't give up pursuing our prey and in the end it didn't get away from us. The poor wretch recognized his fault and made his confession with many tears. I sent him to the town of Damão, which is held by the Portuguese. There he abjured the Mohammedan sect and was reconciled to the Church by the officers of the Inquisition.

78. A Few Comments on the Town of Surat and My Four Months' Stay There

I'LL NOT undertake to speak about the commonwealth of the Mogul, who is well enough known through the historians who have written about him. He is called the Great because of the greatness of his wealth and the extent of his domains. He puts fearsome armies into the field numbering 4,000 to 5,000 men, which he often employs in making war on the king of Persia. Furthermore, his kingdom extends from Persia as far as Bengal, which means he is actual king of all India, although a few other princes claim the same title for themselves in view of a few localities they hold along the seacoast, which is nothing compared to the rest of India.

The two chief cities of the kingdom are Agra and Lahore. The king usually spends the winter in the former and summer in the latter. They are not far apart. Both are said to be very large and beautiful. Our Company has a big college in the town of Agra that a most worthy Armenian called Mizre Zulcharnen founded about thirty years ago. Before that we had a mission there where the great martyr Rudolph Acquaviva labored for a time before going to Salsette where he crowned his holy life by a most glorious death. Reverend Father Francis Xavier succeeded him in this noble employment and remained thirty years in Agra or its environs, always most welcome to the Mogul.

Surat is one of the most important towns in the state because of its harbor, which is one of the most accessible in all the Orient. There I saw merchants from every nation in the world trading in security without having to fear the English or the Dutch, who are forced to keep within bounds because the Mogul, who wants all nations to come to the port with confidence, would drive them quite a distance away if he learned of their incurring the slightest displeasure from those coming to trade.

There one can find the finest stuffs in the world. There are great quantities of diamonds brought from Golconda, which isn't far away and where the most famous mine of these stones in the world is located; silks from China, cottons, all kinds of spices—in a word, all the most exquisite things of the Orient.

In this great conclave of nationalities one naturally finds all sorts of superstitions. Besides, everyone is allowed to live according to his own customs. The prince and almost all his nobles are Mohammedans. Nevertheless, I saw many pagans of a certain type I've never seen elsewhere. They take extraordinary pains to feed dogs, rats, and all the other nasty animals we hold in abhorrence. They are careful never to kill any gnat, ant, or flea. I've often seen them feed rats. One could hardly make them a worse threat than talking to them of killing a rat. There is no amount of money they wouldn't give to prevent the death of this noble animal. I know for a fact that those peddling "Death to Rats" wouldn't be welcome among these people.

Their priests are called *yogis.* They go naked, wear their hair long to the ground, and their bodies covered with mud. I assure you I've never seen anything so ugly or repulsive. They always have large feather fans in their hands that they use to sweep the ground for fear they might kill some gnat or ant. I couldn't watch this without horror and compassion.

I worked as hard as I could at making them see their crazy errors, but I got nowhere because no one wanted to come to the truth. However, before the English ship was ready God granted me a very great consolation in the arrival of our Fathers who came from Goa and stopped a while with me in Surat.

A few days later three of them left for the college in Agra, forty days' journey from Surat. The first was Fr. Anthony Botel, a Portuguese, a man of great worth and great influence destined to become Visitor and Rector of the college in that town, the capital of the entire kingdom. The two others were young men already priests and quite capable of learning the native language: Fr. Anthony Ceski, a German, and Mr. Henry Buscé, a Belgian. The letters I have recently received in Rome tell us of the great fruit that these three Fathers are producing by their work in the Mogul state.

The fourth was Fr. Torquato Parisiano, an Italian who came disguised as an English merchant and was going as far as the port of Suakin on the Ethiopian border to bring help to the poor Christians of that afflicted Church, and was bringing them even some temporal help that Lord Alfonso Mendez, the Patriarch of Ethiopia, was sending them. The English, who were aware of the good Father's plan, approved so highly they weren't satisfied with accommodating him aboard their vessel, but also helped him in every way they could when they were in that country, and knowing the Mohammedans had designs on his life, even snatched him from their hands and set him in a place of safety.

It would be useless to describe how happy we five all were to see one another. After the other three left, Fr. Torquato and I joined forces to battle the idolaters in their errors, but the results were sparse and all our trouble practically futile.

❧ 79. My Departure from Surat for Persia

I THEREFORE WAITED four whole months in Surat for the English ship to get ready to take me to Persia, from whence I had decided to travel overland across the whole of Persia, Media, the two Armenias, and Anatolia as far as Smyrna because, finding no ship prepared to round the Cape of Good Hope, I thought it advisable to go to Europe by a route that was more hazardous, but which would prove shorter.

On taking leave of Reverend Father Zénon, to whom I felt so deeply obligated, and of Fr. Torquato Parisiano, who was waiting for the English ship for Suakin, we left on February 3, 1648, for Persia. This was the third time the English gentlemen received me aboard their ship, where they continued to show me all the courtesy that I could, not expect, but desire. The sailing took exactly one month. We passed within sight of Ormuz and landed two leagues from there, that is to say in Kerman.

As everyone knows, Ormuz is a small island at the entrance to the very heart of Persia, where all the earth is scorched and grows nothing because of the excessive heat. There is only salt, where the sun shining on it burns everything up. There are high mountains keeping the breeze away, so that the temperature of the island is so high it seems almost like a furnace.

But despite the sterility of the land and the unpleasantness of the climate, this island was filled with riches during its tenure by the Portuguese. The harbor is so good and so accessible that the saying went that if the world were a ring, Ormuz would be its precious stone. The swarm of merchants there was incredible, because they came from China, the Moluccas, and all the East Indies. All of Persia, Arabia, and Armenia sent their wares there, and the English, Dutch, and Portuguese found this trade wonderfully advantageous whereby the most precious commodities on earth could be procured. But since the king of Persia took it from the Portuguese with the help of the English about thirty years ago, the island has been entirely deserted. The Persians preferred to transfer all this trade to a neighboring port called Kerman.* It used to be called Bandelké [Bandar Abbas]. That's where we landed at the beginning of March of the year 1648.

I had been there a few days when, running across the good company of a Frenchman and a Belgian going to Isfahan, I joined them and began my overland trek. They were both Calvinists but outside that certainly very fine men. I didn't miss any opportunity of acquainting them with their errors along the way, but I didn't meet with the success I hoped for.

After a few days' travel, before arriving in Shiraz, I made a contact for which I have blessed God a thousand times. I was on foot, reading my Breviary at some distance from those I was traveling with. On the road I saw a very good-looking man, well mounted, dressed as a Persian, wearing turban, coat, and scimitar and the long square beard. I took him for a Persian or an Armenian lord.

Seeing I wore a hat and a long black robe, he realized I was a priest come from Europe. He greeted me very civilly in Latin. His pronunciation told me he was French. I answered him immediately in our tongue. He was so overcome with joy he dismounted. We embraced each other and conversed for

---

* Probably Gombrun, later Bandar Abbas.

about a half hour so happily we contracted in this short time a friendship that I shall preserve most tenderly all my life.

He was a gentleman from Poitou called Monsieur de la Boulaye who only a few months ago published a very fine book about his travels where he related with equal accuracy and clarity the experiences he met with in kingdoms so different. He crossed the greater part of Europe, Asia, and Africa. He found himself among Turks, Arabs, Persians, Armenians, Indians, and other nationalities the most barbarous in the world. He was everywhere possessed of such prudence and virtue he preserved his religion and his conscience inviolate, nevertheless winning the hearts of all and proving that a good Christian and a good Frenchman can circle the globe without making an enemy.

I have met him since in Rome where the Lord Cardinal Capony accorded him the same honors he would his intimates. He arrived in Paris the same time as I, and by excessive good fortune he leads me to hope I shall have the consolation of having him for my companion on the long trip I shall take to China at the earliest opportunity.

Along the way we came to a very large and beautiful city called Shiraz, where the Persian court is said to have held sway a long time. I had the consolation of being able to say Mass there in a little chapel of the Discalced Carmelite Fathers after being unable to say it for three months.

80. Our Arrival in the Capital of Persia, Called Isfahan

AFTER KERMAN we kept traveling by long stages without resting, and still it took us thirty days to reach the principal city of Persia, called Isfahan, which we entered on April

13 of the year 1648. I must say it's one of the largest and most beautiful cities I've ever seen in the world.

There is such a large number of people that all the streets are always jammed. At the time the king was at war with the Mogul, from whom he wanted to wrest a stronghold called Kandahar, on the frontier between the two kingdoms. He had an army of 400,000 men, a great part of which was drawn from Isfahan. Nevertheless the crowds of people throughout the streets were so large I would never have been able to cross them if I hadn't been accompanied by a valet who went ahead of me to break a way through the crowd.

The streets were all straight and very wide. The buildings are magnificent. In the center of town there is a beautiful square like the Place Royale in Paris, but considerably larger. It's certainly twice that of the Piazza Navona I saw in Rome. The houses are all alike, well painted or gilded on the outside, with a large balcony extending all the way around.

But there is nothing more magnificent than a great shaded avenue a good league in length lined with beautiful houses by which one may go from Isfahan to New Julfa, where the king has resettled the Armenians, as I shall relate later. The king of Persia's gardens may be seen there, which are said to be very beautiful, but I had no curiosity in seeing them, any more than his palace, which is in the heart of the city of Isfahan.

In this great conclave of all nations of the world I found so few Catholics, there were practically as many religious as lay Christians. I had the great consolation of seeing three fine convents of religious there who enjoy the free exercise of their faith, each wearing his habit without anyone offering him the slightest affront. The king guarantees them this freedom, as great as they could enjoy in France.

There is a fine convent of the Reverend Augustinian Fathers that the king of Portugal built there, with a very lovely church. The Reverend Discalced Carmelite Fathers have another where there are ten religious who labor with great zeal. The third belongs to the Reverend Capuchin Fathers, who were five at the time, all French. The most Christian king maintains them in this country. They urged me to stay with them. I would very gladly have accepted the favor they were doing me if it hadn't bothered me to have one of their religious moved out to make room for me. I couldn't bear to see them inconvenienced. The Augustinian Fathers, who had more elbow room, received me with open arms. I had the consolation of being in their company until my departure and enjoying their good example.

81. What Hopes of Success There Might Be for Gospel Workers Laboring in Persia

THE GREATNESS of the kingdom of Persia has been so well-known for so long it constitutes one of the nobler chapters of history and was even a subject for Roman stories. I'm convinced that ever so many persons filled with the same zeal that burned in the hearts of the Apostles would be delighted to go expend their blood and their lives in these wonderful lands to preach Jesus Christ, who was driven out by Mohammed, and to revive the Christian faith in this field once watered by the blood of so many martyrs.

But it's taken for granted that nothing whatever is to be gained among all these people, that one couldn't speak to anyone about taking the road to salvation without being immediately run through, that it's by this unfortunate custom that Mohammedans close all avenues to those desiring to show them the light of the Gospel, and that anyone going to Persia can only expect to live in idleness or die straight off.

I feel constrained to express my sentiments on this score and disabuse those who under this false assumption are missing the opportunity of winning splendid crowns by spreading the kingdom of Jesus Christ. Let it therefore be known that I saw in the capital of Persia religious of six different orders walking about publicly in their habits, free to say Mass, recite the Office, and preach as they might have done in the most Catholic cities of Europe.

In the large towns there are innumerable strangers who aren't Mohammedans and who may be converted without the slightest danger. It's true that the king of Persia wouldn't allow those who profess his sect and have reached the age of reason to embrace our holy faith openly, but still he doesn't maintain the strictness the Turks do. He permits religious discussions, and no one is reprimanded or mistreated for condemning the superstitions of Mohammed. This can prove very useful in converting many who leave their country and go to Goa or to other Portuguese territories.

Besides that, when even Mohammedans have very sick children they easily permit us to baptize them. In Isfahan I knew a Discalced Carmelite Father, a Belgian called Fr. Denis, who by this means had sent to heaven forty little children who died shortly after he baptized them. I leave you to decide whether the good Father had wasted his time by delivering forty innocent creatures from limbo who will acknowledge throughout eternity that they owe him their salvation.

And they don't do that only for their children. They too, when they're sick, get themselves carried to the churches where they offer candles and want our priests to read the Gospel over them, and God has often restored these people to health who begged it of Him without knowing Him very well.

But those who can be especially helped are the poor Armenians, who are schismatics and Eutychian heretics. They can be persuaded to relinquish their errors without any fear, and all Persia is so full of them one sees as many of them as Persians even, because the Persian king Abbas,* at war with the Great Mogul, was afraid the Armenians might take his side, and to prevent this made them leave their land to live in

---

* Shah Abbas I.

his states, where he gave them towns. I said above that near Isfahan he had built New Julfa, where there are a very large number of Armenians who have very well-appointed churches and where they enjoy complete freedom of religion.

It's true they are very badly treated as regards their persons and their goods. They are ruined by the taxes they are made to pay, and if they are so poor they have no way of paying them, they are beaten with rods to the point of giving up the ghost or relinquishing faith in Jesus Christ, which, alas, they do only too frequently.

The wretches exert yet another kind of quite unbearable tyranny over these poor slaves. They pick out the most beautiful children they have, lock them up in the king's palace without their even being able to know their parents or make profession of any other religion but Mohammed's.

One must nevertheless admit that these Armenians are most deserving of compassion in their errors and their misery. Most have never heard the Pope mentioned and have no idea they are in error. They are so especially careful to say their prayers and keep their fasts they wouldn't be dispensed for anything in the world.

Nevertheless their fasts are incomparably stricter than ours. They eat neither meat nor eggs nor dairy products, nor even fish or oil. They drink no wine during the whole time. They fast the whole of Advent as well as Lent and aren't content with fasting the day before the feast of certain saints, but the vigil lasts a whole week.

They observe the same abstinence on Wednesdays and Fridays except for the time between Easter and Pentecost, during which laymen are not obliged to abstain from ordinary foods. It has been estimated that even those who are not religious are under obligation to fast six months and three days out of the year. Religious have many more, and all keep them so strictly that if anyone happens to break them, the priests punish him very severely. It's true I noted their fast consists only in abstaining from these foods, for they can eat several times a day.

They accustom their children to this rigorous fasting even before the age of reason, and the sick dispense themselves from it only rarely, as I saw for myself. They say it's the best medicine the doctor could prescribe for them.

So that's what I saw of the Armenians' fasts, which I certainly wanted to tell about, to warn those eager to devote themselves to their conversion that they'll get nowhere with them if they don't make up their minds to keep the same fasts. Let no one think he'll be able to win an Armenian to God without showing him he has the courage to fast as well as he can.

82. How We Left Persia and Crossed the Whole of Media and Upper Armenia

I WAS OBLIGED to stay about three months in Isfahan to wait for a caravan of Armenians, without which I couldn't safely cross the many kingdoms I still had to go through. And even so my friends all wanted me to take off my habit and disguise myself as an Armenian for fear the Turks would offer me some insult when I went through their territory.

The departure date was the twenty-eighth of June, 1648, Feast of the Apostles St. Peter and St. Paul. I certainly needed their protection, being the only Catholic in the entire company of 150 travelers. We nevertheless proceeded very pleasantly, and after a whole month's journey we reached the very beautiful city of Tauris [modern Tabriz] which is, they say, ancient Ecbatana, capital of the kingdom of Media.*

In all my travels I never saw a city larger, more populous,

---

* Actual site of Ecbatana is modern Hamadan. (TR.)

or more mercantile than that one, or where anything was cheaper. I myself saw that for one penny we had as much bread as a man could eat in a week. We stayed there a fortnight and left on the Feast of the Assumption of the Blessed Virgin. After a few days we entered upper Armenia, held by the Persians, and came to the original Julfa that was the capital of Armenia recently depopulated, as I said, by the king of Persia.

Outside the walls of this city, which is now merely a desert, I saw a beautiful testament to the ancient piety of the Armenians. It's a very extensive field where there are at least 10,000 marble tombs marvelously well wrought. On each may be seen a large block of white marble twelve feet high and eight wide, graven with many beautiful figures and a large cross above it. This great quantity of marble is a most beautiful sight.

A doctor famous among the Armenians, of the kind they call *vartabet*,* had built a church on a neighboring mountain and had gained quite a reputation living in this desert spot removed from the doings of men. He had formerly been in Rome, where he is said to have amassed considerable wealth. As soon as he learned I had arrived in Julfa, he came to see me with great courtesy and wanted me at all costs to come visit his church. He urged me to stay a few months with him, promising me he would see me safely to Rome. I declined because I felt safer with my caravan of Armenians. I took leave of him, and I saw where God's very special protection was leading me, because a few days after I left him the Turks, thinking he had come from Rome with his purse well filled, plotted to go murder him for his money during the night. Which they did, killing all who were found in the house. I would no doubt have been one of them if God hadn't inspired me to take no stock in the suggestion the good doctor made me.

We left Julfa a few days later and at the beginning of September of the year 1648 reached the principal city of

* A celibate divine ranking below a bishop.

Armenia, which is called Erivan. It is right at the foot of the big mountain said to be the one where Noah's ark came to rest after the flood, and truly it's so high no one can go to the top without manifest danger to his life because of the intense cold there. It's called No.* The snows there last all year. They say a part of Noah's ark still remains on the crest, but I find it hard to believe inasmuch as they say nobody can get near. No more do I believe what a nevertheless sober person told me, namely that at the foot of the mountain where Noah is said to have offered his sacrifice there is a spot where trees are seen whose only fruit is crosses. The Persians have a fort there near the mountain that the Turks took from them some time ago, but they recaptured it since and have fortified it so well it's considered impregnable.

Thus far I had brought my little Chinaman quite safely, whom I had baptized in Macao and was taking to Rome; however, some of my Armenian friends advised me not to take him farther, because some Turks who were in our company, seeing his very small nose and his complexion rather dark like all Chinese, were convinced he was a Tartar and a Mohammedan and had resolved to hold him when we reached Turkish soil.

I very much dreaded losing this young man, who is naturally so good and wonderfully bright. I learned we had a Catholic archbishop of the Order of St. Dominic in the town of Nakhicheven at four days' journey from Erivan, where mankind is said to have first settled after the flood. I went there to get advice on what I should do in the circumstances so as not to lose my Chinaman.

As soon as the good virtuous Archbishop heard of my arrival he didn't wait for me to come see him at his place, but came to mine with tokens of very great charity and asked me to go with him to a neighboring monastery of the Fathers of St. Dominic, where there are twenty-two religious of exemplary life.

When I told them the reason for my visit and the danger

* Kuh-in-nuh, Persian name of Mt. Ararat.

my Chinaman was in of falling into the hands of the Turks, my lord the Archbishop told me he planned to take a trip to Rome in less than six months and promised to bring my China-man there as safely as he could. I was to leave him in his hands, and the Archbishop would take care of him as he would his own person.

I couldn't have hoped for a better opportunity of keeping the young man safe. I left him in the hands of the charitable Archbishop and the good Fathers, who kept him six full months and showed him all the charity one could desire. They taught him Armenian so well that later, traveling through Turkish territory and appearing before various judges who tried to make him out a Tartar, he always spoke such good Armenian he was thought to have really been born in Armenia. I am under very great obligation to them, because even when my lord the Archbishop couldn't make the trip because of illness, these Fathers took the young Chinese as far as Smyrna where our Fathers took care to send him to me at Rome in very good company. God knows how happy I was to see him there at the beginning of the year 1650, exactly sixteen months after I had left him in Armenia.

❧ 83. About a Famous Armenian Monastery, the Patriarch of Armenia, and How I Stayed behind in Erivan because of Serious Illness

LEAVING MY Chinaman in the hands of those charitable Fathers, I returned to Erivan where I was shown the most famous monastery of religious in the whole kingdom. People came there out of devotion from all over the country, and es-pecially merchants desirous of undertaking some voyage came to this place that they consider holy, to ask God for the graces necessary for its success, and not failing to make fine offerings there.

The monks are very numerous. To tell the truth I saw in them two very beautiful things that led me to feel sorry for the errors in which they are involved. The first is that they rise every night, no matter how severe the cold and regardless of their age. They stay at least five hours in choir, where they never fail to recite the entire psalter, besides several lessons taken from various books that comprise a large part of their Office. The other is fasting so rigorously that they aren't satisfied with the great fasts common to the whole country, but most of them fast practically all their lives with the exception of five or six of the great feast days during the year. These two things make everyone consider them saints. Even the Mohammedans have singular veneration for them, and I was told that the king of Persia allocated large revenues for their maintenance.

I noticed, however, that they are all extremely ignorant. They understand nothing at all of the spiritual life and haven't the slightest tincture of the sciences. I leave you to consider whether the people can be very educated with such bad masters, who are content with knowing how to speak and write Armenian well, and when they know these two things they pass for great doctors.

The arch-Patriarch of Armenia, who is pope for this country, lives at this monastery. He professes to be a Catholic although actually he is enmeshed in all the native errors. It is certainly true that I was told he had made overtures toward union with the supreme head of the Church who is the true Pope, but the native doctors dissuaded him from this good intention. He was already very old and had even chosen his successor, in whose favor he had already resigned his office. I saw him going to church one day in very great pomp. He was returning from a short trip. All the people accompanied him ceremoniously, the clergy going before, and all carried large white tapers, the tallest I've ever seen.

All the bells of the monastery were ringing a beautiful carillon. In fact there are no churches with bells anywhere in the country except for this monastery where the Mohammedans have allowed them. Outside here they don't permit them anywhere on their soil. When he reached the church everyone came to kiss his hand. I saw him consecrate new bishops.

He showed me so much kindness I several times made the effort to discuss his errors with him in order to wean him from them, but for lack of a faithful interpreter my intentions proved futile. As a matter of fact there was an Armenian in this monastery who had formerly taken his degree in Poland, but he would never render me this service because he was extremely attached to the errors of Eutyches and Dioscorus, who pass for great saints in that country.

After waiting for time to leave, at the very moment our caravan was ready to start, God certainly found means of holding me up with a fever so severe I thought no longer of anything but the big trip to heaven. But I still wasn't worthy of it. The good Lord, who sent me this sickness, willed to cure me all by Himself. When I had reached the peak of my fever, four Discalced Carmelite Fathers on their way to Persia luckily arrived in Erivan where I lay sick. As soon as they heard of the state I was in they had the goodness to come see me.

This visit, so unexpected and so welcome, filled my heart with happiness to the point that I felt better almost instantly and entirely cured soon after, so that the next day when the good Fathers came to my room to say Mass and give me Communion, because it was All Saints Day, I had enough strength to say Mass myself, and we continued saying it together during the whole octave except for the last day, on which they left to continue on their journey, and were so humble all four insisted on doing me the honor of receiving Communion from my hands before leaving. We embraced one another cordially, and I assured them I owed my recovery to their holy prayers.

⁓ 84. The Trip through Armenia and the Whole of Anatolia

I HAD TO stay in Erivan three full months, partly to recover my health and partly to wait for company, because we had to cross all Turkey, which was the most hazardous and difficult part of the whole road. After losing my first caravan, which couldn't wait out my illness, God willed that I find another in which we marched very safely across the whole country, which Turkish cruelty usually renders very difficult for travelers.

As we began leaving Erivan snow covered all the fields, and the cold seemed to me far more unbearable than the high temperatures of the Torrid Zone, where I had lived thirty years without ever seeing snow and without feeling any cold requiring me to come near a fire. I had to change my tune and shiver with cold after having crossed the Equator four times.

We left upper Armenia, where the Persians don't treat travelers badly, to enter the territory of the Turks, who were so inhospitable they wouldn't let us enter their towns and made us sleep in the snow in the middle of the fields, which to tell the truth was a very vexing thing, because very often we had the snow both under and above us, thus sleeping between two white shrouds that could certainly have used a warming pan. But to tell the truth, the love of Christ makes all hardships bearable.

After eighteen days we had occasion to enter the town of Erzurum, which is the most beautiful and well-known in all lower Armenia. On this road I noticed a very modest nice-looking young man who was following our caravan on foot and keeping himself at a distance so as not to be distracted from his devotions. I tried to approach him so as to be of service to him in soul and body. I promised to entertain him at my expense and asked him not to leave me.

He was an Armenian, born in Constantinople, on leaving which he had entered an Armenian order to insure his salvation, but being greatly troubled by the devil, his superiors had decided he should take a trip to the country of his birth and there recover his health and peace of mind. Besides, he was burdened with all the native errors and even had others of his own, one of which was that no one could be saved but religious. I kept him with me about forty days, showing him all the kindness I could to win his soul, but he allowed himself to be taken in by some bad advisers who persuaded him to leave me under pretext of his wanting to take another road. I was very sorry to see him thus obstinate. God will perhaps accord him the grace to come to himself.

We were obliged to spend a fortnight in Erzurum. We left there January 11 of the year 1649, and after twenty days' travel we arrived on the thirty-first of the same month at the city of Tokat, now one of the most famous in Anatolia. Many Armenian doctors came to see me and even listened willingly to the talks I gave them on the primacy of the Pope over all patriarchs and bishops of the world. Some seemed to have assimilated my reasoning so well they promised me to set out for Rome.

Our stay in Tokat lasted a whole twenty days because of a problem arising among the camel drivers of the caravan. We left the twentieth of February and once again took up our soft bedding in the snow, which we never changed the whole trip. The Armenians showed us all the kindness they could. We were then beginning Lent in good spirits, which these good people rigidly observed without ever breaking their fast. I tried to do likewise, although I found myself so run down I was bereft of energy, and the regime lasted forty whole days.

After leaving Tokat we came across a town full of Armenians who had all been Christians and had recently abandoned their faith to become Mohammedans, thus wronging

Jesus Christ and their consciences. There were only one good
old man and two very aged women who hadn't bent the knee
before Baal. They had remained steadfast in their faith despite
the bad example of all their compatriots. That whole Church
survived only in these three poor people. All three came to see
me. I received them with love and veneration, regarding them as
souls truly faithful to their Master. I strengthened them as well
as I could in the articles of faith necessary to salvation, without raising doubts in them concerning those which are a matter
of dispute between us and the Armenians, which they were not
capable of understanding.

So it is that these poor Armenians, living in great ignorance
of our mysteries after being separated from the Pope, leave
Jesus Christ very easily and hand themselves over to Mohammed
at the slightest persecution dealt them by the enemies of the
Christian name. Persons worthy of credence have told me that
at one single time 3,000 of these wretched people renounced
their Baptism during the reign of Abbas, king of Persia, who
was urging them to it; later many, on repenting their infidelity,
left the country in order to return to the Church they had
abandoned in such cowardly fashion.

85. My Arrival in Smyrna from Tokat, and from Smyrna to Rome

WE TRAVELED a total of forty days over the territory of
the Turks, who actually never did me the slightest injury. Often enough they asked me to pray to God over their
sick children, which I gladly did, and once, seeing a little girl
who was going to die, I baptized her under pretext of washing
her with a little warm water, pronouncing the sacramental
words secretly. She died soon after. I had the consolation of

having opened the gate of heaven for her through the sacrament.

As we made our way over these open plains I was surprised to see no one in all the villages we came to. I was told that the reason for the great desolation was the war with the Venetians, for which reason the Great Lord had already moved all the people from these lands, having no other means of resisting this powerful republic of which everyone spoke with respect. I was often asked how it was possible for a state so small as that of the Venetians to resist the entire force of the Ottomans so long, and I was assured that since the beginning of this war over 400,000 Turks had lost their lives in it.

It's amazing how since that time the Venetian name is respected among the Turks. I didn't fail to speak well of their strength and worth, giving them to understand that the Christian princes were all at war and were giving no help to Venice, which was beating the Turks on sea and land by its own might alone.

At last, after traveling overland for one year minus one day, I arrived safely in Smyrna on the seventeenth of March of the year 1649, having begun my trip to Persia the eighteenth of March of the preceding year, 1648. It was an incredible joy for me to find our French Fathers there, who have a fine establishment in this city. They received me with such charity I have no words left to convey how indebted I am to them for it. They wanted me to spend Holy Week and the Easter holidays with them. In truth I saw how painstakingly they put themselves at the disposal of all who wished to avail themselves of their services. They taught the little children (who were more learned than their fathers), they visited the sick, went to the prisons, and although they were few in number, their charity filled that great city.

After the Easter holidays were over I found most opportunely a Genoese vessel that carried me safely all the way across the Mediterranean—which seemed a pretty short run compared to the wide oceans I had crossed. On the Archipelago we met the Venetian fleet, comprising twenty fully armed galleys and three galeasses. These were the forces that some time later dispersed and routed the entire Turkish navy and spread consternation all the way to Constantinople.

We skirted Sicily, pased by Messina, where for one whole night we watched with horror the flames pouring in great sheets out of Mt. Lipari. This gave us occasion to think of the eternal fires and to take measures never to be condemned to them. Finally, when we were in sight of Genoa I felt my heart tremble with joy at the sight of the beautiful steeples and the many rare monuments of Christian piety.

But my consolation was much greater still when I came to our house, where I met old friends with whom I had spent my novitiate and studied in Rome. After being thirty-one years without seeing one another we were inexpressibly gratified. I found the same cause for rejoicing in Milan, Bologna, and Loretto, where I found several of my former companions.

It was in that holy chapel that my heart melted entirely for joy at the altar of the Blessed Virgin, whom I held responsible for every success in my voyaging. After thanking my dear Mistress there several days I went straight on to Rome, where I arrived the twenty-seventh of June of that same year 1649. I forego speaking of the consolation that filled my heart on seeing myself come to this place, the most august in all the earth, after three and a half years of travel amid so many dangers on sea and land, such wildernesses, so many barbarians, so many pagans, heretics, and Turks, ever borne on the wings of Providence, which protected and preserved me with such singular goodness that I found myself as strong and fresh for any task as when I left Rome for India thirty-one years before.

Immediately upon my arrival I began acquainting the whole town with the project that had taken me to the ends of the earth. I had the good fortune to speak of it often to our Holy Father, who expressed a great desire to help us. Every day I was at the Cardinals' doorsteps to bring to their attention the new Christian communities that were holding out their hands to them asking the way to heaven. I had to stay three years, partly to attend our three general chapters and partly for the affairs of our provinces, ever petitioning for bishops and missionaries to save so many people from damnation.

After promoting as forcefully as I could the business that had brought me back from the remotest country on earth, I resumed my journey for the third time, but I was careful not to return alone now that I am old and practically have one foot in the grave.

I thought that France, as the most pious kingdom of the world, could furnish me many soldiers for the conquest of all the Orient in order to subject it to Jesus Christ, and especially that I could find there some way of getting bishops for our Fathers and masters in those Churches. I left Rome for this purpose on the eleventh of September of the year 1652, after kissing the Pope's feet.

I came by way of Marseille and Lyons to Paris, which in my opinion is the epitome, or rather the original, of everything beautiful I saw in all the rest of the world.

It was on the road from Lyons to Paris that I again experienced a very special effect of Providence, which has always served me as guide and mother. To make an appearance in France I needed a guardian angel to provide me with preferred entry into the court of the greatest monarch on earth. At Roanne I met Msgr. Henri de Maupas, Bishop of Puy, Abbot of St. Denis, and the queen's head chaplain. He was so kind as to keep me company on this little trip. For eleven days I beheld so many virtues and such goodness in this great prelate that I shall cherish the memory of his worth all my life and consider this meeting one of the most fortunate in all my travels.

I had no sooner preached this mighty crusade against all the enemies of the faith to be found in Japan, China, Tonkin, Cochinchina, and Persia, than right away a large number of St. Francis Xavier's children in 300 kingdoms became fired with the desire to take up their Master's cross and plant it at the ends of the earth.

I received countless letters from our Fathers asking me to enlist them in this glorious army. All five of our French provinces were filled with these generous aspirants. They wrote to Rome, prayed to God, solicited our superiors. They chose twenty out of many, who will leave shortly to go around the world. They are all worthy of this noble work, which they got after praying a long time, inspired by the Spirit of God who invited them into these fine kingdoms. So come, Fathers, Jesus calls us to be instruments of His glory in the salvation of so many peoples the devil has carried off!

I admit myself unworthy of following such great men, but I rejoice to find myself among people so zealous who will repair all the mistakes I made in those lands. Even now the guardian angels of Japan, China, Tonkin, and all the other kingdoms are preparing souls to whom you will go and bring the Gospel. You go like the Rubens, Sylveiras, and Capèches in search of a death beyond the ordinary. You go like the Xaviers and the Bezers to take the light of grace to lands where day is just dawning. I am the one who should admire and imitate your zeal and consider myself fortunate to be able to be of some service to you in this noble enterprise.

This is what is expected of us by the many persons of rank and piety who have undertaken this work as the most glorious France has seen in several centuries: that great queen who has given us more proofs of her goodness than we could ever realize—a group of the most virtuous ladies in Paris who have worked for us with such zeal and have shown by their example that ladies can find ways of preaching the Gospel in India without ever leaving their homes or their households.

This still isn't the crown of all our endeavors. Many high ranking, virtuous persons in Paris are working to secure us some bishops. We hope Rome will have this good news for us at an early date. The lord prelates have taken the matter to heart and have shown by the letters they have written the Pope on the subject that the piety of France's bishops is capable of carrying the Gospel to both one pole and the other. Paris should reap the glory for carrying the torch of Christian truth beyond the seas to enlighten so many people still living in darkness, of seeing bishops consecrated who have no other purpose beyond abandoning themselves to all the fatigues of a long journey and a life of hard work for which the Savior reserves all His crowns.

So many pious persons who have no other design or employment beyond procuring God's glory in every kind of good work have considered this one worth all others. They are working at it so wholeheartedly that we expect to see it completed at an early date, which will be the zenith of all the joy I expect in this life, and the crown of all the objectives I had before me in all my journeying, wherein I have aspired to nothing, nor do I in this whole book, but the greater glory of God.

AMDG

Index

A NOTE ON THE TYPE

IN WHICH THIS BOOK WAS SET

This book is set in Intertype Garamond, a type face considered by many as one of the most successful ever introduced. Claude Garamond, the designer of these beautiful types, was a pupil of Geoffroy Tory, a leader of the Renaissance in France, a university professor, artist, designer and printer who set out to place French on an equal footing with Latin and Greek as a language of culture. Garamond's evenness of color throughout the font is highly appreciated by book designers. The moderately strong fine lines tend to soften the effect, which is decidedly agreeable to many. One thing is certain, Garamond is unusually pleasing and will distinguish much good printing for many years to come. This book was composed by the York Composition Company, Inc., of York, and bound by William Marley Company of Philadelphia. The typography and design of this book are by Howard N. King.